Canadian Peacekeepers
in
Indochina
1954–1973
Recollections

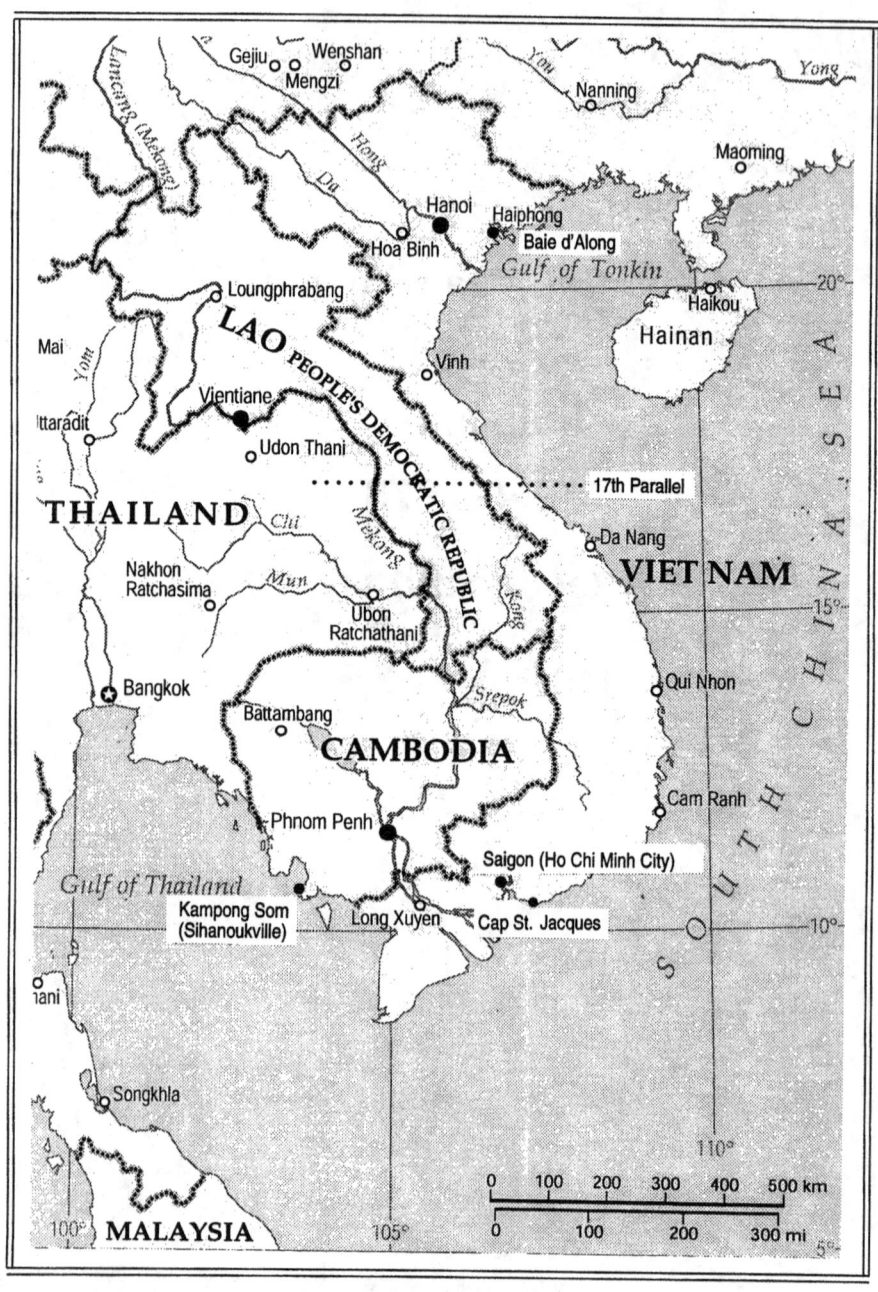

Canadian Peacekeepers
in
Indochina
1954–1973

Recollections

Edited by
Arthur E. Blanchette

Rideau Series no. 2

The Golden Dog Press
Ottawa – Canada – 2002

Copyright © 2002 by Individual Authors.

ISBN 0-919614-96-5

All rights reserved. No part of this publication — other than in brief form for review or scholarly purposes — may be reproduced, stored in a retrieval system, or transmitted, in any form or by any means, electronic, mechanical, photocopying, recording or otherwise, without the prior permission of the copyright holders.

National Library of Canada Cataloguing in Publication Data

Main entry under title :

Canadian peacekeepers in Indochina, 1954–1973 : recollections

(Rideau series ; no. 2)
Includes index.
Includes text in French.
ISBN 0-919614-96-5

1. United Nations – Peacekeeping forces – Indochina – Anecdotes. 2. Canada – Armed forces – Indochina – Anecdotes.   I. Blanchette, Arthur E. II. Series.

JZ6377.C3C35 2002   341.5' 84   C2001-900044-0

Cover design by Jennifer Scott, Toronto.

Typesetting by Carleton Production Centre, Ottawa.

Printed in Canada.

Published by:
  The Golden Dog Press, an imprint of Haymax Inc.,
  P.O. Box 393, Kemptville, Ont., K0G 1J0 Canada

To Michael Gnarowski:

A most valued friend

Contents

Foreword – Hon. Mitchell Sharp, P.C.   ix
Preface   xiii
Acknowledgments   xv
Biographies of Contributors   xvii
Selected photos   between pp. 84–85

1 – The Setting
    1954–1973   Arthur E. Blanchette   1

2 – Learning on the Job
    May 1955 – November 1956   Vernon G. Turner   10

3 – Vietnam: A Year with Uncle Ho
    July 1955 – July 1956   J.H. Taylor, C.M.   15

4 – A Year in Laos
    October 1956 – October 1957   J. Ross Francis   32

5 – The Best of Times and The Worst of Times
    May 1958 – June 1959   Roy MacLaren, P.C.   47

6 – Life Along the Mekong
    June 1958 – August 1959   Arthur E. Blanchette   53

7 – Why am I here?
    April 1961 – December 1962   John Schioler   67

8 – Mission to Hanoi: The Canadian Channel
    May 1964 – November 1965   J. Blair Seaborn, C.M.   85

9 – My War
    1965   Peter Roberts   112

10 – Pearson, Martin, and the Vietnam War
    1965 – 1967   Geoffrey Pearson   117

11 – Memories of Cambodia
  November 1965 – November 1968
                              Louise Pommet-Dyer   122

12 – Assignment to Cambodia
  February 1968 – December 1969   Richard V. Gorham   150

13 – Ma vie au Cambodge
  octobre 1968 – décembre 1969
                              Thérèse Rhéaume-Chabot   170

14 – The Sequel: Canada Does it Again in Vietnam
  April 1968 – May 1973   Daniel Molgat   174

Index   189

Foreword

For almost exactly 30 years following the Second World War, Indochina was the scene of violent hostilities, involving France initially and some years later the United States.

For nearly 20 of those years, Canada was actively engaged in the truce supervision arrangements set up, first, in 1954 by the Geneva Conference on Indochina marking the end of the war between France and her former colonies; and, later, in 1973 as a result of the Armistice signed in Paris in January of that year seeking to end the war between North Vietnam and South Vietnam supported by the United States.

Canada accepted with some reluctance the invitation of the co-Chairmen (Britain and the USSR) of the Geneva Conference in 1954 to become a member of the International Commissions for Supervision and Control (ICSC), along with India and Poland. In terms of their mandates, the Commissions were essentially observation units with no powers of enforcement. In addition, such key decisions as they might make had to be unanimous.

Initially, the Vietnam Commission did have some success in supervising the truce and, especially, in overseeing the large population transfers from North to South Vietnam.

During the 1960s, however, it became almost totally ineffective when it found itself trying to operate in a situation of violent warfare, the result of mounting hostilities between North and South Vietnam, in which the United States had become engaged in support of the South. Personally, I was not involved in any way with the 1954 invitation. At that time I was a civil servant concerned with trade and finance.

Our second commitment began in January 1973, when the two Vietnams, the Vietcong, and the United States signed an agreement in Paris that provided for Canada, Hungary, Indonesia, and Poland to form an International Commission for Control and Supervision (ICCS), created to supervise the terms of the Armistice.

As foreign minister I did not react with enthusiasm, nor did my departmental officials, when I heard from U.S. Secretary of State William G. Rogers that another cease-fire agreement was imminent and that Canada was being considered for membership on another proposed supervisory force. What led me to accept the risks was my desire to help the United States to extricate itself from Vietnam — which we did. As well, I did not want Canada to be blamed for complicating the cease-fire.

This time, as I stated in the House of Commons on January 5, 1973, the government's acceptance was accompanied by a number of firm conditions aimed at making the Commission more effective than its predecessor had been. Also, a time limit for our participation was set, in the event that our conditions were not met.

When it became clear that continuing hostilities in Vietnam were likely to make the new Commission as ineffective as its predecessor, I decided to go to Indochina in order to see for myself how the situation was evolving, what the prospects for peace might be, and whether our continued participation in the ICCS could be justified.

I wanted the question of Canada's continuing participation in the ICCS to be dealt with on a non-partisan basis, so I invited the leaders of the other parties in the House of Commons to nominate Members of Parliament to go with me to Indochina. The NDP (New Democratic Party) and Social Credit parties accepted, and two other Members of Parliament joined me. The Progressive Conservatives did not and thus deprived themselves of useful information about Vietnam.

It was a rapid but intense visit. Between March 13 and 18, 1973, I visited Saigon, Vientiane, and Hanoi, with a working stop en route in Tokyo. During that visit, I tried to probe the minds and intentions of leaders in South Vietnam, Laos, and North Vietnam. I had lengthy discussions with Michel Gauvin, the head of our delegation, who skilfully exploited the "open-mouth" policy we were driven to follow by the failure of the Paris Conference to approve our proposition to have the ICCS report to the Secretary General of the United Nations or to any other internationally accepted political body. I consulted with Vernon Turner, the deputy head of our delegation to the ICCS, General Duncan McAlpine, the head of the high-quality Canadian military contingent, as well as with other Canadians serving on the ICCS.

My conclusions were clear. While the main interested parties, including the leaders of North and South Vietnam, generally agreed that Canada should continue to serve, it was evident that the Commission was not performing the remaining tasks assigned to it under the cease-fire agreement and that there were few if any prospects that it would be able to do so as time passed. The underlying problem was that the East European delegations regarded themselves not as impartial — as Canada did — but as representatives of the North Vietnamese and Vietcong.

That, in my mind, set the stage for Canada's withdrawal from the Commission, with sufficient notice for a replacement to be found. Two months later, on May 29, I announced the government's decision to withdraw. A twenty-year Canadian role in Indochina was coming to an end. After Canada and Michel Gauvin withdrew, the silence of the ICCS was deafening!

The Hon. Mitchell Sharp, P.C.

÷ ÷ ÷ ÷ ÷

Preface

This book is a series of recollections by former Canadian peacekeepers in Indochina between 1954 and 1973.

It emerged from a suggestion made to our publisher, Michael Gnarowski, by Peter Roberts, a former Director of the Canada Council, Ambassador to the Soviet Union and also to Romania. He thought that such a book would make for an interesting read — certainly different from what is usually found in the literature about Canada and Indochina. It also stemmed from his own experience there. As he explains in his chapter below, this occurred in 1965: while en route from a posting in Hong Kong to Washington, D.C., the Department of External Affairs had decided that a few months in Indochina would give him useful information and background for his new assignment by providing first-hand experience of the mounting hostilities between North and South Vietnam, in which the United States was becoming increasingly involved.

In Saigon, Peter was a senior advisor to Blair Seaborn, then Canadian Commissioner to the International Commission for Supervision and Control (ICSC) in Vietnam, and also one of our contributors. He suggested that I, as a former peacekeeper in Cambodia and head of the Historical Division in External Affairs, might try my hand at pulling such a volume together.

It was so agreed and the present book, on the basis of his suggestions, concentrates primarily on what it was like to live and work in Indochina at a time when Canada was actively and directly involved in its affairs. It is more about people than policy, about individual rather than official challenges. Policy matters are not excluded, of course, but tend to enter the picture mainly in order to explain or describe some of the practical difficulties associated with life and work in Indochina. It therefore stresses the personal aspects of assignments, the many difficulties experienced on the ground, and on occasion the humorous and romantic side of things.

The first chapter, "The Setting", explains how Canada became involved in Indochina in the first place, the origin and mandate of the three International Commissions for Supervision and Control created at the Geneva Conference of 1954, of which we became a member along with India and Poland, as well as the problems we faced in Indochina over the years. It concludes with a brief account of the second Indochina Commission (the International Commission for Control and Supervision, ICCS), on which we served with Hungary, Indonesia, and Poland, which resulted from the Paris Agreement, January 1973, between the two Vietnams, the Vietcong, and the United States, and from which we withdrew in July of that year as outlined by former External Affairs Minister, Mitchell Sharp, in his Foreword.

Subsequent chapters offer the recollections of our contributors about their lives and times in Indochina during their assignments there or about their connections with Indochina while in Ottawa at the time. For the sake of convenience, they have been arranged chronologically.

I trust that this approach to an unusual form of peacekeeping in which Canada became unexpectedly engaged in 1954—well before our more successful and more widely-known Suez initiative two years later—will provide readers with new insights into what turned out to be a complex, protracted, and at times frustrating job not only for our people on the ground in Indochina, but for successive governments in Ottawa as well.

Arthur E. Blanchette

÷ ÷ ÷ ÷ ÷

Acknowledgments

The editing of a book of recollections going back nearly fifty years is a complex operation that has required a good deal of assistance from many sources.

To begin with, the contributors themselves were all generous of their time and patient with my many questions and requests for help. In addition, two of them, Ross Francis and Vernon G. Turner, both early veterans of the Indochina Commissions, the first in Vientiane and the second in Hanoi, read most of the text and made constructive editorial suggestions, as did my wife, Marcelle. Their comments and suggestions much improved the final text. Another early Indochina veteran, Colonel Jack Rozee, placed his rich and varied collection of photographs at my disposal.

The subject of photographs prompts me to make a brief mention here of the mothers to whom many young officers posted to Indochina sent photographs with their weekly letters home. These letters, lovingly kept, have now been resurrected a half-century later! Several contributors have used extracts from their letters in order to give first-hand descriptions of what their life and work was like in Indochina. This explains the use of the present tense on occasion in their chapters.

On the technical side, Christina Thiele, Carleton Production Centre, an extremely competent copy-editor and typesetter, assured uniformity and order in a text written by a dozen different hands, each with distinct grammatical and spelling habits.

Finally, the encouragement and enthusiasm of our publisher, Michael Gnarowski, made this book possible.

Arthur E. Blanchette
November 2001

÷ ÷ ÷ ÷ ÷

Biographies of Contributors

ARTHUR E. BLANCHETTE joined the Department of External Affairs in 1947. He was its Indochina Desk Officer in 1953–54, after which he was posted to Egypt and South Africa. During the spring of 1958, while on posting in Pretoria, he was named head of the Canadian delegation to the ICSC in Cambodia. He left Phnom Penh in August 1959. Subsequently appointed Ambassador and Permanent Observer to the Organization of American States in Washington, D.C., he later served as Ambassador to Tunisia and Libya. Four of his books documenting Canadian foreign policy between 1945 and 2000 have been published.

J. ROSS FRANCIS joined the Department of External Affairs in 1954. Subsequent to his year in Laos, 1956–57, he had two more postings in Southeast Asia, as First Secretary/Chargé d'Affaires in Djakarta and then High Commissioner in Malaysia. He also served in South Africa, Britain and Finland, the latter as Ambassador, and was Vice-Commandant of Canada's National Defence College.

RICHARD V. GORHAM was born in Fredericton, New Brunswick. He was educated in the public schools in Fredericton, served for a few months as a merchant seaman, graduated from the University of New Brunswick (B.A.) in 1950, and from Clark University in Worcester, Mass., in 1951 (M.A.). He was awarded an Honorary LL.D by the University of New Brunswick in 1988.

He joined the Department of External Affairs in 1952 and had assignments in Japan, India, Cambodia, and as Ambassador to China, as well as in the department's headquarters in Ottawa.

His assignment in Cambodia was as the last Canadian Commissioner to the International Commission for Supervision and Control, serving from February 1968 to January 3, 1970, at which time the Commission closed.

ROY MACLAREN, P.C., was Minister of International Trade, Minister of National Revenue, and Minister of State (Finance) in the government of Canada and subsequently High Commissioner for Canada in the United Kingdom. Born in Vancouver and a graduate of the universities of British Columbia, Cambridge, and Toronto, he joined the

Department of External Affairs in 1957 and served in Vietnam, Czechoslovakia, and at the United Nations in New York and Geneva. Between 1969 and 1979 he was active in business in Toronto, owning his own publishing company. Today he is a director of several British and Canadian companies. He is also Chairman of the Canadian Institute of International Affairs and of the Canada–Europe Round Table, and a Governor of the Trilateral Commission and the International Institute of Strategic Studies (London).

DANIEL MOLGAT joined the Department of External Affairs in 1959. He was posted successively to Hong Kong, Islamabad, and Washington, and later he was Ambassador to Portugal, Spain, and the European Union. He retired in 1999. He was Director of the Far Eastern Division in the Department of External Affairs when Canada joined the 1973 International Commission for Control and Supervision in Vietnam and when Canada withdrew from that Commission. At the time, he was chairman of the task force that tried to manage Canada's participation and role in the venture.

GEOFFREY PEARSON joined the Department of External Affairs in 1952. After postings to the NATO Secretariat in Brussels and to the Embassy in Mexico City, he served in the United Nations Division in Ottawa between 1964 and 1969. His last departmental assignment abroad was as Ambassador to the Soviet Union (1980–1983).

LOUISE POMMET-DYER joined the Department of External Affairs in 1961. After a posting to Rio de Janeiro in 1962, she returned to Ottawa where she served until November 1965, when she was posted to the Canadian ICSC delegation in Phnom Penh. She remained there until November 1968. Meanwhile, she had married Ken Dyer, an Australian education consultant in Cambodia. They settled in Sydney, where she has lived and worked since.

THÉRÈSE RHÉAUME-CHABOT est entrée au Ministère des Affaires extérieures en 1967 et en 1968 a accepté un poste au Cambodge auprès de la Commission internationale de surveillance et de contrôle, à titre de secrétaire, sous la direction de M. Richard Gorham, Commissaire.

Ce poste faisait suite à des études secondaires et commerciales en Ontario où elle avait exercé son métier dans les services bancaires et d'assurances.

À sa rentrée au Canada en décembre 1969, elle s'est installée à Montréal avec son mari, le Lt.-Col. Luc Chabot, poursuivant des études en traduction et dans plusieurs autres matières de perfectionnement, tout en travaillant le jour comme secrétaire particulière dans diverses maisons d'affaires et à la fonction publique auprès de l'adjoint à l'Ombudsman du Québec.

Son mari et elle se sont retraités la même année, se dévouant beaucoup par la suite au bénévolat dans la région de Montréal.

PETER ROBERTS, a Rhodes Scholar for Alberta in 1951, earned a degree in English language and literature from Oxford University. He joined Canada's foreign service in 1954 and was posted to Moscow, Hong Kong, Saigon, Washington, and Brussels. He served as press secretary to Prime Minister Trudeau from 1970 to 1973, then as Assistant Under-Secretary of State (Cultural Affairs) until 1979. He was Canada's ambassador to Romania (1979–83) and to the USSR (1983–85). He returned to Ottawa as director of the Canada Council until 1989. Since then he has published two books, *George Costakis: A Russian Life in Art* (1994) and *Raising Eyebrows: An Undiplomatic Memoir* (2000). He has finished a third, *Judging Ceauşescu*, and is working on *The Return to the Homeland*, a project of the Centre for Research on Canadian–Russian Relations at Carleton University.

JOHN SCHIOLER joined the Department of External Affairs in October 1959 and served in some 29 positions in a 30-year career, including assignments abroad in Vietnam on the ICSC, Rome, Cyprus, London at the Commonwealth Secretariat, Nigeria, Zaire as Ambassador (1976–78), and Egypt as Ambassador (1983–85). In Ottawa, among other positions, he was a speech writer to the Minister of External Affairs, Director for the Middle East and Director for Personnel Administration and Training. Subsequently, he served in the Privy Council Office as Senior Advisor on Métis and Non-Status Indians (1976–78), and was Director General for Africa and Chairman of the Southern Africa Task Force. He retired in 1989, and served as Director General of the Canada–Arab Business Council from 1990 to 1994.

J. BLAIR SEABORN, C.M., joined the Department of External Affairs in 1948. Before being appointed head of the Canadian delegation to the ICSC in Vietnam in 1968, he had served in The Hague, Paris, and Moscow. On his return to Ottawa from Vietnam, he was Head of the Far Eastern Division until 1970, when he was appointed Assistant Deputy Minister (Consumer Affairs) in the Department of Consumer and Corporate Affairs. In 1974, he was named Deputy Minister of the Department of the Environment and, in 1982, Canadian Chairman, International Joint Commission. He was then transferred to the Privy Council Office as Intelligence and Security Coordinator until his retirement in 1989, when he joined the Canadian Environmental Assessment Agency serving until 1998 as Chairman of the Environmental Assessment Panel on Nuclear Fuel Waste Management and Disposal Concept.

J.H. TAYLOR, C.M., joined the Department of External Affairs in 1953. He was posted, in 1955, to Hanoi as an advisor to the Canadian Delegation to the ICSC in Vietnam. Subsequently, he served in New Delhi, Paris, Moscow, Brussels, and Tokyo, as well as in Ottawa. He was Ambasssador to NATO from 1982 until 1985, when he was appointed Under-Secretary of State for External Affairs. In 1989, he was named Ambassador to Japan, where he served until his retirement in 1993.

VERNON G. TURNER joined the Department of External Affairs in 1954. In addition to Hanoi, he also served in London, Warsaw, Dar es Salaam, New York (UN), and Washington. He was Ambassador to Israel for the period 1982–86, with concurrent accreditation to Cyprus, and Ambassador to the USSR from 1986 to 1990. He retired in 1991.

÷ ÷ ÷ ÷ ÷

The Setting
1954–1973

Arthur E. Blanchette

Indochina was a large question mark for Canada in 1954. It was also a surprise.

In 1954, there was no official Canadian presence at all there. Actually, there was only one federal government office in all of Southeast Asia at the time, that of the Canadian Government Trade Commissioner in Batavia, now Djakarta.

Commonwealth approval of the Colombo Plan in 1951 did, of course, set the stage for a fairly rapid expansion of Canadian representation in the area, but not in Indochina, which was still a French colony, although France's position there was being steadily eroded by the growing military strength of North Vietnam, and also by nationalist movements in Laos and Cambodia. In 1954, Indochina was thus a largely unknown quantity for Canada and, once the decision was taken to serve there, we had much to learn and fast.

Our presence there came about as the result of a series of international meetings in Geneva during the spring and summer of 1954. They dealt with two main subjects: how to wind up the war in Korea and how to deal with the situation in Indochina.

Canada played an active role in the negotiations on Korea, based on our large-scale contributions to UN operations there. As for Indochina, we took no part at all in the discussions since we had not been involved in any way in its affairs.

Relatively little movement occurred at Geneva regarding Korea. The status quo between North and South Korea was largely maintained. Improvement in relations between the two countries would come only 50 years later. Conversely, a good deal of progress was made on Indochina, from which France was actively seeking to withdraw.

The talks on Indochina were conducted separately from those on Korea. They were held under the co-chairmanship of Britain and the Soviet Union, the other participants being China and France, along with representatives from Laos, Cambodia, North Vietnam, as well as South Vietnam, actively supported by the United States. Thus, unlike the negotiations regarding Korea, those on Indochina took place outside the UN system.

Why the Premier of China, Chou En-lai, decided to propose that Canada should join India and Poland as a member of the International Commissions created at Geneva to supervise the truce arrangements agreed upon for Cambodia, Laos, and Vietnam remains unknown to this day. He had studied in France for three years (1920–1923) as a young man and was likely aware that French — a useful language in Indochina — was spoken in Canada. This may have been in the substratum underlying his decision. Another possible explanation is the presence at Geneva — for the Korea side of the conference — of a senior External Affairs officer, Chester Ronning, who spoke Chinese fluently. He had known Chou En-lai for a number of years — they first met in Chungking in 1945 — and they got along well together. Although Ronning makes no mention of the invitation in his memoirs, did he have something to do with it?

In any event, if the answer as to why Chou En-lai decided to propose Canada is unknown, the end product of his proposal is most certainly not. For the next two decades, our acceptance of the invitation resulting from his decision involved us in one of the most complex and frustrating international political undertakings of the twentieth century.[1]

While an invitation to Canada by the Geneva powers had been mentioned in the media on July 19, the official text reached Ottawa only on July 21. Thus, although not entirely unexpected on the basis of the news reports, the invitation did catch the government unprepared.

Issued by the co-Chairmen of the Geneva Conference, Anthony Eden, British Foreign Secretary, and V.M. Molotov, Soviet Foreign Minister, it proposed that Canada should become a member of the International Commissions for Supervision and Control (ICSC), to

---

[1] An exact explanation of the circumstances affecting Chou En-lai's decision — if put on file at the time — will have to await research into Beijing's archives for the period, if and when released. Incidentally, France would have preferred Belgium, but went along with Chou En-lai about Canada.

give them their full name, set up to supervise the peace arrangements that had been agreed upon at Geneva for Indochina.[2]

Cabinet consideration of the invitation was conducted mainly by the then Secretary of State for External Affairs, Lester B. Pearson, supported by Paul Martin, Sr., Minister of National Health and Welfare at the time, who had an abiding interest in foreign affairs. Between them, they persuaded a very reluctant Prime Minister Louis St. Laurent and Cabinet to agree.

Acceptance, despite many misgivings, was based primarily on the hope that our participation would help the cause of peace in the peninsula. Disillusionment set in fairly soon, as we found ourselves in a quagmire of toil and turmoil, of crises and frustration, that came to an end only in 1973.[3]

The international supervisory arrangements created for Indochina at Geneva were, in part, a device to allow France to withdraw from the peninsula without too great a loss of face after its defeat there at the hands of the North Vietnamese; and, partly, also a means for the international community to come to terms with the new political realities brought about by that defeat. These arrangements were largely set up and financed by Britain, France, China, and the Soviet Union.

There were three "Agreements on the Cessation of Hostilities in Indochina" agreed to at Geneva, one each for Cambodia, Laos, and Vietnam. They were all concluded on July 21, 1954, but the representatives of South Vietnam dissociated themselves entirely and vehemently therefrom. Each agreement called for the creation of an International Commission for Supervision and Control in each country.

The agreement on Vietnam was the most complex and difficult of the three, that for Cambodia the most straightforward, while the one for Laos emerged, somewhat uneasily, in between.

---

[2]For Ottawa's reaction to and acceptance of the invitation, see "From Desk Officer to Acting Commissioner", pp. 35–37, by the editor (then External Affairs desk officer for Indochina), in *Special Trust and Confidence*, edited by David Reece (Carleton University Press, Ottawa, 1996).

[3]For the full text of the Geneva Conference invitation (July 21, 1954), that of the Government's acceptance (July 27, 1954), and of its statement of withdrawal from Indochina (May 31, 1973), with background notes, see *Canadian Foreign Policy 1945–2000*, by the editor (Golden Dog Press, Ottawa, 2000), pp. 54–58.

In Cambodia, a politically stable situation had emerged under the government of Prince Norodom Sihanouk. He had resigned the kingship of his country in favour of his father and had created a political party of his own that easily won the general elections called for under the Geneva Agreements. He thus became Prime Minister of Cambodia. The country was at peace and ICSC Cambodia was able to accomplish its mandate fairly expeditiously. By 1958, its basic work was done and it should have withdrawn. However, Prince Sihanouk viewed it as an insurance policy against outside intervention in Cambodia and, as a result — at his strong insistence — it continued to exist, albeit on a much-reduced scale.

As for Laos, internal political difficulties aggravated by Royal family leadership rivalries soon made it difficult for the Commission to operate effectively. Elections of sorts were held in May 1958 and, under prompting from the Laotian government, ICSC Laos adjourned *sine die* in July of that year. The internal political situation continued to deteriorate and outside forces became increasingly active in the country.

At the request of Britain and the Soviet Union, as co-Chairmen of the Geneva Conference, ICSC Laos was reconstituted in 1961. A cease-fire came into effect and the co-Chairmen convened a fourteen-power conference in order to try to establish the basis for a new peace in Laos. This conference, also held in Geneva, included the three Commission members, as well as Burma and Thailand, along with the original countries present at Geneva in 1954. Despite the conference's recommendations, conditions in Laos remained uneasy and quarrelsome. Its border with North Vietnam, astride the Ho Chi Minh Trail used to supply the Vietcong in South Vietnam, was bound to cause problems. The reconvened Commission was not particularly effective but, as Laos was a relatively minor player, it understandably received less attention than Vietnam over the next few years, although at one point U.S. bombing in Laos became highly intense and destructive.

From the very outset in 1954, the Agreement on Vietnam caused the most trouble. It called for a cease-fire between France and North Vietnam and the regrouping of their armies on either side of a demilitarized zone running along the 17th parallel of north latitude. This resulted in the *de facto* partition of the country. The Final Declaration adopted by the Geneva Conference anticipated the eventual unification of Vietnam as the result of free and general elections to be held under the supervision of an international commission composed of representatives of the ICSC for Vietnam. Elections did not take place and partition was increasingly resisted by the North.

Nevertheless, ICSC Vietnam did have some success at the outset of its operations, particularly its monitoring of the cease-fire and, especially, its supervision of the massive population movement from North to South Vietnam that followed the cease-fire. This was a large and complex operation. Between three-quarters of a million and a million people, mostly Catholics, moved south. Understandably, Hanoi was not pleased at this massive display of opposition to its rule and became increasingly uncooperative in dealing with population movements.

However, it was the issue of the unification of Vietnam that caused most of the turmoil besetting Indochina and international relations related to the peninsula for the next 20 years. The question was finally resolved when North Vietnam defeated and occupied the South during the 1970s.

Thus, apart from the strictly peacekeeping complexities of their mandate, the Commissions soon found themselves subjected to political pressures that went well beyond Indochina. Although Britain and France receded into the background fairly soon, the Soviet Union and China continued to vigorously support North Vietnam, while the United States came increasingly to the aid of the South, to the point that it eventually found itself involved in a particularly pervasive and violent war against the North. Because of these international political ramifications, Ottawa decided that External Affairs rather than National Defence would be the lead department regarding Indochina.

The Geneva Conference had stressed that the Commissions be set up urgently. Accordingly, Canada and Poland were invited by India, as chair, to send representatives to an organizational meeting in New Delhi from August 1 to August 6, 1954.

The three countries agreed that the Commissions should be established and operational on August 11. It was also decided that, initially, Canada and Poland would provide about 160 to 170 peacekeepers each. Polish delegations tended to be somewhat larger than ours because of a need for interpretation from English, the ICSC working language, to Polish. The Indian contingent would be more sizable and complex because, as chair, India would be providing administrative, secretarial, and other support services to the three Commissions.

It was also agreed that the Commissions would have parallel structures in each country. Headquarters in Vietnam would be located in Hanoi, with a sub-office in Saigon, while headquarters in Cambodia and Laos would be set up in Phnom Penh and Vientiane, respectively.

As to actual work in the field, it was decided that each Commission would have Inspection Teams: both Fixed and Mobile. Their mandate, in theory, was to check out developments, investigate complaints, and so on. The 26 Fixed Inspection Teams, agreed upon by the three countries, would be located primarily in provincial towns and cities. Each one would have two officers. The 26 Mobile Teams would have one each. As their name implies, they were to move about the countryside for their investigative work.

All this looked fine on paper, but it must be stressed here that, in terms of the mandate and structure given to the Commissions at Geneva to monitor the uneasy peace in Indochina, they were hamstrung in their work from the outset. Under the Agreements they were defined as *supervisory* bodies, but had absolutely no powers of enforcement. Essentially observers, the Commissions had no real clout, certainly none of the executive powers one would normally associate with a supervisory function. In fact, they could only try to persuade, provided that the parties concerned were prepared to be persuaded. Moreover, key recommendations had to be *unanimous*. Given the diverging political philosophies of the participants, unanimity was rare indeed. Minority reports, of which Canada tabled quite a few over the years, could be submitted to the co-Chairmen of the Geneva Conference, but were largely ignored.[4]

During the second week of August, the scramble for personnel to staff the Canadian delegations began. To begin with, Commissioners and/or Acting Commissioners had to be found for the delegations

---

[4]For a detailed analysis of Canada's role and problems in Indochina, see *In Defence of Canada: Indochina* (University of Toronto Press, 1983) by James Eayrs; and also *In the Interests of Peace* by Douglas Ross (University of Toronto Press, 1984). A more recent account *The further shore: Canada and Vietnam* by Robert Bothwell is carried in the Canadian Institute of International Affairs' (CIIA) *International Journal*, Toronto (Winter Issue 2000–2001), LVI (1): 89–114. John Holmes' *Shaping the Peace, 1943–1957*, vol. 2 (University of Toronto Press, 1982) deals comprehensively with the Geneva Conference.

accredited to each Commission. Political and military advisors, as well as civilian and military support staff, were also required. Personnel for the Fixed and Mobile Inspection Teams had to be provided as well.

The first Canadian peacekeepers to reach Indochina consisted of an advance party of about 70 armed forces personnel airlifted to Hanoi from Korea. The remainder were soon flown in from Canada. Senior External Affairs officials were quickly sent out to head the three Commissions. External Affairs also provided personnel to serve as political and/or legal advisors for each one. Assisting the civilian and military officers on each Commission were a number of courageous and spirited secretaries from External Affairs, who volunteered to go to Indochina despite the difficulties of daily life there, especially in Hanoi and Vientiane. In addition, several enterprising women officers from External Affairs served as political or legal advisors both in Cambodia and in Vietnam, particularly after Commission headquarters moved from Hanoi to Saigon in 1958. Overall, about one-third of the Department's officer personnel served on the Commissions between 1954 and 1973, along with a proportionate number of secretaries and other support staff. Indeed, Indochina was by far the single biggest administrative and posting problem faced by External Affairs at the time.[5]

Warfare in Vietnam became increasingly violent during the 1960s and early 1970s, as American military support for South Vietnam grew. Many countries friendly to the United States, including Canada, expressed mounting scepticism and doubt about the war. At one point during the spring of 1965, Prime Minister Pearson suggested a suspension of the U.S. bombing campaign against North Vietnam. This occasioned a fair amount of unpleasantness for him with President Lyndon Johnson, who took strong exception to the suggestion.[6]

---

[5]For a good account of the personnel and administrative burden placed on External Affairs by the ICSC commitment, see *Canada's Department of External Affairs*, vol. 2, pp. 115–121, by John Hilliker and Donald Barry (McGill-Queen's University Press, 1995).

[6]See *Canadian Foreign Policy 1966–1976*, pp. 122–126, by the editor (Gage, Toronto, 1980, *Carleton Library Series* 118) for the full text of Prime Minister Pearson's statement, as well as *MIKE III* (University of Toronto Press), pp. 138–144, for his own account of President Johnson's reaction. His son, Geoffrey, provides further details in his chapter below.

Although the bombing continued, the suggestion did not go entirely unnoticed in the United States and, as hostilities increased, it was a contributing factor influencing American public opinion, which was slowly beginning to turn against the war. These international and domestic considerations, accompanied by growing North Vietnamese success on the ground, eventually led to an armistice among the belligerents: North and South Vietnam, the Vietcong, and the United States. It took the form of an Agreement signed in Paris in January 1973.

One of the provisions of the Agreement was the creation of new truce supervisory arrangements under an International Commission for Control and Supervision (ICCS), set up in an attempt to deal with the new situation.

Canada was invited to join the ICCS, along with Hungary, Indonesia, and Poland. We accepted, but on the basis of our earlier experience we laid down strict conditions for participation this time, especially that the Commission have some real supervisory powers. We also set a time limit for our membership.

Hostilities continued as North Vietnam increased its hold on the South, so that the work of the ICCS proved largely ineffective. As pointed out in Mr. Sharp's Foreword, Canada withdrew at the end of July 1973. (We had withdrawn from Laos and Cambodia in early 1970.) Hostilities ceased with North Vietnam's victory and occupation of the South in 1975.

Thus, for nearly two decades, Canada found itself in the incongruous position of trying to supervise, amidst increasingly large-scale hostilities, peace-keeping arrangements set up much earlier and long-since broken down. In retrospect, the question might well be asked here why we stayed on so long at so hopeless a task.

However that may be, service in Indochina did turn out to be a professional plus for External Affairs. There was no parallel for this experience anywhere else in the world at the time, either in the UN context, NATO, or other venues. In those cases, unlike the Indochina Commissions, negotiations were conducted with the most advanced equipment available, in generally comfortable surroundings, with at least some allies around the table.

In the process, the Department acquired a reservoir of officers and staff who had had to develop skills in unusual management techniques and in the art of negotiating under the most trying conditions, while having to learn how to handle complex questions quickly in difficult circumstances. There is no doubt that its experience in Indochina was to stand it in good stead later on as the Cold War developed and it had to deal with such complex issues as East-West relations, disarmament and nuclear proliferation, the Law of the Sea, the international aspects of federal-provincial affairs, and problems with France.

In conclusion, a situation entailing increasingly violent warfare over the years could not but affect the daily life and work of Commission personnel, particularly in Laos and Vietnam. Complicating the equation, Indochina was a largely underdeveloped area where health conditions were poor, the climate hot and humid. Disease was rampant, particularly malaria, but amoebic dysentery, diarrhea, and other intestinal disorders, were widespread. The number of pre-posting inoculations required for the assignment was daunting. Even such simple things as a cup of coffee, a pot of tea, a shave could pose problems. Water, such as it was, could be made safe only by thorough boiling; in most parts of the countryside the only source of heat for cooking food or boiling water was firewood.

It is against this complex and difficult political and physical background that the recollections of the lives and times of our peacekeepers in Indochina should be projected and read.

÷ ÷ ÷ ÷ ÷

Learning on the Job
May 1955 – November 1956

Vernon G. Turner

When I joined the Foreign Service in 1954, I suppose I had visions of drawing rooms in London and Paris and grand conferences in Vienna. It is hard to be sure. What I did not envisage was 16 months in Vietnam as a very junior member of the Canadian delegation to the International Commission for Supervision and Control (ICSC).

My qualifications for this first assignment abroad were deemed appropriate by the Department of External Affairs: six months in the old Information Division, dispensing paper flags (the red ensign) to our bemused posts abroad; four months as document shuffler to the NATO desk officer; and no knowledge of Indochina. Learning on the job was to take on real meaning in that distant place.

The long trip by air from Ottawa in May 1955 was uneventful as was arrival in Saigon — until I reached the dusty quarters of our small Canadian office at *Camp des Mares*, a former French military base. Since I was to stay there only a few days before departing for Hanoi, I was given the mimimum possible amount of space and equipment — an elementary school desk, a hard chair, a pad and a pencil. If I had any confidential papers, I was told, I could put them in the adjacent Chubb safe. But I was not to open the bottom drawer because "Jack is in there". This was a reference to Jack Thurott, a former colleague who had been killed in a jeep accident in Laos several months earlier. He had been cremated in Saigon but the disposition of his ashes remained undecided. I never did learn of their final resting place.

In the light of this introduction to Indochina, leaving Saigon did not seem such a bad idea. As the least experienced Canadian civilian officer at headquarters in Hanoi, I was appointed secretary of the delegation. This involved attendance at almost daily Commission meetings, the taking of voluminous notes, which made my hand ache, followed by the preparation of voluminous telegrams, which made my head ache. My reports were patiently scrutinized and judiciously amended by the deputy head of the delegation, Saul Rae, whose sure touch always improved the product. What I could not understand, then or later, was why such long telegrams, even when improved, were accepted and sent. There seemed to be a view in the delegation that Ottawa needed and indeed deserved to know every detail about every event, dispute and debate. Perhaps it was our way of getting even with "The Department" for sending us to Hanoi in the first place.

As several of my contemporaries can testify, life in Hanoi was extremely circumscribed, to say the least. It consisted largely of reading and writing reports and briefs in the delegation office at the Burmah-Shell building, regular attendance a few blocks away at Commission meetings, and three meals a day at the *Métropole Hotel* where we all, except for the Commissioner and the senior miliary officer, resided. For a diversion, we could stroll around Hanoi but the empty streets tended to have a dispiriting effect. By the spring of 1955, all the private restaurants and most shops already had been closed under the stern rule of the new Communist administration in the North.

Delegations of all three Commission countries, regardless of political orientation, were condemned to live in the same confined conditions and did not normally complain. In the circumstances, it came as a surprise when the Liaison Officer of the People's Army of Vietnam (PAVN), our main contact with the regime, suddenly announced one day, in a diplomatic note, that for the benefit of all honoured members of the Commission, a lemonade stand had been opened at the edge of Le Petit Lac in the centre of the city. We were, of course, grateful.

In the midst of this excitement, I took delight in an unexpected discovery — a music store where a disconsolate merchant squatted in the gloom of his surroundings hoping against hope that somebody — anybody — would grace his premises and take off his hands one of his remaining inventory of musical instruments from France. For the reasonable sum of 45,000 Dongs (45 dollars), I purchased a beautiful new flugelhorn made in Lyon and a few days later, for a much lesser amount, obtained a handmade leather case to put it in. To the surprise of my colleagues, I also occasionally played this instrument, my best solo being "Cherry Pink and Apple Blossom White", a tune much favoured in those days by Filipino bands in the dance halls of Southeast Asia. On one occasion in Hanoi, I had the pleasure of fronting a small group of ageing and frightened Vietnamese musicians who had emerged out of the woodwork for the delegation's Christmas Party.

The PAVN, having provided a lemonade stand for the International Commission, did not again rise to this level of concern and generosity. Thus there was no improvement in the cuisine at the hotel in my two periods of residence there. Chicken in every guise was offered—*poulet bouilli, poulet rôti* and, alarmingly, *poulet farci*— but it always seemed to be the same fowl which had just completed a route marche and fought for its life before succumbing to its fate on our plates. Tough chicken with rice for the main course, with the occasional alternative of tough meat, presumably water buffalo, followed by a dish of yoghurt, is what I remember. Not impossible fare in the short term but the complete lack of lettuce, spinach or any green vegetable was definitely unhealthy. After my first six months in Hanoi, I was diagnosed as suffering from malnutrition.

I retain a vivid memory of my room in the *Métropole Hotel*— the bed with its suffocating mosquito net, the very tall windows, the ever-revolving fan, the small lizards on the ceiling, the table and chair where I wrote endless letters to my astonished parents, and the wash basin and bath. To this day I resent the fact that, as a result of my lowly status, I was given a room with no adjoining W.C. As a consequence, I was obliged to saunter frequently from my room down the hall to the common facilities. It was at such times that I wondered whether the diplomatic life was meant for me.

The hotel arrangements subsequently seemed quite luxurious by comparison with what awaited me in the remote village of Yen Van, where I passed a couple of days and nights as the Canadian representative on a Mobile Team investigating an alleged infringement of Article 14(d), the freedom of movement of civilians provision in the Geneva Agreement on the Cessation of Hostilities in Vietnam. Arguing with the hard-nosed representative of People's Poland, remaining patient with the painfully non-aligned and easily offended Indian representative, enduring the PAVN's obvious intimidation of witnesses—all this was challenge enough during the daytime. But tip-toeing by the light of a misty moon in a straight line along a narrow dike, with a water-filled ditch on both sides, to a primitive loo, where I was serenaded in my solitude by an abundance of insect life, made the challenge of the investigation process seem tame.

It was rare for a civilian from any of the delegations to participate in an investigation conducted by a Mobile Team but it was certainly instructive. I experienced first hand the discomfort of travel by jeep over rough roads under a blazing sun in a journey that consumed most of a day in each direction. As for the investigation, I felt deeply the frustration that any Canadian would encounter trying to determine the objective truth when confronted with a Polish representative whose purpose was diametrically opposite while PAVN interpreters, on whom we were totally dependent, made certain that testimony from the hapless complainants was suitably modified to ensure that nothing critical of the local or state authorities reached our ears. As a consequence, it is not surprising that our Mobile Team's report was benign. It did not find fault because it could not obtain uncoerced testimony on which a finding of violation of the Geneva Agreement could be based. The most useful results of my foray into the unreal world of ICSC investigations was a deep appreciation of the determination and staying power of the Canadian military, whose exposure as members of Fixed and Mobile Teams to obfuscation and procrastination while attempting to supervise implementation of the Geneva Agreement was a regular experience, not a one-time adventure as in my case.

After a period in Saigon in early 1956, I was recalled to Hanoi for another four months or so. The Commission met less frequently, the office routine remained unaltered, the menu at the *Métropole* unchanged. Life was still circumscribed. During this time something happened which gave me pause.

While out for a solitary walk one evening, I encountered a new member of the Polish delegation who had arrived in Hanoi only a few hours earlier. Speaking in French, he said that he was lost. Could I direct him to the "Happiness" Hotel, which was our nickname for the less desirable alternative to the *Métropole*, where some of the ICSC delegates were lodged? I did so and was about to stroll away when I realised that he was looking at me very intently. This made me uneasy. Sensing that something was still bothering him I stopped. He then struck me dumb with the following question.

"Dites-moi, monsieur, vous êtes vietnamien?"

Now, I acknowledge that somebody coming from one closed society to another might be unaware of the wider world. And I admit that the encounter in question occurred at dusk and that the Hanoi streetlights were dim at best. Still, this was a shock. Much as I admired the Vietnamese people and respected their culture, my Polish colleague's question suggested that I should move on. A few weeks later, in November 1956, I left Vietnam for good.

*   *   *

Or so I thought.

Just over 16 years passed and, in January 1973, I was in Vietnam again. On this occasion I rejoiced in the position of Senior Political Advisor to Michel Gauvin, head of the Canadian delegation to the International Commission for Control and Supervision (ICCS), headquartered in Saigon. This newest, slightly differently named Commission was established under the Paris Agreement on Ending the War and Restoring Peace in Vietnam. The new Commission facilitated the withdrawal of troops and exchange of prisoners much as the first Commission had done. In 1973 this enabled the Americans and their allies to recover their personnel and withdraw, as the French had been able to do in 1954, i.e., with a modicum of dignity. Once these essential tasks were completed, however, the Commission found it just as difficult to investigate alleged infractions of the Paris Agreement in South Vietnam as the old Commission had found it to identify violations of the Geneva Agreement throughout the whole of Vietnam. While wiser heads than mine drew their conclusions, one thing was clear to me. If any more commissions were set up in Indochina, I would refuse to go.

÷ ÷ ÷ ÷ ÷

Vietnam:
A Year with Uncle Ho
July 1955 – July 1956

J.H. Taylor, C.M.

From the moment the Canadian government agreed in 1954 to serve on the three International Commissions for Supervision and Control in Indochina (ICSC), every young and healthy bachelor in the Department of External Affairs knew his days were numbered: it was only a matter of time before he would be sent to serve in Cambodia, Laos or Vietnam — especially if he spoke French. Quite apart from a large military component, the Commissions required a foreign service staff roughly the size of the staff in the embassy in Washington. But since the tour of duty was nine months — later extended to a year — it was as if Canada had decided to open three embassies the size of its largest one on no notice at all.

The Department resorted to all the obvious expedients to meet this unprecedented demand. It called in its officers on loan to other parts of the public service, of whom I was one. This took several months to organize; by the time I had been retrieved from the Cabinet secretariat, it was too late for me to make the first team sent to Indochina. Since an assignment to the second team seemed inevitable, I spent my remaining months in Ottawa waiting for confirmation of my posting and making prudent preparations — among other things by having four impacted wisdom teeth extracted.

The axe fell, as expected, in the spring of 1955. I was assigned to Hanoi, then the headquarters of the ICSC for Vietnam. At the time, it was supposed to be the worst post in the service. I consoled myself that I had nowhere to go but up, got my shots, and departed in July, via Calgary, Vancouver, Tokyo, Hong Kong and Saigon. For the following year, I lived in the *Métropole Hotel* in Hanoi and worked several blocks down the street in the Canadian delegation's offices, formerly the property of the Burmah-Shell Oil Co. The civilian members of the delegation were pretty well confined to the city. (The military members travelled more, usually to places even less desirable, because they were rotated between the various Fixed and Mobile Teams deployed around the country.) In a year, I was allowed to go outside Hanoi only once in North Vietnam — to Haiphong, the port at the mouth of the Red River. It was another 45 years before I saw anything of the rest of the half of Vietnam north of the 17th parallel which was assigned to Communist rule in 1954.

Luckily, the Commission visited the southern half of the country from time to time at this stage of its existence. Those of us otherwise trapped in Hanoi took it in turns to go south with the Commission during these periodic visits. By hitching rides on the ships and aircraft that supported the Commission's Fixed Teams in South Vietnam, it was possible to see a good deal of the southern half of the country. In this way, I managed to see Gio Linh, Hué, Nha Trang, Cap St. Jacques and Tan Chau — a number of the ports of entry from the demilitarized zone at the 17th parallel down the coast and around to the border with Cambodia. In addition, the normal route of the Commission's courier aircraft, operated by the redoubtable *Aigle Azur*, permitted stopovers in Cambodia and Laos en route from Saigon to Hanoi. This allowed me at different times to visit Phnom Penh and to see the marvels of Angkor Wat; to stop briefly in Vientiane and Luang Prabang in Laos; and even on one occasion to cross the Mekong in a *pirogue* to Nong Khai in Thailand.

The logic of the cease-fire agreement[1] we had been sent to supervise was straightforward and sensible: stop the fighting; separate the combatants into two zones, North and South; exchange prisoners; allow civilians 300 days to change zones if they wished to; and, by the terms of an accompanying Declaration, begin consultations between the Communist and non-Communist halves of the country with a view to holding national elections two years after the cease-fire. By the time I arrived in Vietnam in July 1955, much of the work that could be accomplished under the Geneva Agreements had already been completed. It was to become clear in the coming months that not much more was going to be done.

On the constructive side, the cease-fire was holding. The regrouping of forces into two zones had taken place. Prisoners of war

---

[1] "Vietnam: Agreement on the Cessation of Hostilities", IC/42/Rev. 2, dated July 20, 1954, reprinted in *External Affairs Supplementary Paper* No. 54/22.

had been released. The French had withdrawn from the North in accordance with the timetable set out in the cease-fire agreement. In 1954, they had undertaken, moreover, to withdraw their forces entirely from all of Indochina at the request of the local governments. In the course of 1955 and early 1956, they withdrew from South Vietnam at southern request.

Above all, as provided for in Article 14(d) of the cease-fire agreement, there had been a spectacular exodus of civilians from the North to the South, numbering close to a million people. Despite the efforts of the Commission, this movement had been thwarted and obstructed by the authorities in the North, who were alarmed by such a dramatic demonstration of how many of their countrymen had no desire to live under Communism. Although the original period for civilian movement specified in the cease-fire was extended by two months, it was evident that, one year after the cease-fire, there were still thousands, if not tens of thousands of people, who would have left the North had they not been prevented by the authorities from doing so. We guessed—although there was no way of knowing—that a million and a half people would have gone south if the Communist authorities had implemented Article 14(d) as they were supposed to. When the extended period ran out in the summer of 1955, these would-be refugees had no recourse but to come to terms as best they could with their fate. The Commission might protest, but it could do nothing for them: they had to stay in North Vietnam.

Article 14(c) of the cease-fire also caused endless difficulty. This was the article designed to prevent reprisals. It read as follows: "Each party undertakes to refrain from reprisals or discrimination against persons or organizations on account of their activities during the hostilities and to guarantee their democratic liberties." Given the political realities in both halves of Vietnam, it was hard to know what was meant by guaranteeing democratic liberties. Neither in the North or the South were the authorities in full control of the territory assigned to them.

Although the Communist hold on the northern half of the country was the more complete, the evidence of the huge flow of refugees made it plain that support for Communist rule in North Vietnam was far from overwhelming. The extent of opposition became more evident as the administration in the North initiated a land reform program so brutal that even they subsequently admitted, when it was too late to do any good, that it had been a mistake. This opposition existed despite the enormous prestige Ho Chi Minh and his associates had earned as the successful leaders of the anti-colonial revolt.

In the South, the situation was even more confused. Ngo Dinh Diem, as nationalist as he was anti-Communist, had come to power. He faced the daunting task of replacing the departing French colonial power while establishing effective control over the southern half of the country. He was in consequence engaged from 1955 onwards in a protracted and violent struggle to eliminate his rivals: first the puppet emperor, Bao Dai; then the so-called sects, of which three controlled large areas with their private armies; and finally, the Communist Viet Minh (later Vietcong), who were still active all over the South, and who controlled extensive regions that the French in their day had never succeeded in penetrating.

In short, there were intense political struggles and formidable problems of public order everywhere in the country. Both regimes were accustomed to dealing with such problems with a heavy hand. They were not by nature inclined to guarantee anybody's democratic liberties—not even the liberties of their own supporters, let alone those of their opponents.

The authorities in the North managed, however, to extract a propaganda advantage from this situation, while drawing attention away from their own oppressive record. This they did by invoking Article 14(c) of the cease-fire agreement and embroiling the Commission. With their excellent intelligence network throughout the South, the Communist authorities in the North were quickly informed of any moves to stamp out Communism in the southern zone. Whatever the truth of a particular incident, it was simple for the People's Army to complain to the Commission that one of their former partisans, living innocently in the South since the cease-fire, had been the victim of some unprovoked act of repression on the part of the Diem regime. A complaint in these terms required investigation as a possible violation of Article 14(c); the Commission was obliged to transmit the accusation to the southern government and demand a response.

A sufficient response would have been to counter that the supposed victim, far from being a peaceful innocent, had in fact been guilty of some criminal act since the cease-fire, and was being prosecuted accordingly. This was how the North dealt with such accusations on the rare occasions when the shoe was on the other foot: they simply replied that the person in question was guilty of arson. The South, however, was slow to respond, so that a mountain of unanswered accusations piled up against it. In what was essentially a propaganda game, the North emerged the winner.

This Northern success said nothing about the true state of democratic liberties anywhere in the country. Reprisals against political opponents were common in both parts of Vietnam. Neither the Communist nor the anti-Communist regime was a model guarantor of the rights of the citizen. The apparent superiority of the Northern record arose instead out of a fundamental difference in the relationship of the two sides to the cease-fire agreement itself. The North was a full party to the cease-fire. It was prepared to exploit the terms of the agreement whenever it saw an opportunity to do so. In the South, on the other hand, there was, strictly speaking, no party to the agreement once the French had left. This bizarre situation arose because the South Vietnamese refused to sign the agreement in 1954 and refused thereafter to accept responsibility for its implementation as the legal sucessors to the departed French High Command. While they promised practical co-operation, their attitude to the Commission was ambivalent.

Thus it was that the head of the South Vietnamese Liaison Mission — whose smile, someone said, was like the opening of a box of Sobranie Black Russian cigarettes: all black and gold — constantly repeated that, despite his government's position on the principle of refusing legal succession to the French, "Sur le plan pratique, il n'y a pas de problème."

This, however, was not totally reassuring. The government of India led a public campaign to press the Diem government to make a formal commitment to the Geneva Agreements. The South refused to budge. The consequence was that we were never sure whether the Commission would survive from one month to the next. We should have been mightily surprised in 1955 to be told that the Commission would not only survive, but survive for almost twenty years more, outliving in the process disasters far worse than the original refusal of the South Vietnamese to accept formal responsibilities under the Geneva Agreements.

The second year of the agreement, which was supposed to have led up to national elections, departed completely from the plan of 1954. Although the cease-fire still held, there was no political dialogue between the two Vietnamese governments. Ho Chi Minh and Ngo Dinh Diem remained bitterly and totally opposed. In the event, neither side had the control of its own zone that would have allowed free elections to have gone ahead easily. However much they may have benefitted from the cease-fire and the departure of the French, the South Vietnamese were clearly going to have nothing to do with the rest of the Geneva scenario. July 1956 came and went, and with it the prospect of the kind of political settlement envisaged in 1954.

At this point, the governments on the Commission might well have said to the co-Chairmen of the Geneva Conference, to whom they reported, that they had done all that could reasonably be expected of them under the terms of the cease-fire and that it was now time for them to withdraw. They did not do so. Indeed, Canada stayed on almost two more decades, through a second and much worse war, a second cease-fire and a second commission, before the Vietnam commitment at long last came to an end. It was a convincing demonstration that international organizations are almost impossible to kill.

My time in Vietnam coincided almost exactly with the ICSC's second year. The frustration of working on Article 14(c), for months my principal responsibility; the tedium and discomfort of life in Hanoi; the excitement of brief trips to the South; the uncertainty about the future of the Commission; and my anxiety to serve my time, take home leave and get on to my next posting are reflected in more than 50 letters that I wrote to family and friends in Canada at the time. These were returned to me years later and I have been able to check my memory against them.

Here, for example, from a letter dated December 22, 1955, is a commentary on the problem of impartiality in the Commission.

> ... So long as the regrouping of forces was still going on, and freedom of movement was a major problem, it was easy to square an entirely impartial attitude with a defence of the interests of the South Vietnamese. Since July 20 [1955], of course this has been much more difficult, because of the conflict between behaving as impartial international civil servants and at the same time behaving in a sense as lawyers for a client who

refuses to have anything to do with the Geneva Agreement in its present form ...

The physical appearance of Hanoi, and some of the problems of living there, are described in a letter dated July 25, 1955:

... The temperature range seems to be about 85° to 95°[F]. But you sweat all the time, with even the smallest exertion drenching your clothes. It is a five minute walk from the hotel to the office, along a shaded avenue. Yet at eight o'clock in the morning, you arrive at work with your shirt sticking to your back. We do use lined pads, but as you guessed [because I wrote home on unlined paper] your forearm lifts the ink off the paper. Everyone has prickly heat, some even have the rash from head to toe, swelling into little red lumps ...

... Hanoi itself is a very French city, and a very modern and beautiful place. The buildings are new, large and handsomely adapted from French models to suit the climate ... The streets are wide, well-paved and shaded, as in France, with plane trees. At the same time, the atmosphere is almost weird. There is virtually no motor traffic, although there are traffic cops on every corner ... Traffic is mainly bicycles or "pousse-pousses", which are pedicabs. The main buildings — including both the hotel I live in and the office I work in — have guards dressed in the shapeless drab tunic and trousers of the Vietminh, and wearing helmets covered with the same material. They are all armed with bayonetted rifles (of half a dozen types) and carry grenades. The only colour in the city, apart from the buildings themselves, is provided by innumerable banners and posters and pictures of Ho Chi Minh ...

Another letter describes the rice-growing countryside of the Red River delta, as seen during my solitary trip outside Hanoi to the port of Haiphong:

The highway between Hanoi and Haiphong is about one-and-a-half lanes wide. It is built on a dyke, running through rice paddies all the way. The railway runs parallel to it on another embankment and at every bridge the two come together, with road and rail running across the same spans. Rice is grown here by traditional methods. The land, which is about knee-deep in muddy water, is ploughed by water buffalo, driven by ten- or

> twelve-year old boys who can even sleep on the broad backs of the buffalo. Water is transferred from one field to another by a man-powered water wheel, or by swinging wicker buckets ... We drove along by these paddies in a white Commission car, a battered Citroën provided originally by the French. The car, like most we use, is in bad repair and there are no more spare parts to be had. We blew a tire about halfway and, when we got out to look, found that it had a tear in the casing about eight inches long, through which a boot, made of another old tire, was protruding. "Tout fini", observed our driver sadly, putting on the spare, an equally ancient tire through which. the tube could be seen. This tire also had a boot in it which bumped so badly that the wheel bolts (on which the threads were probably half-stripped already anyway) kept coming loose. Every ten kilometres or so we stopped and tightened the wheel back on. However we made it to Haiphong and back.

Haiphong was the last city in North Vietnam to be transferred to the Communists. It was "liberated" on May 22, 1955.

> Since it was a port, it was probably always seedier than Hanoi, but even so there are already signs of rapid decay. The port and wharves are deserted, except for sampans and junks, and the only colour in the city is provided by the inevitable posters of Ho Chi Minh, Mao Tse Tung, Marshall Bulganin and others of the hierarchy, and by banners and slogans which are everywhere.

Hanoi is repeatedly described in the letters as deathly quiet, except for the occasional burst of political activity:

> ... Hanoi itself is a little gayer (or less dismal) than usual. There is to be a national celebration on September 2 [1955] and already everyone from the age of five up has been out practicing marching in step, banner-waving, slogan-shouting, patriotic song-singing, and all the other manifestations of socialist highjinks. Here is another slogan for you: DANG LAO DONG VIETNAM MUON NAM. The People's Party of Vietnam Forever.

Work on the Commission was often unattractive, as a letter of September 13, 1955, explains.

> In my own department there has been very heavy traffic recently in murder, beatings, torture and arson. If half the accusations

people make about each other in this country are true, then the Vietnamese are certainly capable of great cruelty. It begins to get you down after a while, to come to the office every morning and find a few more murders waiting for you ...

Distractions were few: reading, listening to records, swimming at the *Cercle Sportif*, before it closed down, and doing domestic chores:

> ... I spent a quiet afternoon brushing the mould off my belongings, which were beginning to make my cupboard look like a penicillin factory. Everything moulds, even plastics. I'm sure human beings would too, if they stood in the same place long enough. Mould removal is an art all its own. For shoes, there is no answer, except periodic cooking on top of a light bulb. For suits, brushing and hanging up under a fan (we have an ingenious arrangement of unbent coat-hangers for this) — produces a drawn battle over a period of time. Finally there is dry cleaning at the one cleaners left in Hanoi. The price is roughly $3.00 a suit. With all this people bit by bit write off their wardrobes. We have one poor officer in a Highland regiment who is struggling to preserve a kilt.

Occasionally the limited social life produced something of greater interest, for example the following:

> ... the same charm [of the Vietnamese] is one thing people notice in Ho Chi Minh himself, who I suppose is one of the most single-mindedly dedicated communists a colonial country has ever produced. Yet he is a friendly, gracious and cultivated man, who speaks about eight languages and has a wonderful sense of humour. I've seen him at a party, which is quite an honour, for he appears in public only on rare occasions. Although only a few Canadians have had the opportunity of speaking to him, they agree that it is easy to understand why the people feel towards "Uncle Ho" (which is what everyone calls him), the same way many Canadians feel towards "Uncle Louis". Mary Stock [administrative officer of the delegation] had a long chat with Uncle Ho at a reception only a few days after we arrived here. He just picked her out of a group and asked her to sit and chat with him. All of this surprised the Vietnamese who were present or at least the lesser lights. To them Uncle Ho is a sort of living legend, and they rarely have a chance to see him.

Periodic brief visits to South Vietnam provided a relief from the limited life of the Commission in Hanoi and revealed the extent of South Vietnam's problems as Ngo Dinh Diem took over from the French. These visits began in the autumn of 1955 and continued at intervals into the spring of 1956. This is what one team site looked like in October, 1955:

> ... Tan Chau is a seedy little port on the Cambodian border, located at the point where one of the Mekong's tributaries enters the main stream. I flew there in a Grumman Goose, a neat little four-passenger amphibian. It takes about an hour from Saigon. The French pilot made a perfect landing on the river, which is brick red, about half-a-mile to a mile wide and very swiftly flowing. Tan Chau looks like a set for "Rain", or a Conrad novel — flat paddy fields, rusting river boats, a village of bamboo huts, and a down-at-the-heel hotel. There are a few Europeans about, mainly bearded French sailors from a gunboat anchored in the river. It rains heavily every day ... the two Canadians there were quite cheerful and sane although glad to see familiar faces. We had a very good lunch with the team, which consists of a Pole, a Canadian, an Indian, a French liaison officer, a Vietnamese interpreter and two other interpreters, one Polish–French and the other Polish–English. This is a standard procedure for the Poles, who outnumber the other two delegations on every team with this dodge ...

A trip by land from Saigon down to the mouth of the Saigon River in the same month is described as follows:

> ... The most interesting part about Cap St Jacques is the trip there, since the road passes through rubber plantations, the first I had seen, and more important, through Binh Xuyen country. You may remember that there are three sects in South Vietnam, of varying sizes (up to two million) and varying degrees of respectability. The Diem government has to fight them all. The smallest and least respectable is the Binh Xuyen, who used to run the rackets in Saigon until Diem kicked them out. They are now holed up in some rough country between Saigon and the coast, and the government has to go after them with a full-scale campaign. For miles along the road there are patrols out on the verges on either side, and every few kilometres, a log and mud fort flying the National Government flag. At night the road is closed, and you can hear the whump of mortars at work. When

> we went through the driver put his foot down to the floor and didn't stop for anybody ...
>
> ... coming to Saigon [in January 1956] has been a pleasant change. There has been unlimited cheese and orange juice, and shorts-and-knee-socks weather. I've been on one excursion, down the Saigon R. to Cap St. Jacques on a French landing ship. The country we went through was all flat, dull and marshy. Up until several months ago, it was dangerous, because there were posts of the Binh Xuyen sect along the banks. These have all been cleared up, and the trip was thus quite uneventful ... Saigon, as usual, is hectic in the daytime and very expensive. At night it is becoming quieter all the time. The opium dens, gambling parlours and "dance halls" are all being closed down and the streets are very quiet by about 10 p.m. President Diem is communicating his own austerity to the place ...

Another letter records the closing of the *Palais des Glaces*, reputed at the time to be the largest brothel in Asia.

> ... Friday and Saturday [March 1956] I spent at one of the team sites on the coast, called Nha Trang. Nha Trang is a sort of Vietnamese Riviera. The mountains come down quite close to the sea and circle a large bay which is edged with wide beaches of white sand. The weather was perfect blazing heat, a powder-blue sky and an aquamarine sea—and nothing to do but lie on the sand or go swimming ...
>
> ... This morning [April 27, 1956], I was down at the port [of Saigon] again, watching the ships for half an hour after work. There was the usual complement of tramp steamers and river boats, and two big ships as well. The big French steamship line which runs passenger ships between Indochina and France is called "Messageries Maritimes", and it runs a fleet of handsome, single-funneled cream-coloured ships of about 15,000 tons. One of these, the *Cambodge*, was in harbour this morning. The other big ship was a French aircraft carrier, the *Lafayette*, which is the flagship of the French Far Eastern fleet. Admiral Jouzan, the senior French officer here, reviewed his officers on the flight deck last night. It was the last formal review before the disbanding of the French High Command, which takes place tomorrow. I noticed in the *Times* that M. Bidault, in his testimony during the official secrets trial which is now going on in Paris, said there was nothing French left in Indochina now, except the ruined Pasteur Institute and the tombstones ...

> ... Cholon [Saigon's twin Chinatown] is quiet now [May 1956] but less than a year ago it was still the headquarters of the Binh Xuyen. Their camp still exists, half disused and surrounded by rusting barbed wire strung on concrete posts. The restaurant where I ate the other night, called the Arc-en-Ciel, is the only one left I have seen that still has a grenade cage. Like a French restaurant it has a terrasse, and this is completely surrounded by a heavy grill of crisscross wire, so that people in the old days could sit outside without being hit by bombs ...
>
> ... Mr Diem disposed of the last of his enemies in the South the other day [April 1956], when Ba Cut was captured. Ba Cut was the last of the leaders of the sects, who was still in open rebellion against the government, and he was the most formidable military leader of the lot, although he is only about 35. He is a very slippery character who came to terms five times with the French. His name means "cut finger", and was given to him because he chopped off one of his own fingers as a gesture of defiance against the authorities. After months of chasing him the government's troops captured him while he slept. What a country.

Of course Ba Cut was not the last of Diem's enemies; he was simply the last of the leaders of the sects in revolt. There was still the entire army of the supporters of the North who had gone to ground in the South, whom we knew as the Vietminh and who became, during the American war, the Vietcong. Diem never did master them. In January 1964, almost eight years after those letters were written, and three months after Diem himself had fallen from power in a bloody coup, *Time* reported that "the Viet Cong still reign supreme in 13 of the country's 43 provinces".

Boredom and anxiety to leave Vietnam increasingly mark the last letters:

> ... This morning [May 9, 1956] I attended the 300th meeting of the Commission. Most of the time was spent discussing an issue which arises every few months, and which is discussed in exactly the same terms every time it does. This was the fourth time I had listened to the identical debate. Being an international civil servant is really pretty dreary — at least in Vietnam.

Then, on May 30, "Six weeks from tomorrow I leave Hanoi for ever. How sad for Uncle Ho."

And on June 13:

> ... About the same time as I leave, there will be a whole contingent of Army officers leaving courtesy of the RCAF. It will take four flights to get them all back to Canada. Just as an indication of how keen people are to get out of North Vietnam, you might be interested to know that the Army has posted a schedule on our notice board, divided into two columns. The first column is headed "Flight No. — ", and the second "Days to Go". Every day, the entry in the "Days to Go" column is reduced by one. Some people have calculated down to the hour how much longer they have to stay.

My last memory of Hanoi, which is not recorded in my letters, is of an incident that took place a few days before I left perhaps on or about July 1, 1956, because the office was closed for an official holiday. I was upstairs in my office when a request came from the Canadian guard on our door to come down and talk to a Vietnamese caller who was trying to explain something to him. I did so, to discover that this courageous and desperate visitor had learned that there were foreigners in Hanoi who helped people go South. Could we help him? I had to tell him that the days for moving South had long passed; that unfortunately we could not help him to leave; and that the longer he stayed talking to me in the lobby of the Canadian delegation, the harder it would go for him with the police when he left. Finally, he walked out into the street. A black police Citroën was parked opposite our building, waiting. The police let him get as far as the corner before they pulled over and hauled him in. I have forgotten if we protested to the authorities; if we did, we were probably told he was arrested for arson.

A few days later I left Hanoi myself. I did not return until forty-five years later, in March 2001.

* * *

The boom of the 1980s has transformed many cities in Asia. The skyscrapers, shopping malls, subways and skyways of Bangkok, Jakarta, Singapore, Kuala Lumpur and Hong Kong make Toronto's a modest entry in the competition for worldclass city.

Hanoi, too, has changed in the last generation. The highways from the airport to the city and from Hanoi to Haiphong are now, if not six lanes, at least four. Foreign investment has financed a few high-rises, including the luxurious 20-storey hotel on the Grand Lac, built by Singapore money, where my wife and I stayed in 2001. The city is several millions larger than it was 45 years ago. The streets are crowded and lively. But none of this change is on the same scale as that of other centres in Southeast Asia.

The Vietnamese economy is still subject to excessive controls, despite years of economic reform. Foreign investment is relatively limited, as the regime itself complains. For all its strengths — among them a highly educated and vigorous population and an impressive stock of natural resources — Vietnam remains a Communist country with a half-reformed economy and an unreformed political system. Rice farming, as my long-deferred trip into the countryside of North Vietnam revealed, has not changed the landscape markedly from the prospect of water buffaloes and wicker-basket irrigation I saw in 1955. The traffic in the cities is dense but it is not yet automobile traffic. The bicycles and pedicabs are still there, as they were forty-five years ago; the difference is that the young people have graduated to Honda motorbikes. Private cars are rare. Buses and trains are old and battered, trucks rusted and smoke-spewing. The system on the highways is that bicycles keep to the verges, motorcycles monopolize the slow lane, and the passing lane is reserved for trucks, buses and the few private cars.

Somewhere in this picture lies the explanation for the fact that, for example, Vietnamese rice sells for $30 a ton less than Thai rice. Even so, the Vietnam countryside is still beautiful, and Hanoi, rather than being destroyed by progress, has been preserved to a great extent as it was 50 years ago. It shows few if any signs of wartime damage. The avenues in the centre of the city look much as they did, tree-lined, with low cream or ochre buildings and only the occasional high-rise. A good deal of restoration and renovation has been done, some of it by foreign governments taking over old villas as diplomatic properties, some by entrepreneurs seeking to attract tourists.

The *Métropole Hotel* has been splendidly renovated and extended. It is now so expensive that I startled a waiter when we went there for a drink by saying I had lived in the hotel for a year; he assumed this must mean I was enormously wealthy to have afforded a room for that length of time at $300 a night. The dining room where we struggled with stringy chicken is now called the *Beaulieu* ($120 a couple; wine extra). Down the street, the *Hoa Binh Hotel*, which was also a Commission hostel in the 1950s, has been restored to its art deco state of about 1925, and houses an excellent but empty French restaurant.

The Opera House has undergone a dazzling and costly restoration. The Burmah-Shell building where we worked is now a Vietnamese ministry. There are no longer armed guards on the doors (the military presence has largely faded away from the city). I walked boldly up the stairs to my old office. Nobody had polished the handrail on the staircase for years.

The shower in the corner of the office, one of the amenities we inherited from Shell, had been replaced by a modest waiting room. The civil servants at work where I had sweated under the fans, writing briefs on Article 14(c), were mildly startled to see a foreigner appearing suddenly on their threshold. I received more respectful recognition, however, when I told the young woman in the travel agency which was organizing our excursions to the country that I had actually met Ho Chi Minh.

To her, Uncle Ho must be a near-mythical figure. For many years now, he has rested in his Lenin-style mausoleum, near the Canadian embassy. The mausoleum sits across the square from the *Cercle Sportif* where we used to swim. The *Cercle* is now closed to outsiders and reserved for deserving cadres. My wife and I lined up to pay our respects to Uncle Ho: this involves sitting through an obligatory film about his life before the visitor is allowed in to see him. We were told the mausoleum is shut every September for two months, to permit the body to be shipped to Moscow for annual maintenance. The respectful crowd was large but not overwhelming. Elsewhere, slogans and portraits of Ho are still evident, although less omnipresent than in the first hectic days of the Democratic Republic. The deification of the dead leader creates problems for all Communist countries eventually. On the whole, I thought the Vietnamese were coping with the legacy of Ho Chi Minh better than the Russians do with Lenin's or the Chinese with Mao's.

In every village there is a war memorial with the names of the dead inscribed on it. All the Democratic Republic's wars are honoured in this way. Apparently the longest lists of casualties date from the Vietnamese occupation of Cambodia. Another reminder of the past is Dienbienphu Avenue in Hanoi. General Giap, the victor of Dien Bien Phu, still alive in his eighties, is the last survivor of Ho's generation. In a sense, it was Giap's victory over the French that brought us all to

Vietnam in the first place. We were told that his back is straight, and that he still goes jogging in the gardens of the Presidential Palace.

I puzzled over what all this means to the laughing and attractive young people crowding the streets on their smart little Honda motorcycles. Sixty per cent of the population of Vietnam has been born since the end of the war with the United States. To have known the war with the French, people must be at least in their seventies. No doubt as in other countries, the old in Vietnam worry about how to keep memory of past sacrifices alive, while accusing the young of ignorance, materialism and ingratitude. The young, meanwhile, are wondering when those in charge are going to change their Honda bikes into Mercedes.

* * *

One of my mentors, the unforgettable Charles Eustace McGaughey ("McGuff"), once warned me, when I had questioned the point of some project our ambassador had assigned to us, "Go back to first principles in this business and you're lost." While I was working under orders this was sound advice. In retirement, however, there is both time and temptation to go back over the past and ask what was the point of whatever it was we were doing.

One thing that has always struck me about the Canadian experience in Vietnam is that we were not serving a clear and specific national interest. We had, as a country, no experience in Indochina, no knowledge of that part of the world, and no particular interest in acquiring any until the invitation to serve on the Commissions. Had it not been for that invitation it would probably have been a generation or more before Canada would have scraped together the resources to provide a presence on the ground even in Vietnam, let alone in Cambodia or Laos. In fact, we were not invited to serve in Indochina because of our interest, but for precisely the opposite reason, because we were thought to be disinterested. And yet Canada, in a part of the world where we had no interests, managed to acquire more experts in a few years than we had on any other area. A third of the Foreign Service of my generation served in Indochina at one time or another. It was an enormous distortion and distraction. It leaves one puzzling over the theory, popular in Pierre Trudeau's day, that foreign policy-making consists of tracing those extensions of the national interests that lie abroad, and then deploying resources as a function of the interests in order to advance them. If only it had been that simple. We could have spared ourselves all the fussing over whether we were supposed to be disinterested international civil servants or interested national ones. In fact we wouldn't have been in Indochina at all. No wonder the Canadian government had so many misgivings about agreeing to serve!

Once we were there, we probably did some good in keeping the Commissions constructively engaged and on a reasonably balanced course. Some worthwhile things were done by way of reducing the level of violence in the area in the early years, although there always was some violence. Sometimes there was a great deal of violence. In the last analysis, the Geneva machinery could not have prevented, nor did it prevent, the eventual renewal of full-blown war. The hundreds of thousands who fled North Vietnam because they did not want to live under a Communist government were spared Communist rule for twenty years, although their escape was temporary, except for those who eventually fled Vietnam entirely. Canada was of some service to its French ally in helping, along with others, to provide a respectable exit from Indochina after France's bitter defeat, as it was to be for its American ally twenty years later in similar circumstances. But these are actions for which it serves little purpose to wait for thanks.

The Canadians who served in the Commissions were left without illusions about the determination and ruthlessness of the Communist forces and the weakness of the various forces opposed to Communist rule. It was widely believed in 1954 that the cease-fire in Vietnam simply amounted to giving to Ho Chi Minh by peaceful and superficially respectable means in two years what he would have won by violence in a single year anyway, had the war continued. The survival of South Vietnam, under Ngo Dinh Diem and all his equally flawed successors, was an uncovenanted miracle for as long as it lasted. Miracle or not, a divided Vietnam was never part of the Geneva covenants. It was not surprising that the Democratic Republic of Vietnam, cheated as it believed it was of what it thought it had won at Dien Bien Phu, eventually went to war again against an opponent even more formidable than France, in order to complete its victory.

A Year in Laos
October 1956 – October 1957

J. Ross Francis

When I joined the Department of External Affairs in 1954, Canada had just agreed to membership on the International Commissions in Indochina. As an expendable bachelor I should have realized that I was likely to be asked at some point to fill one of the many staff positions there. Nevertheless, it came as a shock to be assigned as junior political advisor in Laos in 1956, not least because I was taking out an attractive fellow Foreign Service Officer, Ardath Matheson. I obviously lacked the organizational skills of a colleague in similar circumstances who proposed, was accepted and had a formal wedding, all within a week. We became engaged, but decided to keep the engagement secret in the hope (vain as it turned out) that Ardath might also be posted to Indochina or elsewhere in Asia so that we would not have to spend a year apart. The posting would have one major advantage: because all of my living expenses in Indochina would be paid by the Commission, I should be able to save a fair proportion of my salary and allowances. This would mean starting our married life on a sound financial basis. So I flew off to Laos with mixed emotions.

First, I stopped in Hong Kong to spend my tropical clothing allowance. The Chinese tailor recommended by my predecessors provided what he considered to be an appropriate wardrobe of linen suits, white dinner jacket and black trousers, long shorts, white shirts and discrete ties. Since he sold exactly the same assortment of clothes to all of us, Canadian political advisors throughout Indochina appeared to be clones. Fortunately, dress standards in Vientiane were not high. Towards the end of my posting I showed up at a diplomatic meeting wearing what by then were distinctly tatty linen trousers, a shirt left over from the night before and a black polyester tie borrowed from my Commissioner, since we were theoretically in mourning for King Haakon of Norway. As I looked around the room

I realized that, despite my scruffy state, I was one of the best dressed men there.

Once in Vientiane I reported my initial impressions in letters home. In the warm, dry late October climate the city felt like a popular beach resort but looked like nothing I had seen outside of the pages of the National Geographic. Solid French provincial buildings stood next to Buddhist temples, houses on stilts and little wooden huts. My arrival coincided with a festival of sorts, apparently intended to raise funds for the temples. Unlike most church fund raisers at home, the activities included Thai kick-boxing. I was particularly impressed by the exotic music accompanying the fights until I realized that it consisted of "Marching Through Georgia" played at double speed on the upper register of an out-of-tune clarinet. There were also boat races, conducted in pairs of enormous primitive dugouts, paddled furiously by perhaps two dozen in each. They looked quite unstable, and in fact were, as one of them sank, to the immense satisfaction of the onlookers.

I was fascinated by the crowds—the beautiful, the ugly, the young, the old, the numerous small children, some of them carrying even smaller ones, the soldiers in uniform, the *bonzes* in their orange robes. They seemed more orderly than the crowds at the Central Canada Exhibition in Ottawa. They were curious about us foreigners, but not obtrusively so. (Although when I went out in my shorts one day a small boy darted across the street to feel whether my legs were really as hairy as they looked and dashed back to report to his friends.) Unusual sights abounded. My favourite was of a man running down the main street after a mud fish which had escaped from his bicycle basket and was trying to flop its way to freedom.

Initially, I was assigned a room in a crumbling French hotel with intermittent water supply, inadequate electricity and a resident lizard. The lizard was fortunately less monstrous than the one that lived behind the portrait of Governor General Vincent Massey in our mess. I learned to turn on the tap whenever I came in, so that I could have a hasty shower and fill a pail if by any chance the water came on. Of course if I forgot to turn it off again when I left, I risked a flood, as one or two of my colleagues discovered. Later, I moved to a new but badly constructed hotel where I was lulled to sleep every night by the sound of termites chewing their way through the woodwork. At either hotel, we were bound to share our rooms with any visitors who might show up. This was easier if they came from outside Laos or from one of the team sites in the south. Officers coming down from the northern team sites tended to be like lumberjacks emerging from the woods at the end of the logging season and were much noisier companions.

The two political advisors and the two delegation secretaries became members of the army officers' mess a short walk from the hotels. We ate all of our meals there. The food prepared by a French-trained Vietnamese cook was usually quite good, and we learned to put up with water buffalo disguised as beef. Breakfast was a bit of a hazard. The cook would start our individual meals when he saw us walking towards the mess. As a result I had a cheese omelet every morning for six months. I broke the string by going on mid-term leave, and followed this with six months of toasted peanut butter and banana sandwiches. At one point our caterer threatened to cut off our supplies if his bills were not paid more promptly. I became briefly interested in the Commission's arcane financial procedures. Fortunately, the money came through on time, and we did not have to join the *bonzes* with their begging bowls on the streets of Vientiane. Apart from meals, the mess also became the centre of our social life. Having graduated only two years earlier from an Oxford college, I found the total lack of a private life less disturbing than an older officer might have done.

Our office was an informal building on stilts, with water buffalo grazing nearby and occasionally sheltering beneath us. They loved the rainy season when they could wallow in the mud which surrounded us. None of them tried to come up the stairs, but we once discovered a goat in the washroom. Neither our accommodation nor the office had air conditioning, but we learned to put up with the heat even when the temperatures rose to over 40°C. The Ottawa public service rules for closing offices when the combined temperature and humidity reached a certain level would have shut us down for weeks at a time.

Communicating with other offices in town was always an adventure. We had to go through any of four loosely interconnected telephone systems, all of which used live operators, some with only a passing knowledge of either English or French. These included the Commission's own system, staffed by Indian signalers, the French Army's, the American Embassy's and last and least the Laotian PTT.

Sending messages by hand would usually have been faster except, that in the absence of street addresses and a city map, it was difficult to tell the messengers where to go.

By the time I arrived in Laos, the Royal Laotian government and the Communist Pathet Lao had complied with the first requirement of the 1954 Agreement for the separation of forces and the consolidation of the communist troops in the two northern provinces of Phong Saly and Sam Neua. The two royal half brothers, Prince Souvanna Phouma for the government and Prince Souphanouvong for the Communists, were negotiating the terms of an agreement by which these two provinces would be reintegrated with the rest of the kingdom, the Communist forces would be absorbed into the Royal Laotian Army and a coalition government would be formed to pursue a neutral foreign policy. Although there were occasional skirmishes and considerable suspicion about North Vietnamese activities in the north east, both parties chose not to register formal complaints with the International Commission. Under the circumstances, there was little for the Commission to do except watch developments, offer unofficial encouragement and, on one occasion when it appeared the talks might be breaking down, express official concern.

Since the two parties refrained from making complaints, the Commission's Political Committee on which I served, like its sister Military Committee, had as its only formal task the preparation of the Third Interim Report on the Commission's activities. Because our activities were negligible this should have been a simple job, but it proved impossibly difficult. The Indian political advisor who chaired our committee was intelligent and fair minded, anxious to complete the draft report if only the other two delegations would agree. The Polish political advisor, however, was an unreconstructed Stalinist, loathed not only by us but by the rest of his own delegation. He would make speeches about the need for cooperation and compromise, but then insist on a completely one-sided interpretation of events. We, for our part, may have been more inclined to criticize the Pathet Lao than the Royal Laotian government, but we tried not to distort facts, at least not too blatantly. After some weeks of stalemate the Polish Commissioner came up to us at a party with what he termed good news: his political advisor had suffered a nervous breakdown and was being repatriated on medical grounds. He was succeeded by the delegation's interpreter, an intelligent man who was cooperative to the point where we wondered whether he might be jeopardizing his future in the Polish foreign service. By then, however, we unfortunately had a new Indian committee chairman whose arrogance was matched only by his stupidity and who stood in the way of completing the report even when we and the Poles were in agreement. He had been seconded from one of the domestic departments, and I could imagine the glee with which his superiors realized that by lending him to the foreign service they would be free of him for a whole year. When the Indian Commissioner finally decided that the report really must be produced before the end of his own assignment, he took the draft out of his political advisor's hands and quickly reached agreement with the Canadian and Polish Commissioners along the lines we had been advocating. (Since I might be thought to be exaggerating the Indian political advisor's incompetence, I should add that when the new Indian Commissioner arrived, he asked to borrow my services to help with his correspondence. I was surprised, but glad to help.)

My contribution to the delegation's political reporting was comparatively marginal, even after I was promoted to senior political advisor towards the end of my stay. Our Commissioner, Peter Campbell, had excellent and frequent access to Laotian ministers and other senior political leaders. They provided him with a richly detailed account of the complex political maneuvering among the elite. (They also provided more personal advice. He was particularly amused when the Minister of Health recommended the best opium den to go to when the Commissioners made a trip to Xiang Khouang in the heart of the poppy growing area.) At any normal mission (including all of those at which I subsequently served) I would have expected to support the Head of Mission by developing contacts among lower-level politicians, senior officials, professional and business leaders, academics and journalists. In Laos, however, people at this level scarcely existed. My best contact was the local *Agence France Presse* (AFP) representative whose secretary was allegedly the mistress of one of the senior ministers. He was an unrivaled source of gossip, much of it accurate. Of course like diplomats everywhere I also compared notes with colleagues from other missions. This revealed a division of opinion among the Americans, with some preferring a continued division of Laos to an agreement which would lead to a neutralist government. In retrospect, I failed to realize how influential this group was and how harmful their views would be to the future of the kingdom.

We needed all the help we could get in trying to make sense of political developments in a country where personal and family relationships were at least as important as party or policy considerations. When the government resigned in May after being defeated by a vote of 13–11 in the National Assembly, one of the ministers told us that he had been relieved to find that the Prime Minister's principal opponent, the outgoing Vice-Premier, had only eleven supporters. One of us suggested tentatively that surely the vote proved he had thirteen. Oh no, we were told, the Prime Minister's supporters voted against his policy in order to give him an excuse to resign and form a new government with a different Vice-Premier. The Vice-Premier's men therefore voted for the Prime Minister's policy in order to force him to stay in office. They lost. At one point the former Vice-Premier came within one vote of receiving National Assembly approval to form a new government. Some members of the diplomatic corps speculated that by one means or other he should be able to persuade an additional parliamentarian to support him on a second attempt. My AFP friend assured me that if he did pick up another vote, one of his previous alleged supporters would fall ill or be called unexpectedly out of town, so that he would always be one vote short. And so it proved.

After more than two months, Prince Souvanna Phouma was finally able to present a new cabinet to the National Assembly. I had the misfortune to be ushered by mistake into the VIP gallery just before he rose to speak and was obliged to remain there while he explained, at an hour's length, the policy he hoped to carry out, all in Laotian. Fortunately, I managed to obtain a copy of the French translation, which had been my reason for coming to the Assembly, so that I was able to follow what he was saying. The crisis had been fascinating while it lasted, for it gave me an opportunity to study the Laotian political system in action. I learned more about it than I had during the previous seven months, when the play of influence was hidden beneath the surface. The lengthy delay in forming a new government inevitably slowed the negotiations with the Communists. I had unrealistically hoped for an early agreement which might have led to the International Commission's adjournment. This would probably not have led to my early return to Ottawa and my fiancée, but might have meant a transfer to the Vietnam Commission, which was far more active than ours.

At one point we received a message from the Canadian UN delegation asking why, if the Laotian government was working towards a neutral foreign policy, their representative in New York was the only member of the Afro–Asian group to vote with the French against a resolution condemning their policy in Algeria. We explained that the representative was a member of the opposition who had agreed to leave town for a while in return, presumably, for a generous expense allowance. We doubted that he received instructions on how to vote, or would have followed them in any case. He obviously felt free to cast his vote in any way which he considered to be to his personal or political advantage.

I contributed what little economic reporting the mission attempted. I vividly recall a meeting with the Laotian director of economic planning, at which he vigorously contested the view that Laos, in the vocabulary of the time, was an underdeveloped country. Holding his hands at chest level, he said this represented the developed countries. Underdeveloped countries came up to his knee caps. But Laos, he said, pointing to the floor, was not developed at all. He had a point. Apart from whatever money came into the country from smuggling opium, Laos derived its foreign exchange almost solely from foreign aid, principally American money intended to bolster the Laotian armed forces. The most visible results of this injection of funds were the Mercedes parked beside or underneath the houses of influential politicians and army officers, symbols of prestige and influence rather than of any practical utility since there were virtually no roads. The Americans also ran a token program of rural assistance, but the projects, although interesting to visit, were on too limited a scale to win the hearts and minds of the average Laotian, at whom they were directed. I reported that "conditions in villages immediately within walking distance of Vientiane are extremely primitive and in the more remote parts of the country the standards of sanitation and hygiene and the working methods must be much the same as those prevailing centuries ago."

I also ran a small Colombo Plan program. My first attempt to acquaint the Laotian government with the Canadian scholarship program, in a note carefully composed in French with the aid of my francophone secretary and a major from the Van Doos, led to a phone call from a French advisor asking whether I would mind resubmitting it. Was it unintelligible or had I made errors? No, he replied, but it didn't sound really French. With his help I rewrote it to conform with proper French bureaucratic jargon. I was less surprised, when the Laotians nominated appropriate candidates, to find that I had to get their school records from the French Embassy. We provided a technical expert from Quebec to help set up a small saw mill. (One of my first unusual sights in Vientiane was of two men sawing planks by hand, looking like figures from a nineteenth-century Japanese print.) A French advisor to the appropriate ministry told me in a rather condescending manner that our expert was very popular with the mill's employees because he was actually helping them operate the machinery — not something, I was given to understand, that a true Frenchman would have done.

Unlike our colleagues in Vietnam, we did not have enough work to fill up our days, let alone our evenings. This left us plenty of time for exercise. We played tennis and badminton. We swam in the Mekong, choosing a beach up-stream from the city in the hope that it would be marginally less filthy. We were not worried about picking up diseases — no germs could have lived in such dirty water. We walked for miles in town and the surrounding countryside. We had a horseshoe pitch (if you count that as exercise). The Commissioner forgot one day that he was to receive a formal call from the newly-arrived Indian Ambassador. When the Rajah of Khetri showed up he was surprised to see the Commissioner in shorts and sandals playing horseshoes with his driver.

Judging from my letters home, what we really did was party. We celebrated every national day and any religious or secular holiday we could think of, with Christmas and New Year's Eve as highlights. We gave parties to welcome new arrivals, see off departing friends or console any who were staying. The army officers organized formal mess dinners at which the civilians wore dinner jackets, the military wore their formal mess kit and we ate multi-course meals with appropriate wines — followed by very physical games of floor hockey. As he limped away from one of these occasions, the Indian Commissioner told me that he could understand parties where you dressed up and parties where you played games, but he would never be reconciled to parties where you did both.

On a more regular basis we held buffet dinners to which we invited friends for food and films, usually old movies which had been playing the Far Eastern circuit for years, but occasionally new Hollywood musicals. Sometimes we had special occasions, such as the ball which our Commissioner organized for Minister Paul Martin Sr. and his wife when they passed through Laos on their way to a Colombo Plan conference. At one of the parties, our Commissioner accidentally locked himself in the upstairs bathroom. He stood on the toilet seat and shouted and waved out the window to the mess staff in the courtyard below. Always cheerful, they shouted and waved back. We, of course, could not hear him down below. It took about half an hour before anyone realized there was something wrong and went to his rescue. This incident became part of delegation folklore, celebrated in story and song.

Our serving staff were not too efficient or perhaps they themselves entered the spirit of the parties too freely. On one occasion the American Counsellor's wife had two separate trays of drinks dropped on her. She came to our next party wearing a plastic raincoat, just in case. Fortunately, she had a sense of humour. She told me that she was having a shower one day when she noticed a Laotian staring through the window at her. What really upset her, she said, was that he didn't look very interested.

As our own first attempt at organizing a diplomatic reception, my secretary, Janine Caron, and I had three dozen people in for drinks in honour of the senior political advisor, Jim Langley, when he left for Canada just before Christmas. I felt quite grand, snapping my fingers at the staff and having them open more champagne. We then all charged out to the airport, only to discover his plane being taken apart by rather dubious-looking mechanics, who seemed to be arguing about how to put it back together. The party which had been planning to see him on to the plane by singing "For He's A Jolly Good Fellow" slowly evaporated as people returned to their families for lunch. With one or two others I stayed to the end, when the plane was finally put back together with Scotch tape and baling wire and headed shakily off towards Bangkok. We were relieved to learn that he eventually arrived back in Canada.

One of the pleasanter parties I attended was a picnic given by the American Ambassador for his daughter. He hired a boat and took about twenty of the younger diplomats several miles up the Mekong to the mouth of a little stream which flows into it. There we found an attractive waterfall and pools of cool clean water to swim in. I was fortunate to miss a British party which tried to build on this success. Their expedition went down-stream from Vientiane instead of up, so that when the boat's motor broke down the party were drifting away from the city instead of towards it. I was told by members of the party that they wondered whether they might reach Saigon.

The Polish delegation were as keen party-goers as we were. They appeared to have a natural ability to sing traditional Polish songs in four-part harmony. They put our delegation's feeble off-key attempts at "Alouette" or "Vive la Canadienne" to shame. Except for the senior political advisor, they became noticeably closer to us during the period when it appeared that the Soviet Army might intervene in Poland as it had in Hungary. One evening I noticed that one of their secretaries had been left behind at a party after all but the Polish Commissioner had gone back to their quarters. When I offered to walk her home I was surprised to have him wink at me. He had come to us with a reputation as a hard liner from a previous posting as political advisor in Vietnam, but had apparently mellowed in the different atmosphere of Laos. At the reception he gave for his National Day, one of the Polish captains slugged him, but this appeared to be the result of general joie de vivre rather than real animosity, and the officer was quickly hustled out of harm's way by his Canadian friends. Thirty years later I unexpectedly ran into the former Commissioner at a conference in Helsinki, where he was representing a Norwegian peace studies institute. We fell into one another's arms and reminisced about Laos, but I never did learn how he had developed a Norwegian connection.

On evenings when there was no organized party several of us might go to one or other of the rather seedy local night clubs, where our two secretaries were much in demand as dancing partners. When one of the Polish secretaries enquired how she had been chosen to serve on the delegation, my secretary claimed she had simply been asked whether she could dance and whether she enjoyed parties. When we took a newly arrived secretary, Jean Smith, dancing on her first evening in Vientiane she assured me that she also knew how to take shorthand and type. The favourite local tunes appeared to be "Rock Around the Clock" and "Jingle Bells", but I also learned to dance the *Bal Musette* and the *Lam Vong*, a graceful Laotian dance in which partners do not touch but there is much graceful waving of arms. I had never considered this a possible life skill, but I was a hit years later in Malaysia when I danced it with a Laotian group who showed up at a conference organized by one of the universities.

In the spring there were two occasions when the whole of Vientiane became a giant party. For three days, at Laotian New Year, it was hardly safe on the street, since everyone was throwing water at everyone else, from small children with water pistols to soldiers on fire trucks. Pretty girls were, of course, the principal targets, but anyone else was fair game. On the first day our Brigadier started off for his usual walk from the office to the mess. We warned him that he would get soaked, but he assured us that anyone who was well dressed and looked determined would be spared. When he arrived at the mess sopping wet he told us that at least the soldiers had saluted and called him "Sir" before emptying buckets over his head. On the second day, having had enough of being a target, I joined in and, armed with a jerry can, shared a station on the top gallery of the hotel, soaking those who passed beneath. The third day, although a Monday, we all gave up and took off for the river with our bathing suits to immerse ourselves at the source.

A few weeks later we had the fertility festival, about which various stories had circulated through the Department in Ottawa. The first event was more of an Arbour Day. We followed about 100–200 orange-robed *bonzes* to the largest *That* ('monument') in Vientiane for the most confused tree planting I had ever attended, before adjourning to the mess for brunch. The next day was more lively. A rocket-launching platform had been built on the edge of the Mekong — a shaky affair of bamboo about 40 feet high. Numerous societies had made rockets, elaborately constructed and painted to resemble dragons or other mythical beasts, some more than 20 feet long. These were paraded to a position near the platform where they stood in long ranks to be admired. Throughout the afternoon and evening they were fastened to the platform and touched off, some to fizzle out immediately but the majority of them to take off with a reassuring swoosh and a few actually to reach Thailand across the river. The successful ones would prompt the launchers, including those at the top of the platform, to break into informal drunken jigs. Considering the fire, the explosions and the height of the platform,

I was not sure why no one was killed. However, I was not there all day, and perhaps someone was.

But stories about the rockets were not what had produced the snickers back in the departmental cafeteria in Ottawa. The festival got its renown from the groups of men who wandered, dancing, drunkenly through the crowd. In groups of about eight, many costumed and painted, some as women, all of them sloshed to the eyeballs, they staggered along the river front, banging on drums or old kerosene tins and blowing reed pipes. They sang in leader and chorus fashion what were undoubtedly obscene songs and were probably impromptu. (When I walked by one group with one of our secretaries they were obviously singing about us, judging from their expressions and the word "American" which I caught.) They carried or wore a most surprising assortment of obscene objects: phallic symbols of all descriptions, pornographic photographs and drawings, and animated models of men and women bobbing up and down in assorted poses—immediately dubbed training aids by my military colleagues. All of this was taken as a huge joke by everyone, including *bonzes*, venerable ladies, small children and (fortunately) Canadian secretaries. I gave a rapid tour by jeep to a Canadian who came in from the airport between planes. He asked what was going on in the tents along the river. You can imagine, I said. Evidently he could, as his eyes lit up. I didn't have the heart to tell him that they just housed games of chance, played for very low stakes.

As basically an overgrown village, Vientiane was understandably a cultural backwater by either Western or Asian standards. We did enjoy a mini-festival sponsored by the Thai Embassy. This included a splendid dance group which made the Laotian court's dancers seem very provincial. A talented theatre company managed to overcome the language barrier, with the comedians a particular success. With the arrival on our delegation of a future Canadian Commissioner of Official Languages, D'Iberville Fortier, we ourselves began a program of play readings in both English and French. I was allowed to take minor roles in English, but was encouraged to specialize during the French evenings in passing drinks and applauding the others.

I visited colleagues in Hanoi, Saigon and Phnom Penh on the Commission courier plane. In Phnom Penh my colleague, Lois Hill, took me with her to an American party. There I told our host how much I enjoyed the city: it had attractive buildings and parks, lots of things to do, interesting shops, excellent food. Where the hell did he come from, my colleague was asked. Her answer — "Vientiane" — explained everything.

Of more direct relevance to the work of our own Commission, I also visited the military officers at several of the team sites scattered about Laos. Since they were never asked to conduct the investigations for which the teams had been set up, they had even less work to do than those of us in Vientiane. They therefore welcomed visitors, especially those prepared to help with the cooking, join them in games and listen to their stories. The most exotic of the sites was Communist-controlled Sam Neua in the mountains bordering North Vietnam. I flew there in a *Dragon*, a little pre-war twin-engined biplane. This inevitably conjured up visions of the adventures of Saint-Exupéry, as we descended through the mountains to the valley and landed on a runway which had been badly damaged during the war and left unrepaired. My major activity for the weekend was walking up to Houei Thao, where Sam Neua had a sub-team, staffed by officers alternating a week at a time. Three years previously the Laotian Army had dropped a parachute company on this mountain top in the heart of Pathet Lao territory and there they still were. Their numbers had been reduced by gunfire, mines and disease, but the remainder had clung to the position, supplied by air and determined to remain, more for reasons of pride than of military strategy. The Commission team was present to ensure that the post, which was entitled to be there under the terms of the cease-fire agreement, would not be removed by force. When I came back down that evening, I attended a party for the Indian colonel who was about to return to Vientiane.

The next day the Colonel and I walked to the airfield, along with most of the other team members and waited for the plane. There was a strong wind blowing up the valley, and to our horror the pilot was unable to put down on the truncated runway in time. He attempted to pull up in order to circle around and try again. He failed to gain enough altitude and crashed into one of the mountains surrounding the airfield. He and his two passengers, the incoming Indian colonel and a French military helicopter crew member, were killed instantly. I flew back to Vientiane in an *Otter* aircraft with the three bodies. Over the next few days, I attended the cremation of the

Indian colonel, an airport ceremony for the helicopter crew member whose body was being flown back to France and a funeral mass for the pilot. I was acutely conscious of how lucky I was that the accident had not happened on the previous flight with me on board.

I left Vientiane to return to Canada a year and a day after my departure, to marry Ardath and proceed to our first posting together in South Africa. (There I met our editor, Arthur Blanchette, and was able to brief him on living conditions in Indochina when he was unexpectedly cross-posted to Phnom Penh.) Shortly after I left. Prince Souvanna Phouma finally reached agreement with his half brother and formed a coalition government with Prince Souphanouvong as Minister for Planning, Reconstruction and Urbanism and another Communist leader in the even less plausible role of Minister for Religion and Culture. The Commission agreed to adjourn *sine* die a few months later. Unfortunately, this did not prove to be the end of the country's problems. With CIA encouragement, a group of army officers, supported by conservative forces from southern Laos, set out to destabilize the coalition government and after some skirmishing toppled it in a coup. Fighting escalated and eventually led to a major confrontation between the United States and the Soviet Union. A second Geneva conference resulted in the restoration of a neutral coalition government, again under Prince Souvanna Phouma, and renewed the mandate of the International Commission. The new coalition was even weaker than the one established in 1957, and was completely unable to resist North Vietnam's use of Laotian territory to send supplies and troops to South Vietnam along the so-called Ho Chi Minh Trail. In a vain attempt to block the trail, the United States dropped more bombs on Eastern Laos than it had on Germany during the whole of the Second World War. When South Vietnam finally fell to the Communists in 1975, Laos followed within days. Our work on the Commission in Laos seemed even more futile in retrospect than it had appeared at the time.

* * *

For my family, there is a postscript. Forty years after I left Vientiane, my son Charles, aided by his wife and accompanied by his then seven-year-old daughter, went to Laos to conduct a survey of bats and other small mammals in eastern Laos on behalf of the Wildlife Conservation Society. To make up for missing school, our granddaughter kept a diary of their activities. From her we learned that several children in the village where they were staying had been severely injured when one of the many millions of cluster bombs dropped by the Americans years before had blown up. The fighting which the International Commission had been powerless to prevent was continuing to claim innocent victims many decades later.

÷ ÷ ÷ ÷ ÷

The Best of Times and The Worst of Times

May 1958 – June 1959

Roy MacLaren, P.C.

It was, to quote Dickens, the best of times and the worst of times. It was the best of times for someone who, not nine months before, had joined the Department of External Affairs as a probationary Foreign Service Officer. It was not that Saigon was an unknown destination. The French Indochina war and Canada's subsequent participation in the tripartite International Commission for Supervision and Control ensured that every school child in 1958 knew where the newly minted—and divided—Vietnam was. Rather, it was that, brimming with the peculiar Canadian idealism of peacekeeping, well established at Suez and earlier still in Kashmir, the aspirant diplomat was going to where all good—and bachelor—young Canadian Foreign Service Officers went. And what an initial posting it was! Graham Greene in *The Quiet American* had foretold something of what awaited in the divided Vietnam: a tropical former French colony, full of colour in bright sunlight, when not monsoon-drenched, and exoticism of a bewildering variety, animal, vegetable and mineral.

But it was also the worst of times. By 1958, a mere four years after the fragile Geneva Agreements which, following the French defeat at Dien Bien Phu, had ended the long agony of the Indochina war, it had become increasingly evident that few really wanted the agreement to succeed. Certainly no-one envisaged that free elections throughout Vietnam leading to reunification (as provided for in the Geneva Agreement) would be held in the foreseeable future. And no-one believed that the United States was not going to do everything to advance its puppet, South Vietnam, while China and the Soviet Union were variously promoting North Vietnam.

A "demilitarized zone" (DMZ) separated the two hostile parts, but just behind the DMZ, South Vietnamese troops, trained and counseled by the U.S. Military Assistance Advisory Group, were no great distance from the heavily-armed units of North Vietnam, complete with their Communist bloc advisors. It was, in short, a vulnerable truce, rendered even more so by the widespread conviction that both sides were clandestinely introducing yet more modern weaponry, in contravention of the Geneva Agreements. And the dispiriting conviction had taken firm hold in the Commissions that they could do little or nothing about arms violations or indeed much else.

One part of the difficulty was that the United States, while endorsing the Geneva Agreements, was not a signatory to them (that dubious distinction having been left to France and China and, less relevantly, to Britain and the Soviet Union). A second problem was the tripartite Control and Supervision Commission set-up itself. It was, to paraphrase the cliché about the Holy Roman Empire, neither controlling nor supervisory nor a commission. The root cause was that neither side in the Cold War wanted the Commissions to succeed (other than possibly a post-colonial, war-exhausted Britain). We on the ground could toil as we wanted, but the Commissions would clearly go nowhere and reunification recede into never-never land unless the so-called great powers agreed upon what the future of Indochina should be. Even the three nations composing the Commissions, India, Canada and Poland, consciously or unconsciously, saw themselves or were at least seen by others in conflicting roles: the Indians piously neutral, the Poles representing the Communist East and the Canadians as surrogates of the West. One result was that the three delegations were frequently working at cross-purposes, effectively paralyzing Commission work (although the Canadians and Poles did agree on at least one thing: a mutual dislike of the Indians).

The Commission in Vietnam, both at its headquarters (recently moved to Saigon from Hanoi) and at the distant sites of its military observer teams, continued to go through the motions. Petitions alleging abuse of human rights (then still something of a novel term) or DMZ border violations or the illegal entry of modern arms abounded. Although they were all solemnly recorded, the puppet governments of both North and South Vietnam ensured that in every case they were either stillborn or aborted.

Yet it was also the best of times. Having made a seemingly endless and noisy flight from Vancouver on a Canadian Pacific Airlines propeller-driven DC-6 via the Aleutians (craning to see where the Japanese had invaded North America), and eventually to Tokyo and Hong Kong, I was deposited in all my Hong Kong tropical finery in what was still essentially a French military airfield, proximate to the novel stench and steam heat of Saigon. I spent the first few months of my year in Vietnam (1958–1959) in Saigon, living in the well-shuttered prewar *Continental Hotel*, sometimes doing no more in the enervating heat than lying naked on my back within my mosquito net watching the overhead fan slowly rotating and the geckoes moving about the high white ceiling, seeking an unwary insect.

On weekdays I would be in no less heat, although more fully clothed, at the headquarters of the Canadian delegation, housed with the Polish and Indian delegations in the small former French army camp near the centre of ever-restless Saigon (appropriately named the *Camp des Mares*). Whether attempting to carry out my ill-defined duties at the Commission headquarters achieved more than observing the industry of the geckoes at the *Continental Hotel* is a moot point.

I spent part of my time on non-Commission work, trying without much success to determine what South Vietnam might want or require from our proffered development assistance (administered then by the External Aid Office). Replete as it already was with consumer if not productive goods, the motor scooters clogging its streets, Saigon attested most visibly to the seemingly endless U.S. largesse.

The remainder of my time I spent attempting to make head or tail of various allegations reaching the Commission headquarters of supposed abuses of the Geneva Agreements (abuses that always somehow achieved a remarkable balance between North and South). Although invariably frustrated and impatient at the charade, I was not in fact surprised at the futility of what I was doing. The scant formal briefing that I had received before leaving Ottawa in May 1958 (eight months after joining the Department) had vainly attempted to mask that basic futility, but the Indochina veterans whom I had met were also both cynical and angry about the uselessness of it all, consoling themselves at best with the doubtful supposition that, without the ICSC in place, North and South might be going at it hammer and tongs (assuming that the United States or China–the USSR authorized them to do so).

In any event, farewell the well-stocked French restaurants and bars and the more distant beaches of Saigon, the endless urban bustle and the companionship of junior Western diplomats. Greetings to the austerities of the decidely more temperate Hanoi. I soon found that, despite scrawny chicken, rice and small bananas three times a day, I welcomed my transfer to the North as the temporary head of the small Canadian delegation office in the former Burmah-Shell office building, with an army captain and a corporal's guard supporting me in my new do-nothing role. The austerities of Hanoi, underpinned by the grim Communist earnestness of the true believer, was at least orderly if wholly repressive, but as long as one was not on the receiving end, it was decidedly more tranquil than the non-stop artificiality of President Diem's raucous Saigon — sometimes likened to being in a nightclub twenty-four hours a day.

Ho Chi Minh and the more ubiquitous General Giap were also austere enough, although an occasional glass of chilled champagne at the Swedish or British consulates or even more so at the ambiguously designated French Commission seemed to go down well enough. From time to time I saw something of both Ho and Giap at receptions, although I had at first wondered if I would ever be invited back when I, upon my initial introduction to Ho, carelessly grasped his tiny claw-like hand in a vise-like grip. Certainly I saw more of them and their colleagues than I ever did of President Diem (and his notorious brothers and sister-in-law in the South). But whatever the level of contact with North Vietnamese officials, little or nothing was ever forthcoming of any relevance to a truce commission, nothing but bland assurances that the North consistently behaved in an exemplary fashion in the face of "endless provocations from lickspittle American lackeys in a belligerent South".[1] Accordingly, I set out on various perambulations, strolling along the sylvan but

---

[1] The surveillance to which we were endlessly subjected (Indians and Poles as well as Canadians, both in the North and South) was forty years later to have a sequel. During a 1996 official visit to Hanoi, Prime Minister Chrétien introduced me, his Minister of International Trade, to Le Duc Anh, the President of the Socialist Republic of Vietnam, and Do Muoi, the Secretary-General of the Vietnamese Communist Party and long-time comrade-in-arms of General Giap. Chrétien referred to my service with ICSC almost four decades before. Le responded, to my surprise, that I was widely known as a "vrai ami du Vietnam", substantiating his intended compliment

heavily guarded Chinese border with the local ICSC team, idly contemplating my recent sojourn at Cambridge and revelling in my vivid recollections of the relentless slanging matches of C.S. Lewis and F.R. Leavis and their perfervid acolytes of less than a year before. From Haiphong, a dilapidated Commission launch would carry me northward among the cormorant-equipped fishing junks and the conical islands of the hauntingly beautiful Baie d'Along.

Having completed several months as the commanding officer of my corporal's guard in Hanoi, I returned to Saigon on one of *Aigle Azur*'s C-47 Commando planes, the single air link between North and South Vietnam — for Commission members only. Raffish French veteran pilots shuttled us, in our bucket seats, among Saigon, Phnom Penh, Vientiane and Hanoi.

Awaiting my return to Saigon was an invitation from the Canadian Commissioner of the day, that affable ex-gunner Tom Carter, to reside with him in the Commissioner's modest French Riviera-style villa near the *Camp des Mares*. For my repose, there awaited me the bloodstained bed-frame in which Lucien ("Brodie") Canon had been murdered some little time before, plus a pack of the most surly domestic servants on which eyes had unfortunately ever clapped. Consolation was, however, in abundance in the presence of Lee Mitchell, a Third Secretary at the sprawling U.S. Embassy, whom I had first met — and adored — before departing for Hanoi. Her sparkling new white Thunderbird took us to the deserted beaches near Cap St. Jacques. In that pressure cooker heat we accomplished one thing above all else: Lee and I agreed to marry in London upon completion of her pending tour in Washington and mine in Vietnam.

Following Lee's departure for Washington, everything else became anti-climatic. The frenetic Saigon became strangely lonely. The regiments of chirply little ladies of the night along the rue Catinat — their *ao dai*s cut to their armpits — might have provided some light diversion, but I left their several ministrations to our military, mostly well-weathered veterans of the Second World War, and instead concentrated my final months on the then largely intact Angkor Wat, Luang Prabang, the hill stations of Cochin, and beyond to the still-British Singapore, Hong Kong and Kuala Lumpur.

---

by readily reading from what was clearly the 1958 dossier of the North Vietnamese intelligence service about one Roy MacLaren.

Back quickly to Ottawa in June 1959 (with a mandatory side trip to the Montreal Tropical Medicine Institute to ensure I was not unduly infested with intestinal parasites, hepatitis or other more social afflictions), only to be greeted by several colleagues in the Department who kindly enquired whether I had been away. Certainly no-one — other than John Holmes — was interested in what I thought of the whole Indochina show. But who cared?

Lee would soon meet me at the altar of Holy Trinity, Brompton Road, in London. Prague, our next posting, awaited with another variety of Communism, more sophisticated perhaps, but no less baleful for that. But Prague is another tale.

Vietnam had proven to be a story of both futility and instruction in an exotic and profoundly alien land, of *Wanderlust* in the best and worst of times.

÷ ÷ ÷ ÷ ÷

Life Along the Mekong

June 1958 – August 1959

Arthur E. Blanchette

I have smoked only once in my life and that was opium, along the banks of the Mekong, in Phnom Penh in 1959.

The French Ambassador had been informed that the *Restaurant Rajah*, in which Prince Sihanouk had a personal interest (he enjoyed good food and wine), had just received a shipment of prime, well-aged, beef from France along with a selection of choice cheeses.

So, he decided to invite the Australian Ambassador and me out for what he called a bachelor evening. Both their wives were absent and I was alone, since External Affairs did not allow wives to accompany their husbands to Indochina at the time (it was only during the early 1960s, as the pool of available personnel dwindled, that families were sent out).

My French colleague was probably the best informed diplomat in Phnom Penh. He had been there a long time, having been seconded from the French colonial service to the Palace and royal household where he had served Sihanouk for many years. When Cambodia became independent, he was appointed ambassador to the new country. He knew all the ins and outs of the situation. His information about the culinary and other aspects of life in Phnom Penh thus tended to be accurate. This would therefore be an invitation well worth taking advantage of. I accordingly accepted with alacrity, without however knowing just how he defined a "bachelor" evening. I was soon to learn.

After a superb meal of perfectly prepared and served *châteaubriands*, accompanied by some excellent red wine, topped off with a selection of fine cheeses and some surprisingly good coffee, which was not a strong point in Phnom Penh at the time, the three of us were all feeling at ease with life and the world.

It was at this point that his definition of a "bachelor" evening became somewhat clearer. "Chers amis! On ne peut terminer une belle soirée de la sorte sans une visite chez Mme Chaum."

My Australian friend looked at me. I looked at him. We both looked at our host. What was this all about? Was he inviting us to a high-class bordello? He noticed our quizzical looks and immediately reassured us. "Ne vous inquiétez pas, mes amis. Ce sera tout à fait correct. Tout ira très bien."

So, off we went to Mme Chaum's. We eventually reached a fine villa with a nice garden in the suburbs of Phnom Penh. It was very quiet and also rather dark inside. We went in and I remember being struck by a wave of heavy smoke that I did not recognize. We were in a *Salon de désintoxication*. In theory, opium addicts could come to these establishments in order to detoxify themselves, to ease themselves slowly out of their bad habits.

Mme Chaum recognized our host and received us warmly. She was a middle-aged Eurasian, somewhat stout, who in smooth and elegant French, invited us in. The atmosphere was rather opaque and fuzzy. The villa had been divided into a number of cubicles of varying sizes, equipped with comfortable low couches. To these cubicles were assigned a bevy of lovely Vietnamese girls, so graceful in their long silken *ao dais*. Their role was to prepare and serve the pipes that the reclining clients were smoking. These were mainly Chinese locals, along with a few Europeans, some Vietnamese, and the odd Cambodian. The girls were lovely, but there was absolutely no hanky-panky going on: opium smoking is a serious business.

Escorted to a rather large room, we were asked to lie down comfortably, relax, think pleasant thoughts, and generally take it easy, which I did. The girls brought us pipes, all prepared, and ready to be smoked.

Our host clearly knew the drill. My friend from Canberra and I were instructed to inhale slowly and deeply. He was a cigarette smoker and enjoyed the occasional cigar. So inhalation for him was no big deal. But for me? I honestly did not know what would happen. I had never smoked anything up to that point, let alone opium! However, not wanting to embarrass my friends by a refusal, I followed my instructions.

The results soon came up, quite literally. After the third or fourth deep puff, my whole fine supper emerged! The girls screamed and giggled about the mess on the couch and the floor. Mme Chaum was tolerant, but clearly not amused. My French colleague had a somewhat pained look on his face, while I got some sympathetic, but rather wry, smiles from my Australian friend. As for me, all I wanted to do was to get out of there fast, which I did. For some time thereafter I was the butt of some sly, but generally well-meaning, jokes.

Clearly, these Confessions of an Opium Eater are not in de Quincey's or Coleridge's class.

* * *

Life, on the whole, was rather placid in Cambodia when I was there in the late 1950s. Phnom Penh was quiet. The countryside was generally serene except for some internal uneasiness in the northwestern areas, where the *Khmer rouge* movement was just beginning to be heard of. The roads, built by the French, were tolerable and I was able to visit Angkor Wat by car quite readily on a number of occasions. During one of these visits, I remember climbing about the ruins with the German actor, Kurt Jurgens, who was there with a girlfriend. He and I had the great monuments pretty much to ourselves.

It was also possible to drive to Saigon on quite good roads at the time and to move peacefully about South Vietnam as well. Saigon was a large, lively, sophisticated, city compared to Phnom Penh. The French had obviously put a good deal of thought and effort into its development. I would look forward to visits there. In particular, the beaches at Cap St. Jacques, south of Saigon, could be reached quite readily. They were much better than those around Kampong Som or Kep in Cambodia and in addition had good restaurants and hotels.

It was during one of my visits to Saigon that I picked up the following delightful description of the differing traits, characters, and outlooks of the three peoples who share the Indochinese peninsula.

> The Vietnamese plant the rice; the Cambodians watch it grow; the Laotians listen to it grow; and the Vietnamese harvest the rice!

France had granted independence to Cambodia in 1953. Not long thereafter, Prince Sihanouk abandoned the kingship in favour of his father, Norodom Suramarit, and founded a political movement of his own — the Sangkum party. It easily won the general elections held in 1955 that had been called for by the Geneva Conference and he became Prime Minister of Cambodia.

He ran a tight ship when I was there. Cambodia was peaceful and its economy was developing slowly but steadily. By 1958, the Commission had accomplished the mandate given to it at Geneva, but Prince Sihanouk was determined to keep it in place. He viewed it as a form of protection against outside intervention. Ottawa was reluctant about this, but went along. However, it did reduce the size of the Canadian delegation; Poland did likewise, and so too did India (but its delegation and secretariat still remained by far the largest of the three).

This situation of peace and tranquillity was to deteriorate sharply some ten years later, when fighting between North Vietnamese/Vietcong forces and those of the United States/South Vietnam spilled over into Cambodia's eastern border zones. As hostilities intensified, Prince Sihanouk sought vigorously to defend his country's neutrality against growing outside interference. He was ousted in 1970 following a coup d'état organized by Cambodian army officers, led by General Lon Nol, who had been aided and abetted by the Americans. Prince Sihanouk sought refuge in Beijing, where he lived for a number of years and whence he supported the *Khmer rouge* movement in opposition to Lon Nol. When the United States withdrew from Indochina in the mid-1970s, the Lon Nol government fell and was followed by the horrendous *Khmer rouge*/Pol Pot regime. Meanwhile, Prince Sihanouk had returned to Phnom Penh, where he managed to survive the Pol Pot years confined incommunicado in the Palace. When Pol Pot in turn was ousted, the wheel of Sihanouk's fate came full circle — he became King of Cambodia again!

When I was in Phnom Penh in the late 1950s, conditions were calm and peaceful. There was relatively little strictly Commission work to be done. We usually met about once each month. It was during these rather sporadic meetings and my frequent personal contacts with the Indians and the Poles that I got an insight into their work habits, outlooks, and mindsets. (My previous postings had been in Mexico, Egypt, and South Africa.)

Canadians serving on the Commissions fully expected the Poles to be intransigent and rigid in their support of North Vietnam. For instance, not once when I was in Phnom Penh did they take a neutral or even mildly anti-North Vietnam stand. Nevertheless, I found that they tended to approach questions, to justify their positions, in terms of logic and thinking processes that were essentially Western. Also their daily lives, their general deportment, their dress, reflected Western patterns and practices. I, for one, found them to be much more like us than I had expected.

My Polish opposite number, Michalski, took some pride in proclaiming himself to be an old Socialist, not a Communist. He spoke excellent French, but no English. He was a minister in rank and close to retirement. His staff was roughly a generation younger. Many were not Communists at all but devout Catholics, particularly the secretaries and interpreters, who went to mass and took Communion regularly at the Catholic cathedral near the *Hôtel Le Royal* where many ICSC personnel were lodged. In age I was somewhere in between Michalski and his staff, but rather closer to the staff's.

Not long after my arrival, both he and his staff began to approach me about personnel matters and office problems affecting their delegation. Administratively, the Poles (at least those in Phnom Penh when I was there) tended to run their delegation somewhat like ours, but rather more stiffly. Neither he nor his staff got along very well together, probably owing to age differences and divergent outlooks on life generally. Perhaps even for underlying religious reasons? In any event, both sides soon began to approach me and ask that I intervene on their behalf with the other in order to try to improve things! This went on for several weeks, particularly on the staff side. Where they got the idea that I was a whiz at personnel administration, I do not know. I knew no Polish, but we all spoke French, so perhaps it was a question of language? In any event, their problems were none of my business. While Warsaw might have been able to solve some of them, if it so wished, there was nothing that I could do even if I had wanted to. So I refused quite emphatically to become involved in their affairs and eventually they stopped asking me. Nevertheless, these approaches left me rather puzzled. I often wondered why this had happened and whether my predecessors had been so approached. I was never able to find out. One of the Polish staff was a very pretty blonde. Was all this a devious way to try to compromise me?

As for the Indians whom I came across in Indochina, I found their thought processes and their way of approaching things to be quite different from what I had expected. They tended to deal with Commission business more convolutedly, more indirectly. This doubtless reflected the complexity of their long historical connection with the peninsula and also its importance as a facet of their regional interests. Also, it probably derived from the way in which they had been brought up to approach questions, to solve problems generally.

In addition, caught between the Canadians and the Poles on the Commissions, the Indians would sometimes agree with them and sometimes with us. However, as ICSC Cambodia was on the whole generally inactive and quiet, we did not experience the persistent tensions experienced in the other Commissions.

Our chair — Major General Ghanshyam Singh — was a career officer in the Indian Army and close to retirement. I sometimes wondered what fate had befallen him; clearly, a major general was far too high a rank for the size and work of our Commission.

He was a decent chairman, who moved things along reasonably well when there were things to be moved along. Despite the gap in our ages and in our professional ranks, we got along very well together and I rather liked him.

As for his dealings with his fellow Indians on the Commission, that was quite another matter. With them he tended to speak only to God. The following incident is a fairly good example. One morning during a Commission meeting, he needed a file. "Subahdar!", he shouted towards the next office. "Get me file number such-and-such!" The subhadar came in, clicked his heels sharply, saluted smartly, got down on his knees, opened the right bottom drawer of the desk behind which our chair was seated, drew the file, stood up, placed it on the desk, saluted smartly again, and said: "Sar! (sic). File number such-and-such". He did not even get a nod of recognition or a thank-you. Almost simultaneously, my Polish colleague looked at me and I looked at him while all this was going on. We both raised our eyebrows and stared at the ceiling, while struggling to keep our faces straight! Our chair looked at the two of us with no little puzzlement as we proceeded to study file number such-and-such.

Thus I, for one, found that, on balance, despite our sharing common parliamentary institutions and democratic government, as well as the English language, the Indians turned out to be much less like us than I had expected.

Nevertheless, rather to my surprise, our chair would sometimes consult me quite seriously about some of the more mundane aspects of life. For instance, he seemed to think that I was an expert on automobiles! What sort of car should he buy for his impending retirement, he would ask, adding rather dolorously that it would be his last car. After considering his description of India's road network, car servicing available, the market for used cars, his family background, his rank, and so on, we came to the conclusion that he should get a Mercedes. He took it all in very soberly and eventually did buy a Mercedes.

Of such were some aspects of daily life with the Indians and Poles on the ICSC in Cambodia!

* * *

Reflecting Ottawa's decision to downplay the Commission in Cambodia, I was an Acting Commissioner and therefore the junior of the three heads of mission in age and professional rank. Nevertheless, for Commission business I was, of course, their equal and they would listen quite attentively to my explanations of Canada's position on such few items on our agenda as required a vote. Mainly, these concerned issues or initiatives that Sihanouk would try to get the Commission involved in so as to achieve certain domestic political objectives of his own. The Poles and Indians went along with this, but my instructions from Ottawa were firm: I was to vote against any and all such initiatives. I did so, of course, knowing full well that my opposition would annoy Prince Sihanouk far more than my Commission colleagues; without unanimity there could, of course, be no Commission involvement.[1]

As for my staff at "Candel", as our mission was called, it reflected Ottawa's approach to the Commission and was minimal: a military advisor, Major Roy Oglesby, a career officer and veteran of World War II, who had a small staff from National Defence; and myself, as Acting Commissioner, with a secretary and an administrative clerk. Roy and I got on very well together in Phnom Penh and we have maintained friendly relations with one another over the decades ever since.

Actually, daily work at Candel resulted far more from Canadian Colombo Plan programs, then getting off the ground in Cambodia, than from our Commission connection. Canadian fisheries technicians and education consultants were arriving, thanks to the External Aid Office, as the Canadian International Development Agency (CIDA) was then called. There was even a Canadian rice expert from

---

[1] For details regarding some of Prince Sihanouk's reactions to my negative votes, see *Special Trust and Confidence*, Chapter 3 (pp. 43–45), cited in Chap. 1, fn. 2 of this book.

the UN Food and Agriculture Organization (FAO) on the scene. He was from Sudbury, Ontario, of all places. Scholarships to Canadian universities and other educational institutions were on offer and suitable candidates had to be found. These activities were interesting and kept us reasonably busy. In addition, on-site visits to Canadian projects in the field and to those of the many other countries offering aid to Cambodia at the time were a pleasant change from office routines.

By the late 1950s rivalries in the aid sector between the Soviet Union and the United States in Cambodia, as well as China, France, Japan, among others, including Canada, had become intense. Aid had become a very big business indeed in Cambodia and Prince Sihanouk nursed it zealously. He would frequently play one country off against another in order to get what he wanted. Admittedly he could, in the process, be extremely emotional and mercurial. Indeed, some observers thought him to be quite mad in his machinations. Yet, clearly, as I reported to Ottawa at the time, there was a good deal of method in his madness; he was managing to get large amounts of much needed outside help to improve the basic economic infrastructure of his country. Cambodia survived not too badly when he was in office. Tragedy struck later, after he was ousted.

The following gem from the February 14, 1959, issue of *The Economist* by one of its correspondents recently in Cambodia illustrates these aid rivalries and results beautifully:

> Theoretically, it will soon be possible for a lucky Cambodian pedestrian who has been knocked down by a Polish steam locomotive travelling to a port constructed by the French, on a railway built by the Chinese, to be rushed in an East German ambulance, driven by a Japanese-trained chauffeur and fuelled by American petrol, along a highway built by the Americans, to a modern hospital erected by the Russians and staffed by nurses using Czech medical equipment, who have been educated under the Colombo Plan.

Despite the routine of our daily lives at Candel, there could be some quite unexpected surprises. Not long after my arrival in 1958, I got my first one. I still vividly remember the morning when I arrived at the office and saw a cute little red-headed boy with freckles and a light complexion, accompanied by a pretty little girl with light brown hair and blue eyes. They were with their Cambodian mothers in our reception area and spoke only Khmer!

It was then that I learned that Candel had had a family allowance program of its own for some time. The two children were about three years old and certainly did not look like their mothers, who would come in—rather shyly—every month or so for help in raising their children. Nobody in Candel knew who their fathers were or, if they did, they were not talking. My questions revealed that there was no evidence of child support from the fathers, who indeed may not even have known about their offspring in Phnom Penh. So I immediately authorized continuation of the payments to the mothers that had started well before my arrival and to which we all contributed quite generously on a personal basis.

Given their looks, complexions, and background, I am pretty certain that those youngsters would most likely have been killed during Pol Pot's massacres some years later, if they had had to remain in Cambodia.

The next surprise took the form of a saffron-robed *bonze*. One morning, one of the corporals came up to my office to tell me that "a yellow bozo" was downstairs and wanted to speak to "the boss". Could I see him? I agreed and found a young *bonze* in an elegant saffron robe waiting for me. He spoke good French so we continued in that language. It turned out that he was an aspirant young Buddhist monk. The upshot of our conversation was that he wanted to practice his English with us! A rather unusual request for any Cambodian at the time, let alone a *bonze*. I told him that we were a small outfit and that he should try the Americans. He had. They were too big and too busy. No time! What about the Australians or the British? His answer rather startled me. "Leur accent est compliqué." And furthermore, he thought that North American English was becoming far more important and widespread around the world than British English. A fairly perceptive *bonze*. So I agreed that he could come around every now and then and talk with us. He had a talent for language, learned fast, did not abuse of the privilege, and I for one learned a good deal about Buddhism in the process. I sometimes wonder whether he survived Pol Pot.

My driver, Sok Niemh, was a devout Buddhist. He was a courteous and careful driver. He tended to pray regularly, even while driving, and seemed at times to be lost somewhere in the upper reaches of Buddhism. Although he was a good driver, I occasionally had misgivings that his praying might bring us both to our next incarnations rather sooner than expected.

On one occasion he almost did, but not as a result of his praying. We were travelling quite fast on the road south to the coast, rather too fast for the village we were going through, when suddenly a chicken decided to cross the road. Sok Niemh tried desperately but unsuccessfully to avoid it. He plied the brakes so forcefully that I almost went through the windshield. However, I soon discovered that my discomfiture was neither here nor there. I was a bit shaken up of course, but otherwise alright. He, on the other hand, had *killed* a chicken: a much more serious matter. He immediately jumped out of the car, rushed to the chicken, prostrated himself on the roadbed beside it, and tearfully begged its forgiveness. He was inconsolable. For all he knew, he may have killed a friend, a relative, an ancestor, such being the process of reincarnation. I tried to calm him down, to reassure him, and to cheer him up a bit, but it was a melancholy ride south that day.

Sok Niemh could read and write. He spoke decent French and had ably served the upper classes and the diplomatic corps in Phnom Penh for years. Pol Pot's henchmen would certainly not have spared him.

A few weeks after my arrival, I received a letter from Ottawa to be presented to King Norodom Suramarit, a kind of letter of accreditation. Accordingly, I sent a message by hand to the Palace chief of protocol, Prince Norodom Phumisarah, seeking an audience with the King. The Norodom family was a powerful, even legendary one, in Cambodia, going back several centuries and its scions could be found here and there throughout the administration.

His reply, also by messenger, indicated that I should be at my office at 7H30 one morning to be escorted to the Palace, where His Majesty would deign to receive me at 8H15.[2] I found that rather odd; I could have walked to the Palace in about eight or ten minutes, but I was in no position to argue.

---

[2] The state of the Cambodian Ministry of Communications was such at the time that the telephone was seldom used for business. Lines frequently went dead. Messengers were much more reliable, provided that one had a reasonably precise address since streets were not always named in Phnom Penh nor buildings numbered.

And so, dressed in my best white suit, black shoes, white shirt, and black four-in-hand, which was the formal day wear for foreigners dealing with the Palace, I arrived at Candel for 7H30 to be greeted by a spectacle that I could hardly have imagined, even in my wildest fantasies.

Standing before the gate was a huge, extremely ornate, carriage drawn by two large elephants. The chief of protocol, at his most gracious and mellifluous, greeted me: "Comment se porte votre Excellence ce matin? Qu'elle veuille bien monter." I did so and off we went. Clomp. Clomp. Clump. Clump. Elephants, I discovered, are slow and ponderous beasts, yet with a majestic gravity to their stride.

As we advanced along the roadway to the Palace, where vehicular traffic had been banned for the occasion, some spectators bowed courteously. Most, however, prostrated themselves to the ground as we passed. I was quite taken aback, astonished that Canada could command such reverence and respect. Conversely, might I be the cause of it all?

I asked the chief of protocol in essence what was going on, but put much more elegantly of course. His answer startled me. "Votre Excellence ne doit pas s'en faire. Ceci ne la concerne pas du tout. Pas du tout. Il s'agit des éléphants du Palais. Ce sont des éléphants sacrés. Ce sont des dieux!" It was then that I noticed the colour of the elephants. They were a very light grey, almost white. They were very special indeed and, as befits gods, they manifested themselves to the faithful only on special occasions, hence the prostrations. So much for my ego!

I was the first Canadian, as far as I know, to be so escorted to the Palace. I was never able to find out why. I had had a number of lively discussions about Buddhism and other Eastern religions with our *bonze* and also with some Indian members of the ICSC, who were very devout. Cambodian history was a regular topic of conversation also. Perhaps some of these discussions had filtered through to the Palace?

In any event, I was certainly the last one to be so escorted, since shortly thereafter the Palace came down to earth. The Russians gave the Cambodian government a long black Zis or Zil limousine (I am not quite sure which) for protocol purposes and, not to be outdone, the Americans provided an even longer black Cadillac. The rivalry between the two countries was intense. And so, the Palace elephants regained their heavenly abode never to manifest themselves again to mere mortals in such a worldly way.

But to return to my appointment with the King! I found His Majesty on a very elevated throne indeed (he was less than five feet tall), while I was seated well below him on a foot stool on the floor. I was thus forced to angle my gaze upwards quite sharply towards him, as befitted our respective stations in life. He did not deign to look at my letter, but handed it immediately to an aide. He exchanged a few pleasantries with me and in five minutes it was all over. I drove back to the office with a much impressed Sok Niemh, who had been following me at a respectful distance.

Finally, a last episode. One morning I received a message from a very senior official in the Finance Ministry. Could I please have dinner with him and his wife at his home some night. He was from a powerful family and had studied in France. The invitation was unusual and would likely prove interesting. So I accepted right away and showed up punctually on the evening agreed upon. I found myself in a traditional Cambodian house, built on stilts, and luxuriously furnished in the French style. The food was excellent: a mixture of Cambodian and French cuisine. Traditional Cambodian cooking, by the way, is basically Indian, with curries and sauces, reflecting India's long cultural influence in the area. The cuisine of Vietnam, on the other hand, has been heavily influenced by China.

My host was most attentive, his children likewise, but I noticed that his wife who spoke good French did not take part in the conversation. I soon found out why. She was severely deaf.

They had heard that a foreigner had come to Phnom Penh wearing an odd device in his ear and had boiled their search down to me. I had noticed that I was attracting a good deal of attention on the streets of Phnom Penh. People would stare at me quite intently, as I passed by. This rather puzzled me at first, since a Canadian looked pretty much like any Frenchman or other white foreigner there. However, I soon discovered that it was my hearing aid that was attracting the attention. Not me. It was certainly the only one in Phnom Penh at the time, probably in all of Cambodia. In due course, however, I got used to the stares and as time went by the locals got used to me.

My host had managed to track me down in an unusual way: through one of the fruit vendors in the local market where his wife and their servants also shopped! I had acquired a taste for tropical fruit in Mexico, my first posting, and soon discovered that Cambodian mangos, chirimoyas, and guanábanas, were plentiful, fresh and delicious. I used to go to the market once or twice a week and take the fruit back to the hotel for a thorough washing in well-boiled water. *Le Royal* had been built by French interests several decades before. While comfortable enough, it was on the spartan side and lacked most of the amenities usually associated with better hotels around the world at the time. It is still there, I am told, but much improved. On the other hand, the French-built Catholic cathedral nearby is no longer standing.

In any event, my host plied me with questions. What was I wearing in my ear? I explained and was, of course, asked how hearing aids work. Where could they be had? And so on. I said that I did not really know whether they were available in Indochina. Saigon perhaps? If not, possibly Bangkok or Singapore. Certainly Paris. I also mentioned that the real problem would be, not the hearing aid itself, but the piece molded to fit tightly into the ear so as to ensure that sounds reached the inner ear without interference or feedback, which usually produced an irritatingly loud high-pitched whistle.

I offered to do some research for them and also to give madame some lessons as to how to go about understanding conversations as best as she could, e.g., watching lips carefully, paying attention to facial expressions, hand gestures, and so on. My offer to coach her in all this was gratefully accepted and she was a willing student. However, it is hard to teach someone who cannot hear to begin with and French is not the easiest language for lip-reading. It has many nasal sounds and fewer lip movements than English or Spanish, for instance.

My research revealed that hearing aids were not readily available. Cambodia had none, except mine. Possibilities in Bangkok were poor. Saigon, likewise. Even batteries were a problem (mine came in by bag from Ottawa). This was nearly a half century ago and things would certainly have improved in the region since then. The real problem, though, was the lack of otologists and audiologists to determine the cause and extent of her deafness, and correspondingly, the power and special adjustments required for the hearing aid. Also, where and how to have an earmold made.

At my last dinner with them, shortly before my return to Canada, I gave her one of my spare hearing aids, along with a supply of cords, batteries, etc., just in case they might find some way to have an earmold made for her. I never found out whether they did or not. Subsequent correspondence from Canada went unanswered. It most likely never reached them. With their background and connections, they probably ended up in France.

* * *

Most of these recollections of a fairly distant past reflect conditions at the time in Indochina and are unique to my posting there. Not having served in the Far East before and never finding myself there again after Cambodia, it was an experience that in retrospect I would not have wanted to miss.

Fortunately, unlike many others in Indochina, I enjoyed excellent health throughout my stay. This certainly made life more bearable in Phnom Penh, and elsewhere as well. I was able to lead a varied and active life, to venture into the countryside, and also to explore Vietnam, Thailand, and Malaysia. I am glad to have been there.

I was, of course, lucky in my timing. My successors were not so fortunate. I was in Indochina during an interlude of relative calm and peace. One war had just ended. The next one was beginning to get under way. During my time in Phnom Penh, incidents involving North Vietnam and the Vietcong in the South Vietnamese countryside, supplied along the Ho Chi Minh Trail through eastern Laos and Cambodia, were slowly but steadily growing in number. This guerrilla activity would, a few years later, develop into a particularly pervasive and violent war, in which the United States became heavily engaged on behalf of South Vietnam, thus making Commission life and work throughout Indochina both increasingly ineffective and dangerous.

÷ ÷ ÷ ÷ ÷

Why am I here?
April 1961 – December 1962

John Schioler

Mat hai ba, mat hai ba ("one, two, three"), the dulcet tones of the loudspeaker from the furniture factory next door, calling the workers to exercise. It is five a.m. in Happy Hanoi on this steamy day in 1962. I might as well get up myself, as I can't, even after more than a year with this daily ritual, turn over and get more sleep. Still, I refuse to join the "builders of socialism" or to exercise to their 1-2-3 rhythm. Instead, I push myself in the heat to do my Canadian Army 5Bx routine.

Why am I here? I have to remind myself every day, because it often seems pointless. As a bachelor, I am one of the 45, mainly junior, officers, who have been out here in Vietnam over the past eight years as peacekeeping, not cannon, fodder. Officially, I am the Canadian Permanent Representative (Perm Rep) posted in Hanoi to provide a Canadian presence in the North, to maintain liaison with our Commission colleagues, to report on the situation and, unexpectedly, to receive petitions. I flatter myself that at 28 on my first assignment abroad I am a kind of "head of post", a privilege not granted to many Foreign Service Officers (FSOs) of my vintage. Mind you, I have very little authority or scope for action and the only person that I supervise is myself. In the summer of 1962 I have just passed the one-year mark in this role and there is more to come.

My tour in Hanoi results from a Commission decision in February 1958 to move its headquarters from Hanoi to Saigon. A debate ensued about the nature of the presence to be left behind. The Commissioner, Tom Carter, suggested that the Perm Rep should be a military officer, with an FSO visiting for a half or a third of his time. As the post would be primarily concerned with servicing the military teams that pass through on the way to and from the Northern team sites, a full-time FSO from Saigon would be "wasteful". This proposal was overruled by Ottawa in favour of a full-time civilian Perm Rep's spending half his year's posting in the North. If the emptiness of the post had been foreseen, the Commission's original idea might have been re-introduced.

My own extended stay happened by accident, not by design or punishment. I "did my time" here last year for six months (April to October) and moved to Saigon, where I was looking forward to the rest of my year's tour in the South at Commission headquarters as Legal Advisor. In fact, I even asked for, and was granted, an extension of six months. Then the Head of the RVN Liaison Mission was murdered in October 1961 and the decided to undertake a full-scale investigation. As a real live lawyer was needed for the task, I was stripped of my bogus, but much prized, legal title on the delegation and frogmarched back to the North. For a month or so at the beginning of 1962, while the whole rationale for the ICSC was being reviewed in Ottawa, it was thought that the Hanoi post could at last be dispensed with. Alas, the hard decision was not taken and here I am again.

The society I work and live in

It is difficult to characterize this society, since we have little contact and no real interaction. One's impressions risk ending up being superficial and born of great frustration. In addition, the state is a work in progress, having been controlled by the Vietminh for less than eight years. I have to be careful in judging what is best for them and what is best for me.

A well-informed French journalist, Jean La Couture, recently wrote that the North can be characterized as "Monsieur Ho plus bicyclettes". There is a lot of truth in both parts of that phrase. The bikes are everywhere and provide not only personal transport but also heavy duty cartage. Many "carters" are likely preparing themselves for the movement of arms and ammunition along the so-called Ho Chi Minh Trail to the South.

Ho Chi Minh is genuinely respected and even loved. He is venerated for his victory over the French but he is unpretentious in his conduct. As an example, at a public celebration to which some foreign visitors were invited, Ho went about taking unsuspecting visitors by the hand, including me, for a short round of traditional dancing. He was wearing the customary North Vietnamese black sandals made from old automobile tires.

This is a joyless society. Only on National Day are hundreds of thousands seemingly spontaneously in the streets, marching or participating in holiday activities. We call the city "Happy Hanoi" because it most certainly isn't. One exception is gambling. Officially outlawed except for the national lottery, card or dice games are indulged in everywhere by small groups on their haunches at street corners absorbed by this pastime.

They are, to cite La Couture again, living in a "monastic society", elevating self-denial to a national virtue. Their austerity, however, is not all dedication; it is also dictated by the penury of the country. Even though the 1961 harvest was not bad, there is not a grain of rice to spare this year. Rationing is all-pervasive, as are the injunctions to conserve by such initiatives as wearing shorts rather than long pants. Like Henry Ford and the Model T, women can wear any colour as long as the trousers are black and the shirts brown. This is perhaps the most striking contrast with the South, where the *ao dai*, the multi-hued dress of the women, is a delight. Another noticeable difference is the order, calm and quiet of Hanoi compared to the bustle of Saigon.

The Vietnamese in general are dedicated first and foremost to the cause of unification, and only secondarily, to socialism. We foreigners debate among ourselves whether that ordering of priorities might be true of Ho himself.

The Vietnamese are enormously industrious. As far as I can see, they do not need to be exhorted to do exercises twice a day as so many of them are engaged in manual labour, as attested to by village women everywhere with two loads attached to a pole across a shoulder moving quickly with a characteristic gait.

Recently, there were references in the local press to corruption. Some Western commentators took this to mean that the system itself was venal. While I am the first to rail against the bureaucratic inefficiency and bloody mindedness of the regime, I see little evidence of general corruption. The honesty of the party cadres is a strong weapon that the leaders use in their "hearts-and-minds" battle to take over the South.

The North is committed to education. The numbers at all levels are exploding and the priority attached to the program are much to be admired even if political indoctrination forms a significant part of the process.

Less admirable are the monolithic character of the society, the curtailment of free expression and the pathological devotion to production. Control by the authorities is complete and surveillance of one's neighbours universal. As an outsider, I find the atmosphere suffocating; it is hard to tell whether the peasant in the field feels the same way.

The French legacy is still evident; not surprising, as they were more or less in control for over a century and only eight years have elapsed since Dien Bien Phu. We see the impact through the physical environment, the use of French as a second language and the existence of a Catholic community of up to a million souls. Yet, we also witness daily the fading of this influence, whether in the deterioration of Hanoi, once called "the Paris of the Orient" or in mounting obstacles to religious practice.

As in many authoritarian societies, personal safety is nearly perfect. No threat here of muggers, bombers or pickpockets. Unlike Saigon, we don't need advice on where to sit in a restaurant in order to reduce the danger of a bomb thrown in from a passing motocyclette. (Admittedly, this is partly because here there are no restaurants or motocyclettes.) On the other hand, a small demonstration against the regime brings immediate intervention. Recently, a man walked into the Commission's offices seeking asylum. The security police quickly entered the building against the express wish of our chairman and hauled the poor fellow off. We protested to absolutely no avail as the authorities claimed that man was insane and that they were actually protecting us.

My work environment

I should say a word about the situation in the region during my tenure here, not as political analysis but to throw light on the working and living conditions in Hanoi that result. Security was deteriorating in the South when I arrived in April 1961. Denying any involvement, the North was in fact stepping up its support for the Vietcong throughout the South to the point where, in December 1961, the United States decided to no longer limit itself to a few hundred military advisors. The number of U.S. military has risen to 15,000. The Americans are convinced, and the Commissioner seems to believe, that the security situation is improving somewhat.

Whenever there is a new development in U.S. and/or Commission policy, the attitude of the regime in the North changes and we are subjected to public criticism, official coldness and sometimes practical harassment. Last year a supposed spy plane crashed on Northern territory and was carried up to Hanoi to be exhibited at a public park, much like an art show. The large number of people who flocked to the park had their hatred of the Southern regime and its supporters re-inforced. Another wave of hostility came at us in June of this year when we and the Indians released a special report that stated unequivocally that "the North is the base for organizing hostile activities in the South aimed at the overthrow of the Southern Administration."

Sometimes, however, cool relations are a help. On Dominion Day, we invited 150 guests, including 30 officials, to our reception at the villas. As we can only accommodate about 90, the absence of all but a token number of officials was a great help. In periods when there is no "provocation", officials will be relatively friendly, if unforthcoming, and I am always personally treated with basic civility.

All of us on the delegation have views on the North/South split and American involvement. There is no doubt that the North is not respecting the Geneva arrangements and in a sense, the Americans, therefore, are justified in increasing their aid to the regime in the South. Up here, I have little idea what the real situation is on the ground; all I see is the mobilization of the people and the all-pervasive propaganda, but I have been telling my family that I have an uneasiness about the prospects for the future of the Southern regime. This is not a moral judgment on U.S. involvement, simply a feeling that their objectives cannot be achieved and that, therefore, they should consider pulling out and not increase their commitment.

My so-called work day

The work day, or should I say, half day, unfolds with great predictability. Groan, it's Tuesday; so it must be petition day, when my Indian and Polish colleagues and I sit in solemn conclave to endure the interminable procession of Vietnamese workers, peasants, students, etc., with their long list of abuses by the authorities in the South. I take some malicious pleasure in the fact that even the Poles find the exercise tedious. Today's session is not too bad, but last week we received over fifty groups. The petition process in the Agreements was not designed for this purpose but we go through it anyway and I, as a Canadian, have to put up with the extra aggravation of being described in banners carried by the protestors as "the running dogs of the American Imperialists". We are left in no doubt that the Commission was deliberately made up of representatives from West, East and the non-aligned world and that we all have our roles to play. We are not peacekeepers in the classic UN sense.

After the petitioners have left, I go for a walk or bike ride around town to pick up whatever incidental intelligence might come my way. I am not taking photos as I do not have permission to do so (although permission was requested a year ago and has been repeated from time to time). To violate such a rule could lead to very nasty consequences even if the object was only a touristic shot of a public building or street life.

After my walk it's time to write my monthly (or a special) report for the Commissioner. It is not profound. Here is how the conditions for reporting are described by my present boss, Frank Hooton:

> Canadians are hampered in their movements in the countryside, are treated with suspicion by the local authorities, have no connection with government officials except through the PAVN [People's Army of Vietnam] Liaison Mission and have few western or neutralist contacts upon which to depend.

To the list of impediments to reporting might be added the playing of the same folk record on the loudspeaker outside the office (one of a reputed 5,000 in the city) for over a week now. I have not yet acquired a taste for Vietnamese music but even if I had, the repetition would still be wearing.

Despite the impediments to official travel, I was allowed to go to Dong Dang, one of our team sites on the Chinese border. This hard-won privilege turned out to be an uneventful and unrevealing journey from an information-gathering point of view (but it did allow me to set my foot unofficially on Chinese soil, an experience few can boast of in 1962). I also went once with the Commissioner to Haiphong, the port for Hanoi, and had a look at the beautiful Baie d'Along, again without photos.

My reports go to the Commissioner in Saigon. I have no control over the use to which they might be put in Vietnam or at headquarters in Ottawa. I know that they are shared with allies to the extent that they contain new or corroborative information. This is not a big deal, as the information in these reports has been garnered by reading official publications with their combination of statistics on the latest achievements of the five-year plan and a rundown on the activities of the leadership, or by simply observing conditions in this nascent bulwark of Asian Communism. I am not engaged in any illicit activity. When in Saigon, I also occasionally speak with members of the American Embassy or correspondents from such magazines as *Newsweek* about the North. To call my activity "spying", however, would be to extend the term light years beyond any reasonable meaning of the term.

My report done, I have to brace myself for one of those diplomatic duties brought on by an event so beloved of authoritative regimes: the interminable official welcome at the airport in the hot sun to greet a "distinguished" visitor. Occasionally, the guest is a little more interesting than the usual vice premier from a friendly socialist country. Today he is Major Titov, the second Soviet cosmonaut, who is feted royally for several days, including a parade watched by as many as 80,000 people. He is hailed as an example of the superiority of socialism over decadent capitalism. I shake his hand and return to town after three lost hours.

Fortunately, I do not have the job of looking after the team site officers or the administration of the post. These duties fall to the military commanding officer, whom I work with, not over, no matter what the terms of reference might say. In my tour in Hanoi, my military colleagues have numbered eight captains, majors or lieutenant colonels, all significantly senior to me in age, service time and experience. The relationship is delicate but positive and we get our respective jobs done. The military staff consists of a sergeant who does office work for me, too, and two corporals as security guards. One curiosity of the civilian/military interaction out here is my role as returning officer for this year's Canadian general election. The army staff votes but, as a civil servant, I cannot.[1]

I understand that all military personnel will receive a medal for service out here—and they deserve it. It would nice to think that those of us who serve in the same theatre of peacekeeping might

---

[1] This regulation was changed some years ago and civilian public servants abroad can now vote. – Ed.

also be recognized for the effort we have made and the risks we have taken in the same cause.²

More experienced colleagues tell me that one of the burdens of diplomatic life is the constant stream of "visiting firemen" who have to be wined and dined, even if they are not adding anything to the relationship between Canada and the host country. From that perspective, I suppose I should count as a blessing the fact that almost no-one comes here, but I think that I would prefer visitors no matter what their reason for coming. When visitors do pitch up, they have to stay at the *Hôtel Métropole*, originally a luxury establishment but since 1954 neglected and rat infested.

A welcome visitor was Bernard Fall, French author of *Street Without Joy*, an account in English of the Vietnam conflict from 1946 to 1954. He was here a week ago researching a new volume, expanding his study to Laos and Cambodia. I had the pleasure of talking extensively with him about the situation. What a break from the usual dry round of contacts! Another occasional visitor is the Commissioner, who meets with the DRVN leadership and incidentally checks to see that I am not up to any mischief. He does not come often or for long since, as he wrote, any "visit should be short in view of the difficulties and discomforts of a lengthy stay". I can say "amen" to that.

Concerning those local contacts, after time off in the afternoon, I have to suit up and prepare for the diplomatic round in the evening. Surprisingly, in a country where frugality and informality are hallmarks of Ho's influence, the cocktail circuit, dominated by the *fêtes nationales* of socialist countries, demands the very Western dark suit, white shirt and dark tie. The heat is almost unbearable at these frequent affairs, but I do my duty and make small talk with all and sundry, hoping against hope that a useful snippet of news will come my way. I fervently pray that these deadening affairs do not reflect what I can expect from official diplomatic social life at posts in other parts of the world.

---

²This has now been done and Indochina civilian peacekeepers are currently receiving a medal. – Ed.

My so-called life

Recounting these official activities, I realize more than ever how pointless the exercise is and how I must redouble my efforts to find satisfaction in the off-hours. It is not easy going. But before listing the lascivious pleasures that I indulge in here, a few comments on the basics of the physical conditions of life and our eating and sleeping habits are in order.

The weather in Hanoi is a serious factor on our pleasure/pain index. Here we have the perfect combination: a Winnipegger who, like all his fellow survivors of Portage and Main,[3] feels compelled to complain about the weather while residing in a place that offers some of the worst you can imagine. Today is particularly hot and unpleasant as the *crachin*, a misty rain, is upon us, with temperatures in the 90s at day break and no relief in sight. The winter is awful, too, when the clammy cold takes over in unheated buildings. Light bulbs burn constantly in cupboards to stop mould from growing overnight. I have no clothes for this kind of thing (except those morning clothes) as I did not expect to be in the North during the winter. I have now come to appreciate to my chagrin that cliché about Winnipeg weather's not being so bad because "the heat/cold are dry".

Our delegation lives in a walled compound of two villas on Mint Street. We are protected at all times by a guard who stations himself across the street, looking at us rather than preventing unwanted visitors from entering. The accommodation is shabby and in need of repair. I occupy one two-storey villa (it is actually the Commissioner's), which includes a reception area and a dining room for meals with the military officers. The household staff (two cooks, two servers and two cleaners) are either informants or, at worst, intelligence operatives. Of course, they are assigned by the Liaison Mission and are no doubt proficient in their primary function, which is to keep tabs on us. Regrettably, they are less capable in their secondary role of taking care of our cleaning and meal service.

Naturally, there is no air conditioning, but we do have ceiling fans. As there are no screens on the windows. I sleep under a mosquito net, which has the second important purpose of keeping the many, full-sized cockroaches out of my bed. When I go down

---

[3] An intersection in downtown Winnipeg reputed to be the coldest and windiest corner in Canada. – Ed.

to breakfast, they scurry away from the table where they have been feeding on sugar or other items not totally cleared away.

I feel very isolated here. Like the Vietnamese, I see myself living a kind of monastic life in Hanoi, albeit at a far higher level of comfort and consumption than any of them. There are only fifty westerners in the city, including several children and seniors. Most are French but we include the Indians in the category because they meet both criteria for membership: they speak English and do not like it in Hanoi.

My isolation is broken from time to time by escape to Saigon on a flight aboard *Aigle Azur*, a small French airline contracted to fly twice weekly among the four Commission offices. It uses a number of Boeing *Stratoliners*, four-engine craft built in 1939 and long out of production. We live from plane to plane as they bring official and personal mail, care packages, information and equipment from Saigon.

Confidence in the plane and its crew (who are served wine during the flight) is never high, but the need to leave overpowers any innate fear of flying. On one occasion, we left Vientiane for Hanoi and turned back because of a very visible oil leak in one of the motors. Our only comfort was that the plane had four engines and supposedly could safely land on three. This proved to be true, as we did make it back to Laos in one piece. Emboldened by this success, the pilot took off again after repairs only to experience an even worse situation, a small flame in the same engine. In 1954 John Wayne in the movie, *The High and The Mighty*, gave meaning to the expression "the point of no return" and we lived that experience before finally landing in Hanoi, the only time that I was very glad to be here.

One visit to Saigon, although enjoyable from every other point of view, unfortunately led through contaminated restaurant food to a year of *amoebiasis*. I am better now but not entirely freed from the effects of the illness. Some experienced colleagues have helpfully suggested that the malady could stay with me all my life, recurring like bouts of malaria when least expected and causing long-term damage to the system. The oft-repeated comment that "all the locals have amoebic dysentery, so don't worry about it" gives me little consolation.

Lunch and/or dinner at the villa consists of chicken and bananas at least once every day. Our Northern army cooks work in a tiny building that straddles the wall between the Indian compound and our own. Luckily, the Indian chairman has a little clout so that on Sunday we can look forward to curry. Of course, it is always *chicken* curry. When I leave here I will swear off chicken and bananas for life. Once in a while we are "treated" to dog as a substitute for pork or beef, of which there is a great shortage at the moment. This is just another experience to go along with raw monkey's brains served with rotten fish sauce, a Vietnamese specialty which I experienced in Saigon. What we won't do for Queen and country!

Before leaving the subject of food, I have to admit that on one occasion, the cooks turned out a very respectable five-course meal of soup, fish, quite tender beef (not water buffalo), fruit and cake, to the amazement of our British guests, who look on tinned sardines as a special treat from overseas. Despite this culinary success, I am not yet ready to invite the French *Délégué général*, whose household establishment is quite lavish, to a similar repast.

One unexpected benefit to being in the North and not in Saigon, with its many temptations, is that I can save money. The daily living expenses are absorbed by the Commission; we are paid an allowance that is based on temporary duty, and there is almost nothing to spend on here. So I have at least been financially compensated for the loss of a year.

The North Vietnamese have never heard the recruiting slogan "join the Foreign Service and see the world". From the day of my arrival I have asked permission to make a tourism visit outside Hanoi, or even to go to the outskirts of the city to see some reputedly handsome pagodas, but no luck for more than a year. They were very worried, I suppose, about my going around not being recognized by the local citizenry, especially as I am 6'3" and Nordic in appearance. It is a measure of their insecurity. Just a few days ago, however, after having given up hope of any permit, I finally did get a tour of the city, but one so closely supervised by a "guide", who provided no information about the sites, that the occasion lost all sense of pleasure. They also gave me permission to take photos but, in the event, no individual subject was allowed, whether person or building. Despite the policy and the potential punishment, I have managed over the months to snap a few shots when the coast has been clear but nothing very intriguing has emerged.

This is my first experience with Third World bureaucracy, where the combination of inexperience, communism and paranoia is lethal to positive action. I ordered a tape recorder from Hong Kong as I was desperate for music. Despite repeated pleas for its release, I did not get possession for four months. (A system with a little bribery — excuse me, a customs release fee — would have been welcome but that is out of the question here.) The second day after the machine's release, there was a power surge in the villa and the thing is now inoperable. At this point, the gulf between this Third World country and most others becomes a reality: here you cannot go to an unprepossessing hole in the wall and have items competently repaired for a pittance by a private entrepreneur. It's not that the Vietnamese cannot do this work. On the contrary, they are very capable, but all their expertise is committed to the public sector and the Five-Year Plan.

One difference between this country and much of the developing world is the lack of communication with ordinary people. To show what I mean — every day I go to a kiosk at the lake to buy a Vietnamese paper to be translated at the office. Every day I attempt to engage the attractive young woman who serves me in a minimal exchange of pleasantries. I continue to go just to see whether after a year she will risk a smile or "hello" in any language. No luck. She is a true believer.

The military support function is very important in the area of morale and keeping in touch. At Christmas, for example, a Canadian plane brings both presents and special food, a welcome change from normal diet. And the wives of the officers send news of Canada, especially sports news. This is most welcome as it is a truism that the farther from home the more we are drawn to things at home that we were not interested in when there, such as the fate of the Blue Bombers.[4] Although I have a strong shortwave radio that picks up information about the rest of the world and I am sent press snippets from Saigon, non-business news about Canada is almost non-existent.

Social graces and other activities

I have a lot of time on my hands here. How to fill it without turning to drink? I decided early on to work on some of the social graces of

---

[4]A Winnipeg team in the Canadian Football League. – Ed.

diplomatic life supposedly required for a successful career: French, bridge, tennis and dancing.

I get to practise French on a daily basis; even though the language of the Commission is English, there is virtually no English spoken outside our office. The knowledge picked up in External Affairs lessons twice a week in Ottawa are clearly insufficient to the task, so, in exchange for French practice, I give English lessons to the children of the *proviseur* at the *lycée*.

When I came to Indochina, I was an avid golfer with a respectable handicap, which I had hoped to lower in Saigon, but I am no longer playing. You can well imagine that there would not be a golf course in this country, which is poor, Communist and short of arable land. There is, however, a tennis court at the French delegation compound and I have taken up the sport with enthusiasm.

The wife of the *Agence France Press* (AFP) correspondent here is a former Belgian ladies' bridge champion. She is a formidable player who unnerves her opponents by dealing the cards with one hand at the speed of lightning. Under her tutelage and criticism I have improved my bridge skills by a power of ten and have moved from Culbertson to Goren. I will leave here able to fill in whenever my ambassador needs a junior officer to fill in at the table. Is that not the expected drill?

The French "colony" makes its own fun here and that includes dance parties. I go dutifully and am acquiring the basics of ballroom dancing. So, you see, I shall leave my Hanoi "finishing school" well prepared to meet all the important challenges of diplomatic life.

I inherited a bike on arrival and, getting into the spirit of things, use it frequently. To maintain that *Bridge on the River Kwai* idea of keeping up standards no matter what the conditions are in confinement and, I admit, to amuse myself with the absurdities of life here, I once wore white tie to a French evening party, but arrived by bike. (By the way, lest the reader think me totally naïve, made-to-measure white tie, tux and morning clothes were all bought in Hong Kong en route here in preparation for the long haul in Europe on cross postings. I was not the stereotypical American tourist arriving in Ottawa with skis in July.)

Speaking of bikes, today I had a major incident that almost led to the withdrawal of the Canadian delegation from Hanoi. Only my seasoned diplomatic *sang froid* prevented a real diplomatic dust-up.

I wheeled out of the compound on my trusty metal steed onto the street, but was accosted by a watchful guard. He accused me of violating one of the basic laws of the land by not alighting from my bike when *crossing* the sidewalk. The penalty was to pay the equivalent of 21 cents on the spot or face the prospect of being led off to a military post for harsher punishment. I thought of standing my ground and fighting the issue right to the top, but opted, at the end of a mutually incomprehensible exchange, to ante up and fly off twenty minutes late. Incidentally, this was the most interesting episode in my life this week.

I am also making a stab at learning Vietnamese, but it is slow going. I have spent the last two weeks trying to master the "ng" sound, to say nothing of attempting to identify and reproduce the language's six tones (which they tell me are one more than Mandarin). It is easier to read, however, as Portuguese priests three hundred years ago created a Western script for it with diacritical marks that make it minimally understandable. It is doubtful that this knowledge will be as useful as tennis, dancing or French, but the effort fills in dead time.

I have begun buying and collecting books about Vietnam. I have had many of them bound in red morocco leather in Saigon for less than a dollar each and now have the largest collection held by a Canadian, a dubious distinction since there is little interest in Indochina at home, where the present big pre-occupation is Cuba. I wonder whether this is a passing phase or the beginning of a lifelong passion for books that will be acquired, admired but not, in many cases, read?

Not tonight, but sometimes when there is no official engagement, I join the Canadian army personnel in their lounge and throw ping-pong balls at the lizards on the walls or engage in a contest of "canfan". This mindless diversion consists of tossing empty cans through the ever-increasing speeds of the overhead fan. The game always ends with a can shooting off to the side at a tremendous rate. We have too little to do! From time to time we are favoured with a new movie such as Laurel and Hardy from the 1930s. As a teetotaller, I endear myself to the military and friends every month by providing sixty bottles of Beck's beer (two bottles per day issued by the Commission, like rum in the navy) and *they* have a party.

Occasionally we have government-sponsored diversions. A while ago I was invited to the opera house, now used mostly for National Assembly meetings and other political purposes, to see Tchaikovsky's *Eugene Onegin*. Needless to say, my Russian is non-existent so that I have never been able to follow the libretto of a performance in the West. Sung in Vietnamese with its six tones, even the musical line became a problem. The conductor, from Bulgaria, did his best but the evening was more interesting than enjoyable in any musical sense. In fact, the sharpest memory of the event was the proximity of the overhead fan to my head while seated in a box usually occupied by smaller Vietnamese. Luckily, the performance did not warrant a standing ovation which would have abruptly ended my tour here.

Now and again I drop by the *petit* or *grand voleurs* who corner the "antique" market here in shops near the lake. Their names do not refer to their price mark-ups, since they both ask exorbitant amounts for goods of questionable value or authenticity. After much deliberation, I have broken down and bought a vase that is not too garish and is reasonably representative of what one might think could be Northern artistry. After all, I have to take something back home to prove that I really have been in Hanoi. It will be an obvious counterpoint to the more modern and much less expensive piece I acquired in Saigon last winter.

Outside Hanoi experiences

More interesting things have happened to me in the few short weeks that I have spent away from the North than in the many months I have spent here. Two examples stand out: to deal with the amoebic dysentery that had plagued me for months, I underwent a very specific cure at the Graal Military Hospital in Saigon under the care of a French physician who was an old hand in the region. The treatment involved injections that were so dangerous for the heart that I was told to lie still in bed for at least a week. I fully intended to obey his instructions but fate intervened.

One morning, February 27, 1962 to be exact (it is imprinted on my brain), the incredibly loud roar of a low-flying jet jerked me from my reverie. A moment later another one screamed by, seemingly close enough to be in danger of hitting the building. Then loud explosions at a short distance. My Hobson's choice was stay in bed and risk being bombed or get under the bed and risk a heart attack.

Hello, floor! When calm returned, the hospital had not been attacked and my heart was throbbing but still functioning. The Presidential palace, a few hundred yards down the road, did not fair so well, as two dissident Southern Air Force pilots had blasted the building, leaving acres of rubble and twisted girders about the palace grounds. Although they terrified me and everyone else in their flight path, they failed in their main goal to kill President Diem, who was elsewhere at the time.

The other incident of interest took place in Laos during a private visit. I went along with our Commission representatives in a helicopter to witness a summit meeting of the three disputing Laotian princes in a jungle village north of Vientiane. The royal delegations arrived from different directions and met under a primitive tin-roofed shelter with a mud floor. Pigs and cows rooted around the building for food. The princes argued acrimoniously through the morning about a permanent cease-fire and formation of a central government and then, as if on a pre-arranged signal, they abandoned their belligerent attitudes and each delegation produced elements of a lunch that they (and we) shared in a most convivial manner. Again the virtual bell rang and they returned to the negotiating table to fight again as enemies all afternoon. We returned to Vientiane in the evening after a diverting day in the forest where history was being made in a new and grand Laotian national debate.

Looking back

Forty years have passed since those dreary days in Hanoi. I never returned to Asia on posting and have never visited Vietnam as a tourist.

They tell me that the old town has changed beyond recognition. Numerous visitors now enjoy staying at the completely renovated and enlarged *Métropole*. Perhaps if I went back, the scene would evoke feelings of nostalgia, but somehow I doubt it.

With the benefit of hindsight, however, I can see that, despite the boredom and frustrations outlined above, I did not really suffer and on the whole was able to create enough activity to avoid rice paddy fever. It was just that sixteen months in the North were too long and were not "cost effective" from either a work or private life perspective.

A major benefit of the posting was to experience a very different civilization for the first time. My extensive travel in Europe with my family as a boy and later as a student at Oxford had not prepared me for Asia or for a Communist society. Vietnam in general and Hanoi in particular were useful lessons at the beginning of a career in the Foreign Service.

I also learned a lot here in Vietnam about an important foreign policy issue that increasingly dominated the news for a decade and is still reverberating through American consciousness today. I have to admit, however, that although I had misgivings, I was not totally convinced until 1964 that the United States had to get out.

Working with the military was an excellent experience as I went to Cyprus on the same day in 1964 as the Canadian UNFICYP contingent to open a diplomatic mission there and even ran into several officers that I had known in the DRVN.

Whatever happened to those social graces I cultivated in Hanoi? Eventually, External Affairs gave me excellent French-language training when French was no longer a social grace and had become essential in the Foreign Service. I continue to play tennis but have never gone back to golf. I do not play bridge anymore and am still a hopeless dancer.

My stomach disorder never recurred; I am still collecting books and finding it difficult to read them all; the cocktail circuit proved to be no more satisfying in other posts; and I have never used a word of the Vietnamese I painfully acquired over those many months.

In 1962 I was very friendly with the Indian Perm Rep in Hanoi to the point where we contemplated writing a book together about the North and our experiences there. In the end, we could not muster the energy to carry out the project when the information was fresh and close at hand. This chapter forty years later is a short substitute for the original idea. If I had known, I would have put down a few more notes at the time and not left this narrative to (fading) memory.

Finally, you would think that after my less-than-enthralling experiences in Hanoi, I would have hoped for a cross posting to one of the great capitals of Europe, such as Rome. Instead, as a bear for punishment, I indicated on Personnel's preference sheet that I would like to go to Lagos in Nigeria to do aid work. No such luck; in December, 1962, on leaving Indochina, I was ordered to put up with the challenges of Rome and *la dolce vita* for three and a half years! It was too good to last. Still a bachelor, I once again had my posting abruptly terminated after only fifteen months and I went off to Nicosia, another war zone.

And I still ask myself about Hanoi: "Why was I there?"

÷ ÷ ÷ ÷ ÷

Commissioner David Johnson (right), Candel ICSC Hanoi, with J.H. ("Si") Taylor (February 1956).

J.H. ("Si") Taylor (left) with Vernon G. Turner, Political Advisors, Candel ICSC Hanoi, at entrance to Canadian offices (early 1956).

The Taylors cruising on the Red River near Hanoi (March 2001).

The editor (Arthur Blanchette) with Major Roy Oglesby (right), Military Advisor, Candel ICSC Phnom Penh, on a trip south to the beaches (May 1959).

Roy MacLaren with Prime Minister Chrétien at the inauguration of the new Canadian Embassy Chancery, Hanoi (1996). Photo courtesy PMO and Hon. Roy MacLaren.

John Schioler (centre) with Commissioner Frank Hooton (left), Candel ICSC Vietnam, and J. Ford, British Consul, Hanoi (1962).

Blair Seaborn, Commissioner, Candel ICSC Saigon (1965). Courtesy Blair Seaborn.

Louise Pommet-Dyer on a *cyclo-pousse*, Candel ICSC Phnom Penh (1967).

Richard V. Gorham, Commissioner, Candel ICSC Phnom Penh, with Prince Sihanouk (1968). Courtesy R.V. Gorham.

Thérèse Rhéaume-Chabot, Candel ICSC Phnom Penh (1969). Courtesy Mme Chabot.

On their way to the office, Si Taylor and Bill Bauer (right) pass a large picture of North Vietnam's President Ho Chi Minh, which adorned the front of the old French Opera House in Hanoi.

Restored Opera House, Hanoi (2001). Photo by Si Taylor.

In the presidential helicopter, President Lyndon Johnson and Prime Minister Lester B. Pearson, with Secretary of State Dean Rusk, National Security Advisor McGeorge Bundy, and Minister of External Affairs, Paul Martin, Sr. Photo courtesy of Geoffrey Pearson.

Mission to Hanoi:
The Canadian Channel
May 1964 – November 1965

J. Blair Seaborn, C.M.

The spring of 1964 was not a propitious time to be selected as Canadian Commissioner to the International Commission for Supervision and Control (ICSC) in Vietnam.

The regime of President Ngo Dinh Diem in the Republic of Vietnam (South Vietnam) had been toppled the previous November by a group of South Vietnamese army officers. The Americans, who had been the chief foreign supporters of Diem, had become disenchanted with him and his army's poor performance in suppressing the Vietcong insurgency in the South, a movement with strong encouragement, direction and support from the People's Republic of Vietnam (North Vietnam). Whether the Americans, and particularly their Ambassador in Saigon, Henry Cabot Lodge, masterminded the coup d'état, or encouraged it, or merely turned a blind eye to it, was a subject of debate. But with the documents now available, it is pretty clear that the coup leaders were sure that Washington would not oppose their efforts.

Glad to see the last of Diem, the Americans were distressed, however, when his overthrow did not lead to a stable and strong government in the South, nor one more effective in fighting the insurgency. Political instability and lack of effectiveness were starting to give rise to that terrible conundrum for the inner circles of the U.S. Administration: we cannot help these people unless they are prepared to help themselves; but we cannot afford, for the sake of America's global interests and status, not to come to their assistance and, if necessary, to take over the defeat of the uprising by our own means.

This was the broad picture, but the much narrower one for the Vietnam Commission on which Canadians, along with Indians and

Poles, were serving was no more encouraging. Having done useful work in the early years following the beginning of its mandate in 1954, the Commission had later become increasingly ineffective and, in the eyes of many, irrelevant. The last bold stand the Vietnam Commission had taken was in its Special Report of 1962, when an Indian–Canadian majority found that the insurgency in the South was indeed aided and abetted, if not directed, by North Vietnam. Since then, Commission meetings had degenerated into endless bickering over evidence of violations of the Vietnam cease-fire agreement of 1954. Military officers at team sites were frustrated in their attempts to do useful investigatory work by the rule of unanimity and by restrictions placed on their movements by the governments of both North and South Vietnam. Morale was low and Canadian participants were asking themselves what greater purpose was being served by their continued service in a difficult and often unhealthy environment, in a land which seemed to have little relevance to Canadian interests.

Be that as it may, I am not sure I had much option but to accept the proposed Saigon posting, as had so many of my friends and colleagues in External Affairs over the previous ten years. And when my wife Carol and our two children announced that they would certainly accompany me there, that clinched it, and I began to prepare for departure at the end of June.

Late in May, however, the assignment became much more interesting. At the end of April, U.S. Secretary of State Dean Rusk paid a quiet visit to Ottawa to speak with Prime Minister Pearson and Secretary of State for External Affairs Paul Martin Sr. The United States, Rusk said, could not simply get out of Southeast Asia, but it did not seek bases or a military position in the area. It did not want hostilities on a higher scale in Vietnam, nor to try for the Korean or "hard" way. The basic Indochina agreements (the 1954 Geneva Agreements) were already in position. What was missing was compliance.

The Americans, said Rusk, getting right to the point, had an important and urgent message for the North Vietnamese and needed to open up a dialogue via a secure and trusted but inconspicuous channel. In effect, they wanted to find out the intentions of the North Vietnamese with respect to South Vietnam. Could the North live indefinitely with a divided country: Communist in the North and non-Communist in the South? If so, Washington and Hanoi could come to an understanding, and Washington might even be able to give economic assistance to the North. If not, the North must be made to understand that the United States would not abandon its South Vietnamese ally and would be prepared to take whatever measures were necessary to prevent the collapse of the South and its takeover by the North.

Could the Canadian Commissioner on the ICSC, asked Rusk, take on this messenger assignment under the guise of regular visits to Hanoi? The deteriorating political and military situation in South Vietnam required that the message be delivered with all possible haste. Pearson and Martin agreed in principle to having me, the new Commissioner, take on the task, subject to working out the details of the message and its presentation. They thought my departure for Saigon could be speeded up.

One can speculate, especially now that so many documents from the period are in the public domain, to what extent this initiative was a genuine attempt to seek a compromise with the North and to limit American involvement in the war in Vietnam, and to what extent it was a cover to justify further involvement if required, as some Americans thought was inevitable. This is not the kind of article for an in-depth analysis, which in any event has been undertaken by many academics in recent years. The initiative was probably a little bit of both, for, as we now know, both currents of thinking were then to be found within the Administration. At the time, however, the question for the Canadian government was relatively simple: if we could help the United States and its adversary in Vietnam to gain a better understanding of one another's thinking and intentions, and if we could thereby reduce the prospect of a deepening and widening war, could we do other than agree to help? Canada did agree, on condition that the Canadian government approve the text of the message to be conveyed, and act as the channel of communication and instruction to its Commissioner.

Late in May, President Johnson spoke personally with the Prime Minister in New York along the same lines that Rusk had used. On the same day, a small but high-powered American team, including William Sullivan of the State Department and Chester Cooper of the CIA, came to Ottawa to discuss the details with senior Canadian officials, including Assistant Undersecretary Arnold Smith, Jim

McCardle, head of Defence Liaison II Division (security and intelligence) and Louis Rogers, head of Far Eastern Division.

There was extensive discussion of the proposed American message which was designed to elicit clarification of Hanoi's goals, to explain U.S. goals and to examine whether there might be a confrontation or a standing down. There was discussion also of the precise channels of communication (Washington, Ottawa, Saigon) and of the Canadian control of the operation. The Americans certainly regarded the 1954 settlement as constituting a virtually permanent dividing line for the two Vietnams. Sullivan and Cooper admitted that there was an indigenous element to the rebellion in the South, but said that it would be manageable without Hanoi's support in both personnel and materiel. China's role in all this, they said, was not crucial or very active. Questioned by the Canadians, they said that the United States could envisage the necessity of air strikes to deter North Vietnamese assistance to the rebellion, but not the commitment of U.S. combat troops.

I sat in on the meetings and dinner, apparently passed muster with the Americans, and prepared to leave in haste for Saigon. I was on my way within a week, leaving Carol to sell the car, rent the house and get herself and the children to Saigon a month later. The Top Secret operation was code-named "Bacon" (by Louis Rogers or by Tom Pope, the desk officer, as in "bringing home the bacon") and the "need to know" about "Bacon" was extremely limited.

To enhance my credentials and to Canadianize the operation as much as possible, Prime Minister Pearson provided me with a Top Secret letter of instruction with respect to the "Bacon" mission, which I was authorized to show to my North Vietnamese interlocutor on my first visit to Hanoi. I carried it in a body belt from Ottawa to Hong Kong to Saigon to Hanoi. To keep things in balance, I had a special letter of introduction from Mr. Pearson to Prime Minister Nguyen Khanh of South Vietnam as well, which said very little and probably baffled General Khanh when I paid the courtesy call expected of new Commissioners.

Arriving in Saigon in early June, I encountered Asia for the first time — its heat, its drenching rainy season downpours, its teeming populations, its vast differences from the European posts where I had served heretofore. I was met at the Tan Son Nhut airport by the civilian and military Canadians on the delegation and the senior

Indians and Poles, all of whom were undoubtedly wondering why I had arrived earlier than first announced, requiring my predecessor Gordon Cox to depart the post rather hastily. I had crossed with Gordon in Hong Kong, where I had stopped briefly to buy tropical clothes, and felt badly that I could not tell him anything of the "Bacon" mission.

The delegation's Senior Political Advisor, Tom Delworth, had been due to depart at the end of his term days after my arrival. But I was able to persuade him and the Department that he should stay on for a few weeks to break me in to the mysteries of the Commission, the delegation and Vietnam. Although I was under instructions to keep my mission to Hanoi under closest wraps I, of course, took into my confidence my Senior Political Advisor, and Tom proved to be an invaluable mentor in any number of ways. Another great support and the soul of discretion was Norma Nadeau, the Commissioner's secretary, who quickly came to know all the details of "Bacon" through typing my reports.

On a sightseeing tour of Saigon the day after my arrival, Tom and I visited the Cholon market, to give me a little local colour. He still remembers me turning a little green on seeing raw meat laid out on the counters, quite unrefrigerated in spite of the heat, and flies lighting on it, to no one's concern. At least it was not as bad as the Vientiane market in Laos, which I visited a few months later and saw a rather mangy old dog lying on the counter beside the raw meat.

Some members of the delegation, including Tom Delworth and David Anderson, the latter to become a Member of Parliament and now Minister of the Environment in the Chrétien government, were housed in rooms in the *Continental Hotel*, in the heart of Saigon, a wonderful old colonial-era building straight out of a Graham Greene novel. Children on the street hawked their wares to the patrons sitting on open balconies almost at street level. Beautiful young Vietnamese girls took drinks with American military advisory officers. Doubtful deals, both political and commercial, were undoubtedly struck at the bar and in the dining room. This, and the *Caravelle Hotel* across the square, were centres of news, misinformation and intrigue throughout the whole period.

The delegation offices for the Indians, Canadians and the Poles were in a compound which had been a French army camp. They were in long, low buildings set among trees, with overhanging roofs, windows shuttered against the sun, and cooled more or less by overhead circular fans. Only the communications room had an air conditioner, and that was for the equipment, not the communicators. Office hours were from 7 a.m. to 1 p.m., and if you had to come back in the afternoon, after a siesta, the heat was pretty unbearable. Everything was rather run down, the furniture was decrepit, and we were quite crowded. There was a faded tropical colonial ambiance to it all.

I was put up for a few days at the *Caravelle Hotel*, new and overly air conditioned and quite devoid of character, while waiting for Beverly Cox to get things packed after Gordon's hasty departure and enabling me to move into the Canadian Commissioner's rambling villa in the compound known as the Cité Hui Bon Hoa (*Camp des Mares*). The senior Canadian military officers had a similar villa nearby. The Indian and Polish Commissioners and their senior military also had villas in the compound. A tennis court on the grounds was much used by the Indians and to some extent by the Canadians. When observing the play in the hot afternoons, one was reminded of the old Noel Coward song about mad dogs and Englishmen going out in the noon-day sun.

The Canadian Commissioner's villa was not without a certain colonial charm, with large rooms, high ceilings and a verandah giving on a small garden with a frangipani tree. It provided little in the way of amenities, furnishings and general comfort, nothing like that of a normal Canadian head of mission's residence. My wife remembers using bed sheets as table cloths. There was a noisy air conditioner in one bedroom (the one where Lucien "Brodie" Cannon, an earlier Canadian representative, was murdered), but ceiling fans did a good job elsewhere. During one dinner party, the Australian Ambassador faced a water rat in the toilet bowl of the downstairs bathroom.

The day after my arrival, I was introduced by one of the Canadian military, Lt. Col. Larry Esmonde-White, at the morning service at the Episcopal Church in Saigon to the formidable American Ambassador, Henry Cabot Lodge. At his invitation, I went back to his residence to have tea that afternoon. He made it pretty clear that he considered this whole message-bearing operation his idea and me as his personal emissary, and that I should be on my way to Hanoi by the next Commission flight. Reading the U.S. documents many years later, I discovered that the message Lodge would have liked delivered was a lot blunter, rougher and even threatening than the one I had been instructed to convey, but had been toned down by State. At the time, I made it clear to him that I was acting on instructions from the Canadian government, that I would get to Hanoi soon but according to a timetable Canada deemed appropriate. I would in due course be reporting to External Affairs, who would no doubt inform the State Department of the results, and they in turn Ambassador Lodge. I would be glad to convey the essence of my report to him once I was sure it had been received by my superiors in Ottawa.

Previous Commissioners based in Saigon had been in no great haste to present themselves in Hanoi, sometimes waiting for the next Commission meeting in that city. I told Tom Delworth and the staff that I wanted to speed up the process. They must press the South Vietnamese Liaison Mission to get me early appointments to call on the senior South Vietnamese personages with whom I must establish myself as the new Canadian Commissioner in Vietnam. They did their best to pass this off as the keenness of an impatient young head of delegation anxious to get going on the job. The head of the Liaison Mission, Colonel Nguyen Van Anh, was clearly suspicious of all this haste ("Why are you in such a hurry to get to Hanoi?"), but he did arrange the appointments very promptly, allowing me to call on, among others, the Foreign Minister, the Prime Minister and the Chief of State. With good reason, given the intrigue and unstable political situation in Saigon, Tom Delworth had some concerns about my personal security if certain elements in South Vietnam were to get wind of the real reason for my early visit to Hanoi. The pressures, the heat, the new food all took their temporary toll on me. As I made visit after official visit in my best new white suit, I prayed that I could complete the conversations and get back to the rather primitive bathroom facilities near the delegation offices without mishap.

After this flurry of activity in Saigon, I took the regular Commission-chartered aircraft, an old Boeing *Stratoliner* with a French crew, to Hanoi via Phnom Penh and Vientiane. The contrast with Saigon — its noise and crowds and motor bikes and bustle, its hustlers and peddlers and garishness, its French restaurants and slender young Vietnamese women in their beautiful flowing national dress, the *ao dai* — could not have been greater. The main sound was the swish of bicycle tires on pavement; cars were few and far between, dress was simple and sombre, the old colonial architecture charming though badly run down. It was like a very quiet French provincial town of many decades before.

I was met by Canada's Permanent Representative in Hanoi, David Jackson, and the North Vietnamese Liaison Officer, Colonel Ha Van Lau. Though under instruction to bring Jackson absolutely minimally into the main purpose of this first visit, I had to enlist his support to impress on Ha Van Lau how essential it was that I see either President Ho Chi Minh or Prime Minister Pham Van Dong on an urgent basis as I had an important and secret message to convey. Ho Chi Minh was out of town on vacation, so it was arranged that I see the Prime Minister. I apologized to Jackson, a very able and discreet officer, for not being able to take him with me on this call, as I would have liked to do, and he took this with professional calm.

My meeting with the Prime Minister on June 18, 1964 took place, as I recall, in one corner of a large, ornate room in an imposing old residence near the centre of the city, formerly the French governor's palace. Pham Van Dong was accompanied only by Lt. Col. Mai Lam, the number-two man at the People's Army of Vietnam (PAVN) Liaison Mission, who was to act as note-taker and, if necessary, interpreter. The Prime Minister welcomed me courteously in impeccable French, and after some small talk about the importance the Democratic Republic of Vietnam attached to the continuing presence of the ICSC, we got down to business. I showed him the letter to me from Prime Minister Pearson, which constituted my instructions for the mission, and set out how the Canadian government saw it. Canada hoped that the use of this channel might open a dialogue between Hanoi and Washington in the interests of peace.

I said that, given the importance of the message from the American government, I would want to convey its text to him pretty well verbatim, in French translation, rather than using my own words to transmit the sense of it. I also hoped that there would be no objection, since I was alone, to my making very detailed notes of his response, as I wanted to be sure to report exactly what was said. Pham Van Dong agreed to both these requests, and listened most attentively to the message. Stressing that he was in no way giving a formal reply, he expounded on the DRVN point of view, with particular reference to the points made by the Americans. After this exchange, I went on with a number of questions and comments of my own, all designed to draw him out on the matter of the proposed "neutrality" of South Vietnam and his understanding of American commitments and intentions. I shall not attempt to summarize the hour and a half of conversation, as my Top Secret "Bacon" reports of the time are now available to researchers in Canadian and American archives and in many publications. The key reports, in fact, from this and my subsequent visits to Hanoi can be found in the *Canadian Forum* of September 1973, drawn from the so-called *Pentagon Papers*, the secret U.S. Defense Department documents leaked by Daniel Ellsberg and published by the *New York Times* in 1971.

I would like to stress, however, that Prime Minister Pham Van Dong listened attentively and courteously to all I had to say and convey, even when he disagreed strongly with it and surely found some of it offensive. He was a highly intelligent and articulate person and an impressive Communist personality by any standards. He died in the year 2000, well into his eighties, almost blind but, according to a Vietnamese source, very alert and lucid to the end.

My call on Prime Minister Pham Van Dong was, of course, the most important part of my first visit to Hanoi. But in addition to conveying the message which laid out the U.S. position with respect to the situation in Vietnam, I had been asked to do some general reporting on the situation in the North, of a kind any diplomat would be expected to undertake. Was there any reflection of the Sino–Soviet split in North Vietnam? Were there signs of war weariness? Were there indications of a North Vietnamese desire for contacts with the West? Were there differences between the political and the military? Was there evidence of alignments or factions in the Party or the Government? What was the nature and prevalence of Chinese Communist influence in North Vietnam?

The Cold War thinking which permeated American and indeed most Western thinking at the time is very evident in these questions. The post-war Communist takeover of the countries of Eastern Europe, the ouster of the Nationalists in China and the establishment of the People's Republic of China in 1949, the outbreak of the Korean War in 1950, the building of the Berlin Wall — all these were still very fresh in Western minds in the 1960s. Foreign policy was dominated by the Cold War, the East–West confrontation and the feared further expansion of Communism, especially in the so-called Third World. It is not surprising that the United States should be preoccupied with resisting a Communist takeover in South Vietnam, not just for its own sake, but also lest "defeat" there should diminish its status as the leading Western nation and, according to the "domino theory", lead to Communist expansionism in neighbouring countries such as Laos, Cambodia, Thailand and Malaysia.

But back to my visit to North Vietnam. I hoped the Americans, in posing their very relevant questions about the situation in the North, did not really expect to get profound analysis on the basis of a three-day visit to Hanoi by someone with no previous direct experience with Asia, let alone Vietnam. I was able to call on a very few Vietnamese officials and some of the few foreign representatives to be found in Hanoi at the time: the French Delegate-General, the British Consul and some Eastern European ambassadors (the Soviet Ambassador was out of the country). Not surprisingly, none of the Soviet bloc representatives bared their souls to me. The Mongolian Ambassador and I found a tiny bit of common ground in that we had both lived in Moscow, myself at the Canadian Embassy, he at the Higher Party School, and we agreed that this gave us rather different perspectives.

My telegram to Ottawa on DRVN attitudes and outlook, with all its careful disclaimers on the paucity of hard evidence and my own limited background in the area, nevertheless came to the following conclusions:

> Tentative conclusion is that we would be unwise at this stage to count on war weariness or factionalism within leadership or possible material advantages to DRVN or kind of Asian Titoism as of such importance to cause DRVN to jump at chance of reaching accommodation with USA in the area. Certainly on my brief visit I detected no evidence to suggest (as some columnists have been doing) that starvation, war weariness and political discontent are bringing regime close to collapse and that they would therefore grasp at any straw which might enable them to save something before country falls apart.
>
> Prospect of war being carried to north may give greater pause for thought. But I would hesitate to say that DRVN are yet convinced, despite USA public statements and moves and private message I have conveyed, that USA would be prepared to take this step, ultimate consequences of which could be start of World War III. I am also inclined to think that DRVN leaders are completely convinced that military action at any level is not going to bring success for USA government forces in SVN [South

Vietnam]. They are almost as completely convinced that [General Nguyen] Khanh government is losing ground on political front and are confident that in fullness of time success is assured for Liberation Front supported by DRVN.

Looked at 37 years later, I have no reason to regret the conclusions I reached. The only regret, perhaps, is that the Americans did not take them more seriously.

On the slow plane trip back to Saigon, I was scribbling furiously to prepare my reports to Ottawa and thinking how, once Ottawa had received them, I should orally convey their gist to the anxiously awaiting American Embassy.

Once the adrenaline rush of this first visit to Hanoi had subsided a bit, and before the next visit in early August, just after the Gulf of Tonkin incident, I had to turn my attention to other more prosaic realities.

One was the fact that I was head of the Canadian delegation to the International Commission for Supervision and Control and had to prepare, with lots of staff help, for the interminable and frustrating meetings of the Commission. The Poles were relatively easy to deal with. They knew and we knew and they knew that we knew that their job was to defend the position of the North Vietnamese and to draw constant attention to the alleged violations of the cease-fire agreement of 1954—not a difficult task given the openness of American society and the press. The Indians were another matter. Their chairman "Ishi" Rahman was a very intelligent and charming Muslim, with whom personal relations were of the best. But the deviousness and unreadability of the Indian delegation on any number of matters before the Commission were almost too much for straightforward Canadians. Their tactics of delay (or so it seemed to us) were masterful, and our frustration in trying to reach Commission conclusions was constant. Given the actions of our Commission partners, and the fact that neither South nor North Vietnam was prepared to allow the Commission any significant activity on its own, it is no wonder that I, like so many of my predecessors after the first few useful years of the Commission, and my successors in later years, said to ourselves and in reports back to Ottawa, "What the hell are we doing here and what good is it doing anybody?"

All this said, the fact was that Canada was a member of the Commission, and as long as it was a member, we all felt that we should in all conscience try to make it work. From our perspective, it was important to have the Commission report, among other things, on the evidence of continuing violations of the cease-fire agreement by the DRVN and the involvement of the North in the insurgency in the South. This latter was not as easy to document as was, evidently, the American support for the government and armed forces of the South. But it was necessary if there was to be some semblance of balance and even-handedness in explaining the situation in South Vietnam. The Canadian delegation laboured away, therefore, in presenting the evidence that did exist and trying to move discussion along within the Commission. We also had it in mind that if ever we were to recommend formally that Canada withdraw from the Commission, we were under an obligation to show first that we had made every effort to make it effective.

Another reality was that my family—my wife and two young children—were to arrive in Saigon in late July, and their well-being had to be thought of. What schools would the children attend and how would we keep them busy and healthy and happy? How would my wife adjust to tropical heat, to the rather ambivalent position of the Commission in relation to the foreign and diplomatic community, and to looking after a family household in considerably less than stable and secure conditions? I could not ask her to share in the arcane frustrations of Commission work and could tell her virtually nothing of the much more interesting "Bacon" exercise.

In the end, it all worked out tolerably well. Our son Geoffrey spent a challenging but probably useful year at the *Lycée Jean-Jacques Rousseau*, and acquired some toughness in the process. Our daughter Virginia was taught by Belgian nuns, who scared the life out of her with their lurid accounts of Vietcong atrocities, but she has turned out a cheerful and well-balanced individual. We swam, took exercises and played tennis at the *Cercle Sportif*, went water skiing through the flotsam of the Saigon River at the *Club Nautique*, took the odd outing to the beaches at Cap St. Jacques (Vung Tau) and a long week-end holiday with Australian friends to Dalat in the hill country. We were only shot at once (in a plane en route to Dalat, with a forced landing at a tea plantation) and the bomb explosion nearest to any of us was at the American military headquarters next door to our daughter's school.

As the war heated up, we could often hear the sound of mortars and bombing in actions not far outside the city. We lived amidst the uncertainties of chronic political instability in Saigon, with its street demonstrations and coups and rumours of coups. When all the U.S. dependents were evacuated following the bombing of the American Embassy, our children found their circle of friends much reduced. As is usually the case, the situation appeared far worse from abroad than it did on the ground, and we said firmly "no" when the Department tried to persuade us to return the family to Ottawa just after Christmas. Rather frantic messages to that effect reached us in Hong Kong, where we were taking a brief break at the splendid old *Repulse Bay Hotel*. Saigon was not the most fun posting, but it was an experience to be remembered, on the whole positively, by all of us.

Our official social life in Saigon was not quite like that of Canadian diplomats in other small posts. A certain amount of it related to our membership in the three-member Commission, with the Indian chairman and the head of the South Vietnam Liaison Mission entertaining us fairly frequently. I shall not forget being served one Vietnamese specialty, large snails of a rubber-like quality which seemed impervious to chewing and eventually had to be swallowed whole lest the host be offended. I often found myself seated next to Mme Anh, the wife of the head of the Liaison Mission. She smiled amiably and comfortably, but her total knowledge of any foreign language appeared to be the phrase "Moi, j'ai onze enfants". Lacking Vietnamese, I could not pursue the conversational opportunities offered by this rather startling statement.

Outside Commission circles, we were treated by other diplomats more or less as a Canadian head of mission, and developped through the social circuit some good friends in the British, American and Australian Embassies in particular. The talk, of course, centred around the increasingly unstable political and military situation in South Vietnam, how the Americans in particular were planning to cope with it, and whether there were any scenarios which might lead out of the impasse. The Americans did not find life any easier when, in July, General Khanh and the head of the South Vietnamese air force, General Nguyen Cao Ky, spoke publicly about the necessity of a "march to the North" in order to deal with the Vietcong insurgency. I was constantly asked about North Vietnam because of my ability to visit there, but with very few exceptions had to avoid saying anything about the messenger role I was playing between Washington and Hanoi.

Early in August 1964, there was a dramatic development in the Gulf of Tonkin which significantly changed the course of American involvement in the war in Vietnam. As it was presented at the time, on August 2 three DRVN patrol boats attacked the U.S. destroyer *Maddox* without provocation as it traversed international waters. The *Maddox* returned fire, but the United States decided to treat the incident as an isolated mistake by Hanoi and contented itself with a warning to the attackers. Two days later, however, it was reported that there had been a second unprovoked attack in the Gulf. And Washington responded by limited air strikes against North Vietnamese patrol boat bases and other targets on the coastline. Of greater political significance was the fact that the Gulf of Tonkin incidents enabled President Johnson to get Congress to pass by a massive majority a resolution authorizing the President to take the necessary action to defend U.S. interests in Southeast Asia. It passed the Senate by 88 votes to 2, and the House unanimously.

It turned out somewhat later that things were not nearly as straightforward as they were presented at the time, nor as I and most others then understood them to be. The *Maddox* was not on an innocent cruise, but was fitted to engage in electronic surveillance along the coast. At the same time, U.S.-directed South Vietnamese units were launching guerrilla raids against offshore islands nearby. The DRVN military could reasonably conclude that the raids and the destroyer's passage were linked. Recent information, however, indicates that the decision to attack the *Maddox* was taken by a local commander, not by Hanoi. It is also all but certain that the second "attack", on the *Maddox* and another destroyer, the *C. Turner Joy*, never occurred. But President Johnson had his very broad authority from Congress and the war had been taken overtly to the North for the first time.

It was in this atmosphere that I undertook my second visit to Hanoi on August 10, instructed by Ottawa to convey a new message from the U.S. government to the government of North Vietnam. Again, I saw Prime Minister Pham Van Dong, on August 13, although understandably he was in less affable and courteous form than at our first meeting.

The message opened with a statement expressing bewilderment at the motives behind the "second attack" on U.S. destroyers, an assertion that the U.S. response was limited and appropriate, and the news that in view of the uncertainty aroused by the "unprovoked" DRVN attacks, the United States was carrying out "precautionary deployment of additional air power to South Vietnam and Thailand." It then went on to reiterate the main thrust of the first message, that Hanoi should cease its support for the insurgency in the South. The message concluded with the statement that "U.S. public and official patience with North Vietnamese aggression is growing extremely thin" and that "if the DRVN persists in its present course, it can expect to suffer the consequences".

Pham Van Dong's reaction was, not surprisingly, one of anger. (The American account of what had happened in the Gulf of Tonkin had been rejected by the official August 8 DRVN declaration about those events, a declaration which had been formally conveyed to the ICSC Commissioners, who were then meeting in Hanoi. Colonel Ha Van Lau had told David Jackson on August 8 that the "second attack" was "sheer fabrication".) I said to the Prime Minister that I regretted that what I had just said was not very pleasant for him to hear, but that I was carrying out faithfully my instructions to convey a specific message. Apparently controlling himself with difficulty, he said that even to deliver such a message to a Prime Minister was not very polite, that it did not merit being listened to, and that he would not deign to reply to "these lies". He gave no indication, however, of being worried by the firmness of the U.S. message, nor of wanting to discuss a way out. He accused Johnson of carrying the war to the North because "there is not a way out in the South", and because of "worries ... about the coming electoral battle." (The U.S. elections were to take place in November.) I reported to Ottawa that, after he had calmed down (I had thrown in a remark about not shooting the messenger, which brought a laugh), the Prime Minister did state that he wanted to keep open the DRVN–U.S. channel of communication. My view, however, was that he was unlikely to use it for some time at least. I concluded that "he is genuinely convinced that things are bound to go his way in Indochina and that there is therefore no need to seek compromises."

Outside on the streets, in contrast with the calm of my first visit, slit trenches were being dug, brick bunkers built, air raid drills held.

The North Vietnamese were taking precautions against further raids on their territory.

All of this, of course, I reported in detail to Ottawa and discussed subsequently with the American Embassy in Saigon, where General Maxwell Taylor, former chairman of the Joint Chiefs of Staff, had succeeded Lodge as ambassador and Alexis Johnson, a career diplomat, joined him as deputy ambassador. They listened attentively, and over the next month or so I was called upon to brief senior visiting Americans about my visits to Hanoi. I recall particularly briefing Secretary of Defense Robert McNamara and top military brass from Washington after a dinner at the home of General William C. Westmoreland, the senior U.S. Army officer in Vietnam. I was also asked to brief Henry Kissinger, who was not to hold official positions until Richard Nixon succeeded to the presidency, but the U.S. Embassy in Saigon had been instructed to look after this distinguished academic well. During his visit to Saigon, he was in the hands of Dick Smyser, an Embassy officer very knowledgeable about the situation in North Vietnam.

The Honourable Paul Martin, Secretary of State for External Affairs, had been a little more hesitant than Prime Minister Pearson about taking on the messenger role when Canada was first approached by the Americans. But once we had taken it on, he followed developments with very keen interest, determined that Canada should do everything possible to encourage a real dialogue between the Americans and the North Vietnamese. He read, I was told, all my reports avidly and insisted on being involved personally in instructions sent to me from Ottawa.

When, therefore, Mr. Martin was to pay a visit to Tokyo in September 1964 for one of the Canada–Japan ministerial meetings, he decided that he wanted to hear from me directly on my visits to Hanoi, my conversations with Prime Minister Pham Van Dong, and my views as to the prospects for reaching a peaceful accommodation between Washington and Hanoi. I flew from Saigon to Tokyo to be available for that purpose. Mr. Martin had a very busy schedule of meetings and social engagements in connection with the ministerial talks, and it was difficult to see when I could be fitted in. I was in due course summoned for a meeting before breakfast to the Ambassador's residence where Mr. and Mrs. Martin were staying, the very impressive mansion built in the 1930s by Canada's first Minister to Japan, Sir Herbert Marler. I was shown up to their suite, but by then Mr. Martin realized he did not have enough time for a proper briefing, and proposed we meet instead at the end of the afternoon, when his meetings were finished.

I returned to the residence as arranged and met a tired Paul Martin saying he had to relax with a swim in the pool in the garden, and why did I not join him and brief him as he swam. I pleaded lack of a swimsuit for not joining him in the pool, but he insisted there must be something for me to wear somewhere in this vast residence. There was, in the form of a pair of bright orange boxer swim shorts once the property of a previous ambassador, Fred Bull, who was about twice my girth. In a cloakroom on the ground floor, I did my best to pull the drawstring tight enough that the shorts would stay on, padded across the elegant front hall wearing nothing but the shorts and a raincoat, and joined the Minister in the pool. For the next half hour, we swam up and down in a leisurely breast stroke while I briefed him and answered his questions. I recall being deeply concerned about the security of the operation and, as evening fell, imagined spies or at least microphones lurking behind every bush around the pool. Mr. Martin was totally concentrated on the subject we were discussing and seemed to find it not at all unusual to get his Top Secret briefing in this way.

My two visits to Hanoi in June and August of 1964 were the most significant of the six visits I made during my eighteen months in Vietnam. During both I had substantive messages to convey from the United States to the Democratic Republic of Vietnam and in both cases I delivered them personally to Prime Minister Pham Van Dong. Thereafter, the American interest in using the Canadian channel appeared to fade.

One reason, of course, is that Washington was increasingly preoccupied by the political instability in South Vietnam, by the lack of effectiveness of the Army of the Republic of Vietnam to cope with the insurgency, and by the question of how far the United States had to involve itself militarily in order to compensate for these shortcomings. Another is that, over the next few months, other channels were being explored or opened, other actors were getting involved in an attempt to seek accommodations and to stave off the dismal prospect of an escalating, bloody and probably prolonged war. The Secretary General of the United Nations, U Thant, was in dialogue with the North Vietnamese and was trying to interest the Americans in what he was hearing. The Americans themselves were in contact with the Communist Chinese through their respective embassies in Warsaw. And the French, who continued to believe that, on the basis of their experience in Indochina, they might have a role to play, were discussing the possibility of accommodation through the North Vietnamese representative in Paris, Mai Bo. It must be noted also that, although Pham Van Dong during both my meetings with him had expressed his desire to keep the Canadian channel open, his government made no move to initiate any response to the messages from Washington which I had conveyed. In Hanoi as in Washington, the preoccupation was increasingly a military one and Hanoi probably hesitated to use the Canadian channel lest it be seen as an indication that it was fearful that it might not be able to stand up to the growing American military presence in the region.

Whatever the explanation, I had no specific American message to convey when I next visited Hanoi in December and saw no one of higher rank than the head of the Liaison Mission, Colonel Ha Van Lau. On this trip north, I took time to visit, along with David Jackson, one of the Commission's team sites at Dong Dang near the Chinese border, with a 100 km "control" trip by jeep to Phuc Hoa on the border. I retain two vivid memories of the visit. One was having to drink, at a team site dinner and no doubt in retaliation for my gift of Canadian rye whiskey, large quantities of the Vietnamese specialty "snake wine", the snake all too visible in the bottle from which the "wine" was poured. The other is of secretly taking a photo from my bedroom window, in spite of grave warnings of the consequences of any photography in such a sensitive area, across the Chinese border to record for memory the steep hills rising straight up from the plain and looking exactly like traditional Chinese landscape paintings.

In March of 1965, the Americans contented themselves with asking Canada to advise the North Vietnamese of what had been said in February by the American Ambassador in Warsaw to his Chinese counterpart. Again, I was able to see only Ha Van Lau, who not surprisingly said that the message seemed to contain nothing new and in any event they had already received a report of the Warsaw meeting from the Chinese.

* * *

I would not want to leave the impression that my messenger role was my only activity during my eighteen months in Vietnam. Certainly it was the most exciting and memorable, but in total it took far less of my time than did the Commission work. There, as I mentioned earlier, the challenge for the Canadian delegation was to give some semblance of balance in our reporting by documenting the violations of the cease-fire agreement by North Vietnam. This was meant to be set against and even help to explain the evident violations inherent in the enormous amounts of materiel being supplied to the South Vietnamese Army and in the rapidly growing American military presence in the South.

The Commission had travelled to Hanoi early in August 1964, just after the Gulf of Tonkin events. At our meeting of August 13, we received a presentation by Colonel Ha Van Lau that gave a very different version of what had happened in the Gulf from that which had been made to the U.S. Congress and to the American people. The Commission was thus formally seized of the matter, and the debate began as to what sort of message should be sent to the co-Chairmen of the Geneva Conference, Britain and the Soviet Union.

Thus began several months of frustrating internal negotiations during which Canada attempted, as it was stated in a memorandum for the Minister, "to set the Gulf of Tonkin incidents into a wider perspective and to present a more balanced and accurate picture of the significant factors in the situation in Vietnam." Canada wanted to make use of extensive work done over several years by the Legal Committee of the Commission to draw attention to the subversive factor and the role played by North Vietnam in the insurgency in the South. I shall not recount the devious twists and turns of these negotiations, carried out in Saigon, in Ottawa and in New Delhi, other than to say that by late January 1965 we still had not managed to find a formula which the Indians and the Canadians could accept.

Early in February, a joint announcement on behalf of the governments of the Republic of Vietnam and the United States revealed that air strikes had been taken against military installations in North Vietnam which "had been employed in the direction and support of those engaged in aggression in South Vietnam". This was in retaliation for a Vietcong attack on a U.S. military base, at Pleiku in the central highlands, which had resulted in significant American casualties. The retaliatory air strikes were to be the prelude to operation "Rolling Thunder", the systematic bombing of North Vietnam which continued over the next several years.

Quite by chance, the attack on Pleiku and the resultant air strikes coincided with the visit to Hanoi of Soviet Premier Alexei Kosygin. Drawing on a recently signed Soviet–North Vietnamese trade agreement, Kosygin pledged increased military and economic assistance to the DRVN, including surface-to-air missiles and other air defence equipment. He condemned American aggression and emphasized Soviet support for the Vietnamese "national liberation" movement. In private conversation with the Hanoi government, however, there is reason to believe that he cautioned against escalating the war and asked about the North's terms for a negotiated settlement. The Soviets were happy enough to see things going badly for the Americans in South Vietnam. But they did not relish the prospect of being themselves drawn directly into a conflict in that area, particularly if there was a risk of it leading to a wider conflagration or even seriously damaging Soviet–American relations.

The Pleiku attack also coincided with a visit to Saigon of National Security Advisor McGeorge Bundy and Chester Cooper of the CIA, who were preparing recommendations for the President on what the future course of action in Vietnam should be. Many years later, it emerged that the Pleiku attack was in all probability launched by a local commander, not ordered by Hanoi. One can only speculate as to whether this fact, if known at the time, would have changed the American decision to begin the regular bombing of the North.

But back to the Commission. The Indians and the Poles decided that, while they had missed the opportunity to report on the Gulf of Tonkin incidents, they could not afford to do so again with respect to something as straightforward as an announcement of attacks against North Vietnam. They prepared a short Special Report to the co-Chairmen, drawing attention to these events and the reaction of North Vietnam to them. They expressed their concern over the gravity of the situation and suggested an immediate appeal to all concerned to take whatever measures were necessary to stem the deteriorating situation.

Canada attached a minority statement saying that the majority report, by concentrating on a very limited aspect of the situation in Vietnam, ran the serious risk of giving a distorted picture of the nature of the problem and its underlying causes. Drawing heavily on the earlier work of the Legal Committee, on the Special Report of 1962 and on more recent documentation provided by the South Vietnamese Liaison Mission, it cited details of the subversion case. It stressed that North Vietnamese support of hostile activities in South Vietnam was a grave violation of the Geneva Agreements and was the root cause of general instability in Vietnam. The Indians and the Poles, in separate brief statements, objected to what Canada had said.

Not surprisingly, what the Commission had to say on the subject had no effect whatsoever on the events which unfolded in the Vietnam drama over the next months and years. The situation had gone well beyond the Commission's power to influence.

After the climax (or anti-climax) of the Special Report to the co-Chairmen, the Commission continued to meet and to try to do its business; but our hearts were not in it. We could only watch from the sidelines as the sad history unfolded. When I arrived in Saigon in June of 1964, there were about 16,000 American "military advisors" in South Vietnam providing equipment and instruction and support such as helicopter and transport units. When I left near the end of 1965, the American military presence numbered over 180,000, including combat troops. A few years later, that number exceeded half a million. The casualties which these troops suffered over the years were an important consideration in the growing anti-war movement in the United States and in the deal finally struck in 1973 between the United States and North Vietnam, a deal which led to the nominal cessation of hostilities and to the eventual re-unification of Vietnam under Communist rule.

As the summer of 1965 approached, my time in Vietnam was drawing to a close. The family was to return to Canada at the end of the school year, the children to go into summer camps (where Geoffrey was given the nick-name "Saigon"), my wife to move back into our home in Ottawa awaiting my return later in the year. My Senior Political Advisor, Bob Hatheway, who had replaced Tom Delworth, was also due to return to Canada that summer, and the Department proposed that Peter Roberts might come over from Hong Kong for a few months to serve as Senior Political Advisor and gain some direct Vietnam experience while en route to his next assignment in Washington D.C. I readily agreed as Peter was a friend from Moscow

Embassy days. He moved into the Commissioner's villa where there was lots of room after my family's departure.

As I prepared to make my next visit to Hanoi at the beginning of June, Washington asked to convey one more message through the Canadian channel. It drew attention to a speech by President Johnson indicating a readiness to enter into unconditional discussions that might lead to a peaceful solution of the Vietnam problem. It expressed disappointment that Hanoi's activities in the South appeared to continue without change and even to intensify. It also expressed regret that a five-day suspension in mid-May of the bombing attacks on North Vietnam, which had been under way for some months, had met with no response from Hanoi, so that the attacks had to be renewed.

Ottawa considered that this message added little to what had been said publicly by the U.S. Administration, and was reluctant to have me seek a high-level meeting solely on that basis. I was instructed instead to emphasize Canadian interest in seeing either the Prime Minister or the new Foreign Minister, Nguyen Duy Trinh. In the event, I saw the Foreign Minister, to whom I expressed Canadian concerns about the situation in Vietnam and said that Canada was willing to play a helpful role if negotiations could be stimulated. I also sought clarification from him of the meaning of the "Four Points" about negotiations which had been enunciated in a speech in April by Pham Van Dong. I was unable to get him to say whether these were preconditions to talks or ultimate goals. In the course of the conversation, I did pass the American message but Trinh showed no interest in it and indeed some irritation at having to listen to this reiteration of the American position.

On the basis of this conversation and those with other Vietnamese and foreign observers, I left Hanoi persuaded that the DRVN was not interested in any negotiations at that time. That was the last use made of the Canadian channel between Washington and Hanoi. On my final visit to Hanoi in early October, Canada was not asked to convey any message.

The "Bacon" exercise began in the spring of 1964 and continued, though in a diminishing mode, until mid-1965. All messages related to it bore the Top Secret security designation, and every attempt was made to keep information about it on a strict "need-to-know" basis. I am sure my Indian and Polish colleagues suspected that my trips to Hanoi, several of them with the full Commission, were related to more than Commission business, and inevitably some countries other than Canada, the United States and the DRVN had at least some knowledge of what was going on. The surprising thing is that at the time so little leaked out to the press and the public.

Early in June, 1965, the Secretary of State for External Affairs, Paul Martin, in a statement in the House of Commons, made mention of my call on Foreign Minister Trinh, stressing Canadian interest in the prospects for negotiations but making no mention of the American message. On June 17, President Johnson commented extensively on Vietnam in a press conference. In the course of it, he referred to "people who were negotiating for us (not members of this government)" and of a recent message from "the same man". He then proceeded to declassify on the spot parts of my Top Secret report on the meeting with Trinh. I heard a report of the press conference on the radio as I lay in bed listening to the late evening news, and my wife remembers me sitting bolt upright and crying, "My God, he's blown my cover!"

"The same man" and his country were not identified, but at a special off-the-record briefing of British and Canadian correspondents the day before the President's press conference, Secretary of State of Rusk said that Seaborn's efforts to sound out the North Vietnamese on various occasions had been deeply appreciated. He did not say that I had been acting on behalf of the United States, but Canadian correspondents put two and two together, and the cat was out of the bag. The amazing thing is that it did not get much play in the Canadian press at the time, perhaps because at least one reporter who proposed to write about my role as "broker" and special emissary was dissuaded by the Department from doing so on the grounds that it could jeopardize my personal security and that of the Canadian delegation in Vietnam.

The correspondent in question was Terence Robertson, who was preparing to visit Saigon and to write a story about the Canadian role in the Vietnam Commission for *Maclean's* magazine. Robertson indeed came to Saigon in September and I had a lengthy conversation with him on the verandah of the Commissioner's villa, sipping *citron pressé*. Keeping in mind the Department's desire not to jeopardize the possible future use of the "Bacon" channel, I gave no details of my Hanoi visits other than the recent conversation with Foreign

Minister Trinh. But I knew Robertson had, through other sources, at least some knowledge of my "Bacon" activities.

The result of the Robertson visit, and the growing interest in Canada about the Vietnam war, was a lengthy article in the November 15, 1965 *Maclean's* issue entitled "Our Man in Saigon", with my photo on the front cover of the magazine. The article as such was not too bad, with no more than a hint that the Americans might have been very interested in my Hanoi visits. But I was embarrassed by the excessive publicity, especially vis-à-vis my friends and colleagues in External Affairs.

Several years later, after I had left External for the Department of Consumer and Corporate Affairs, the whole story of the "Bacon" exercise came out, as I have mentioned earlier, as part of the *Pentagon Papers,* describing "the secret history of the Vietnam War" as published by the *New York Times*. My Top Secret reports were published there and in the *Canadian Forum*. My ready access to the texts at least saved me the trouble of having to get at them via the tortuous avenue of the government's Access to Information procedure. The then Secretary of State for External Affairs, Mitchell Sharp, had the unenviable task (with some background help from me) of telling the "Bacon" story on June 17 to a House of Commons much more critical of the United States than might have been the case in 1964 and 1965.

Since that time, an endless number of articles and books has been written on the Vietnam war, the more recent ones able to draw on the release and publication of a huge number of official U.S. documents. For some of them, and for M.A. and Ph.D. theses, I have been interviewed, even quite recently. And in many of them my small role has been recorded in what my wife kindly refers to as "a footnote to history". I like to think that other things I have done in the course of a 41-year career in the Public Service of Canada may have been of more lasting value. But I have come to accept the fact that the eighteen months in Vietnam and what I was engaged in there are what is most likely to generate positive name recognition, for better or for worse, depending on your point of view.

* * *

In October of 1965, shortly before my final departure from Vietnam, there was a tragic accident involving the ICSC courier plane on a routine flight between Vientiane and Hanoi. As noted earlier, the Boeing

Stratoliners owned by the French company *Aigle Azur* provided regular service to the Commission between Saigon and Hanoi, with stops at Phnom Penh in Cambodia and Vientiane in Laos. They were the only means of travel between North and South Vietnam, primarily for the use of the three Indochina Commissions but occasionally carrying other passengers

On October 18, 1965, *Stratoliner* F-BELV carrying four French crew members and nine passengers, all attached to the various national delegations of the ICSC, departed Wattay Airport, Vientiane at 1505 hours on its normal flight path to Hanoi. On board were Sgt. J.S. Byrne and Cpl. V. J. Perkins of the Canadian Army and J. Douglas Turner, the Canadian Permanent Representative in Hanoi, a Foreign Service Officer who had replaced David Jackson a few months before. At 1520 hours, F-BELV contacted Gia Lam Airport, Hanoi to confirm its departure and give its ETA at Gia Lam as 1644 hours. Gia Lam confirmed receipt of the message and cleared the aircraft for arrival as scheduled. Nothing was ever heard from F-BELV again.

Once it was realized that the aircraft was missing, an intensive air and ground search was undertaken under French and Canadian supervision along the Laotian part of the flight plan. Requests to the North Vietnamese authorities for a similar search along the Vietnamese part of the flight plan were refused. They did not allow the next regular flight of the Commission plane into Hanoi until October 28. The North Vietnamese advised that they had carried out appropriate searches, but had not found the *Stratoliner*.

Repeated attempts over succeeding years to find some trace of F-BELV have produced no results. There have been many theories and much speculation as to what caused it to disappear and its location when it disappeared. The most plausible, to my mind, is the conclusion of a thorough study undertaken by the Department of Foreign Affairs and International Trade in 1996, that "F-BELV's fall from the sky was most likely due to inadvertent or deliberate anti-aircraft fire by a North Vietnamese military unit. Once this became known, there was a deliberate attempt by the government of North Vietnam to conceal the act by not cooperating in the search efforts."[1]

* * *

---

[1] "A Report on the Disappearance of the ICSC Aircraft over Indochina on October 18, 1965," by H.G. Pardy, Department of Foreign Affairs and International Trade, January 11, 1996, p. 22.

I left Saigon in November, 1965, saddened by the fact that the messages I had carried between Washington and Hanoi had yielded no results, saddened much more by the escalating warfare, with no light at the end of the tunnel. Our High Commissioner to India, Roland Michener, had asked me to spend a few days at the residence in New Delhi. Thanks to him and to Bill Montgomery of his staff, I saw something of New Delhi, Fatehpur Sikri, and Agra and the Taj Mahal to counter my rather negative view of India and the Indians which, as in the case of so many colleagues, had stemmed from serving on the Commission. From Bombay, I took ten days on a Messageries Maritimes vessel through the Suez Canal to Marseilles, trying to wind down after the tensions of Vietnam, then by train to Paris before flying home to Ottawa in time for Christmas with the family.

On arrival in Ottawa, there were de-briefings with External Affairs officers and with the Minister, Paul Martin. I was invited to dinner at 24 Sussex Drive late in December when McGeorge Bundy flew into Ottawa to tell Prime Minister Pearson about the American efforts to find a peaceful solution to the conflict in Vietnam. In the New Year, I was assigned back to the Eastern European Section which I had headed before the posting to Vietnam. There I had a brief respite from Vietnam till I was made head of the Far Eastern Division in the spring of 1967 and was once again plunged into Vietnam affairs and the many attempts to move from war into negotiations. Fortunately, the China recognition question was thrown into our laps in the middle of the 1968 election campaign by Prime Minister Pierre Trudeau, and that rather than Vietnam was my main preoccupation (and Trudeau's in the foreign policy field) for the next two years.

In 1984, when I was Canadian co-Chairman of the International Joint Commission, many years after my posting in Vietnam, I ran into Bill Sullivan again at a conference on Canada–U.S. relations in upstate New York, sponsored by the American Assembly and the Council for Foreign Relations. I asked Sullivan whether, in the spring of 1964, there had been an acceptance in official Washington (Pentagon, State Department, the White House) of the inevitability of increased military participation in Vietnam to save the South from collapse. Without hesitation, Sullivan said that there had been no acceptance of such inevitability and that official Washington was looking to all possible solutions to cope with the crumbling political-military situation. The Pentagon was deeply worried about being drawn in more deeply and had no enthusiasm for heavier involvement. The Canadian mission to sound out the views of the DRVN was not perhaps given a great chance of success, but it was a genuine exploration on the part of the U.S. government.

I regret that, apart from a brief visit to Saigon in 1968 following a Canada–Japan ministerial meeting in Tokyo, I have not been back to Vietnam. It would have been interesting to discuss with Colonel Ha Van Lau and with Prime Minister Pham Van Dong in his retirement, what they really thought about my mission to Hanoi, and what might have been had either Hanoi or Washington reacted differently. After Canada and Vietnam had established diplomatic relations, senior Vietnamese interlocutors expressed to Canadian diplomats accredited to Hanoi their gratitude for Canada's role on the ICSC. This may of course have been no more than *politesse*. But on two occasions Ha Van Lau, by then a Vice Foreign Minister, said the Vietnamese appreciated the role I had played in a very difficult set of circumstances. They realized, he said, that my mission was certain to cause controversy and that the Canadian decision to proceed anyway took some courage.

A careful reading of the U.S. documents covering that difficult period, and of the messages conveyed, will show, I think, that the Canadian government cannot be fairly accused of being either the sabre-rattling accomplice of American war-mongers or the innocent and naïve dupe of wily American schemers. Neither we nor the Americans held high hopes for the success of the "Bacon" exercise. But Canada could scarcely have refused to take it on if there was any chance of success. It was not inconsistent with our role as a member of the ICSC, and the North Vietnamese then and later made it abundantly clear that they did not regard our activity as in any way improper. We should also recognize that from start to finish, in Ottawa and in the field, "Bacon" was handled with a professionalism completely consistent with the traditions of the Department of External Affairs. I am glad I was part of it.

My War
1965

Peter Roberts

I got on the *Air France* flight from Hong Kong to Saigon during the spring of 1965. "Take a chance, fly *Air France*", they used to say in those days. I didn't believe them, because they gave you a free drink and the pilot, his door open for all of us to see him, hung a handkerchief over his head to ward off the ferocious south China sun.[1]

The pilot came on the blower. "We have to come down very suddenly because of danger of fire from the ground." I thought, never having been before in Vietnam and knowing it was a forested country like our own, that he meant forest fires. He did not mean that.

My new boss, Commissioner Blair Seaborn, kindly met me (not every diplomatic boss does that). The person I was to replace, Bob Hatheway, was there, too. Blair politely said hello and goodbye, and then sped off in his car to his office in the old French military barracks where I, too, would soon have my own office, with its *ventilateur* and its nest of cockroaches. And rats. Big grey ones.

Hatheway, a genial chap, was supposed to instruct me about my new and unfamiliar duties. It was lunchtime. Bob said that there was an agreeable floating restaurant, not far off, tied up to the wharf in the Saigon River. Let's go there. It was indeed agreeable. At the beginning we had it to ourselves. I found out most of what I needed to know about my new responsibilities as the political advisor to the Commissioner of the Canadian delegation, peacekeeping in Vietnam, etc. What a peace we kept!

At first we were alone in the floating restaurant. The food was splendid. Then a young couple came aboard, speaking French. He had a big artist's portfolio under his arm. We began to talk. He was a pornographic photographer. He had just come back from a big tour

---

[1] This chapter by Peter Roberts is an extract from his book *Raising Eyebrows: An Undiplomatic Memoir* (Ottawa: Golden Dog Press, 2000). – Ed.

of India and Cambodia. The temples, the religious sites. He opened his portfolio. No live pornography, but some of the loveliest things Bob and I had ever seen.

Then people began to arrive. Nearly all Vietnamese. But a few Europeans among them. By now it was 4 o'clock, or perhaps 5. Bob and I had taken on a few beers, and were leaning back, reflecting on the French photographer's art, enjoying the tranquillity of the river, chatting in an ineffectual way about what was happening to our department back in Ottawa and around the world. Soon the restaurant was full of cheerful people having an after-work party.

We left, to join a military "happy hour" party at a nearby hotel. We were only a short distance away when the first blast came. A terrorist bomb, full of nails. Bob and I were not hit. Everyone in the restaurant ran for the gangplank.

The second blast came as many people were on the gangplank. Carefully aimed and timed. Forty-four people died. The two bombs were tied to bicycles, both accurately directed to their targets. Of course, the Saigon police ("the white mice", as they were called, partly for the colour of their uniforms), never found a trace of them.

A little disheartened by all of this, I went back to my hotel. I had arrived in Saigon that very day.

I went to my floor. I saw an open door, looked in, and there was my old friend, Bob McCabe. Far East bureau chief for *Newsweek*. Years together in Hong Kong. But I had no idea that he had been sent to Saigon, as had I, to cover the killing going on there.

I went into his room. He was sitting on his little bed, staring at his shoes. Usually we would have had a drink together. But he had been to the catastrophe from which I had also just come. His shoes were soaked in blood. So I said goodnight, and went to bed.

The origins of the Vietnam War

The Geneva Conference on Indochina and Korea took place in 1954. It was essentially a statement by the French that they were getting out. They had lost the war against the Communists at the battle of Dien Bien Phu. The Vietnamese to this day treasure the French aircraft they shot down (with a lot of outside help) at that battle.

The war ended, more or less. The French went home, except for their considerable commercial interests in Indochina, including banks, hotels, three elegant ships which plied between Saigon and

Marseilles with high-paying passengers on board, and the antique airline which ran the flights from Saigon to Phnom Penh to Vientiane to Hanoi, and back, every week, laden with the members of the Commission set up by the Geneva Conference. A few cases of French champagne to keep the passengers happy, who might otherwise have been disturbed by the absence of the pilots from the cockpit. They too were at the back of the plane, having a stand-up glass with the rest of us. "George runs it," they said over the level plains of northern Cambodia. But when it came to the mountains of northern Laos, they went back to work.

What to do with no more war? Governments and armies abhor peace as nature abhors a vacuum. Let's start another war. A good American friend told me the following story. (He and I had been together several years in Hong Kong, and were close. He had been born and raised in China and was an undeniable East Asian expert, like Chester Ronning, Ralph Collins, John Small and Arthur Menzies, officers of the Canadian foreign service, but younger than them.) What he told me then was a deadly secret; I did not report a word of it even to my bosses in Ottawa. But it is secret no more.

After the Geneva Conference, when the Chinese, the Russians and all the others had gone home, the American delegation held a secret meeting. I can't remember whether it took place in Geneva or in Washington. The chairman of the meeting was John Foster Dulles, Secretary of State, not to be confused with his brother, Allan Dulles, then head of the CIA. The people around the table were all top Asia experts, from the State Department, the CIA, the Pentagon. Maybe thirty of them.

According to my friend, Dulles went around the table, asking each person what he or she thought the United States should do in Indochina, now that the French had bailed out.

The verdict was unanimous, from all these people, well qualified in the affairs of the region. Military, intelligence, diplomatic — all agreed. The United States should in no circumstances be sucked in. Our position in the region is sound, well established on the offshore islands: Japan, Taiwan, Philippines, Indonesia. There was no strategic or political need to plant a foot on the mainland. The cost would certainly be vast, as it has been for the French. They spoke with one voice, and that was their advice to John Foster Dulles.

Dulles, a ponderous man, not a dull one, pondered the advice he had been given by this group of people who knew what they were talking about. "Well," he said solemnly. "We've got this guy Diem in Saigon. Why don't we give him a try?" The answer was unanimous: "No. He won't last a month." But he lasted several years: actually, until 1963, when he was assassinated.

That was how the vast American military presence began in Vietnam. Tens of thousands of lives lost, and not only American. The Vietnamese died too, in huge numbers. Then the war was lost. Wise old Senator Aitken said, "Why don't we just say 'We've won the war' and bring the boys home."

The sequel: Washington, D.C.

My ambassador in Washington, Ed Ritchie, gave a working dinner party. "Working" meant not that we could not eat or drink (we did both) but that we should discuss business. I was there not to talk, but to take notes. I had arrived in Washington, not long before this dinner, from Vietnam. Nobody else in the room had ever been near the place. The two main guests were the Canadian Foreign Minister, Paul Martin Sr. and his American counterpart, Dean Rusk. No wives. There was one item on the agenda: Vietnam. Although Saigon had been my last post before this one, I managed to hold my tongue in the presence of these grand folk.

Paul Martin performed well. He made it clear that, much as we sympathized with the United States, we were not sure what they were up to in Indochina. Were this vast war, and vast killing, necessary? In the same vein as Mike Pearson at Temple University.

Rusk responded at length. Gradually it dawned on me that he believed, really sincerely believed, that his country was fighting a war not with the Vietcong but with China. The Vietcong were mere pawns of the Chinese. Contain them and you contain China. I was almost (but not quite) shocked out of my note-taker's silence.

I had recently come from Saigon. There I had been in daily touch with the experts in the American embassy and before that, with the experts on China in the American consulate in Hong Kong. They knew whom they were fighting. It wasn't China. If there was some great power backing Hanoi, it was the Soviet Union, interested in doing whatever damage it could to U.S. interests anywhere in the world at the time. When we flew into Hanoi on the Commission plane and neared the bridge over the Red River, those surface-to-air missiles glaring up at us were not Chinese. They had come by sea from Vladivostok to Haiphong, which is why the U.S. airforce (which knew what it was doing, even if Dean Rusk did not) bombed Haiphong and caused Pearson to make one of the strongest foreign policy speeches of his life.

After dinner and a good brandy I made my way home, about midnight, and sat down to write my telegram, for the ambassador to sign in the morning.

Before long, China and Vietnam were engaged in a hot war on their common border.

÷ ÷ ÷ ÷ ÷

Pearson, Martin, and the Vietnam War
1965 – 1967

Geoffrey Pearson

There were three dominant factors in the making of Canadian policy towards American intervention in Vietnam during the 1960s: Canada–U.S. relations in general and in particular Lester B. Pearson's relations with President Lyndon Johnson; the efforts of Paul Martin Sr. to satisfy critics that the Government was actively seeking a role as "helpful fixer"; and the nature of the advice from Canadian officials to ministers. This short essay deals with the first two factors; the third has been covered in part by the contributors to this volume.

While I was a member of the UN Division from 1964 to 1967 and recall the debates we had with our colleagues in the Far Eastern Division, who were responsible for advice to the minister on the subject, I have not sought access to the relevant departmental files (no doubt others have done so). There is no question, however, that the weight of official advice, from the Under-Secretary (who had served in Vietnam) down to the desk officers involved (who had also mostly served on one or more of the International Commissions), ran parallel to that of the U.S. perception of North Vietnam as the aggressor and therefore of U.S. policy of support for the South.

Pearson and Johnson

Pearson had six meetings with President Johnson in the span of 17 months, from November 1963 to April 1965, no doubt a record pace for meetings between leaders of the two countries. The first was at the funeral of President John F. Kennedy, with whom he had already developed close personal relations, and the last was after his speech at Temple University, where he had proposed a bombing pause in the war. Pearson's close relations with America's leaders stemmed from his time as Ambassador in Washington during and after the war, and his nine years as Secretary of State for External Affairs, when he both championed and cautioned American leaders about their duties as "primus inter pares". He was especially sensitive to the occasional U.S. temptation to threaten the use of force against China, including the use of nuclear weapons, whenever China itself appeared to threaten one or other of its neighbours. Johnson, on the other hand, came to office looking for advice on foreign policy issues, with which he had had little experience and Pearson was close at hand.

Pearson wrote to the President after their first meeting in the warmest terms, including his "sincere wish to cooperate and be of help in any way I can". The opportunity soon arose for, in January 1964, before they got on to bilateral issues, Johnson was asking Pearson at a White House meeting about France's decision to recognize Communist China. Four months later Johnson asked to see Pearson in New York to talk about U.S. policy vis-à-vis Southeast Asia, and especially the need to open as soon as possible a channel of communication to Hanoi in the person of the Canadian member of the ICSC, J.B. Seaborn, a proposal already put to Ottawa and accepted. The U.S. account of the meeting speaks of the Prime Minister's "entire readiness" to have Canada play this role, and of his agreement that the United States continue to support South Vietnam, provided such support was "carefully limited", i.e., no bombing of civilians. This was the crucial distinction, harking back to Pearson's earlier fears of war with China and of the use of nuclear weapons.

After the bombing of the North began in earnest in February 1965, Pearson seized the occasion of a public speech in Philadelphia on April 2 to return to this subject, suggesting a bombing pause as a way of enticing the North to negotiate. He had discussed Vietnam briefly with Johnson during a visit to Texas in January without apparently raising this idea (the subject was the kind of non-military assistance Canada might provide to U.S. forces). The idea of a "pause" was written into the text of the draft speech by the Department in response to the Prime Minister's request for an "independent" approach, and while he preferred in practice to give advice of this kind privately, he decided to keep it in the text after hearing from a visiting American journalist (Marquis Childs) that the Pentagon was intent on carrying the raids further into the North, perhaps even to China.

The angry reaction of the President to this proposal has been fully described in Pearson's memoirs.[1] The anger may have been due to the fact that he was planning to announce his own proposals on April 7 for an end to the war, proposals which did indicate a greater U.S. willingness to negotiate. In any event, this encounter by no means ended exchanges between the two leaders. In late April, the President let Pearson know that a pause in the bombing "at the right time" would be considered (there was a five-day pause in mid-May). In July–August there was a friendly exchange of letters, initiated by the President, about American intentions, both military and political.

Pearson met Johnson in 1966 and again in 1967, both times in Canada (I was present at the 1967 meeting at Harrington Lake). In neither case did the President expect positive results from third-party intervention, but while he had been relatively optimistic about the military prospects in 1966 he was clearly upset about the stalemate a year later, blaming his critics for not recognizing his willingness to make concessions and to exercise restraint. (An account of this meeting is in the Pearson memoirs.)

By and large, Pearson accepted the American rationale for the use of military force, as long as it was limited to military targets and did not threaten China. But he doubted that it would lead to a political settlement unless there was some form of cease-fire, preceded by halting the air war.

Paul Martin and "Helpful Fixing"

Despite Pearson's resort to public diplomacy in April 1965, he and Martin agreed that Washington was best approached privately if Canada had specific advice to give about ending the war. Accordingly, Martin kept in close touch with Dean Rusk, the Secretary of State, about ways to end the war, based on Canadian contacts in Hanoi. A description of this strategy both publicly and privately came in mid-February 1967, during the resumption of U.S. bombing after a Christmas pause and at a time when public criticism of Canadian policy was on the rise. Two visits to Hanoi in 1966 by Chester Ronning, promoted by Martin, had failed to find a basis for negotiation. There was a need to justify the Canadian "helpful fixer" role.

---

[1]Lester B. Pearson, *Mike: The memoirs of the Right Honourable Lester B. Pearson*, 3 vols. (Toronto: Toronto University Press, 1972–1975) – Ed.

Speaking in the House of Commons on February 13, Martin began by defending diplomatic efforts to end the war as a means of finding a "pattern of steps towards a peaceful settlement". Until this was agreed, the war would continue and public statements would make no difference. Canadian membership in the ICSC gave Canada an advantage as a potential intermediary, either in concert with India and Poland or alone. Chester Ronning remained available to pursue the prospects for agreement. A military solution was neither "practicable nor desirable". A settlement should take place on the basis of the 1954 agreement and would have to involve international supervision, perhaps the current ICSC under a new mandate.

The following day there was a full discussion in cabinet. Martin said public opinion was divided, with a "vocal element" pressing the Government to speak out. But if it did so, it would lose the trust of both the United States and North Vietnam as a "credible intermediary". Most of Martin's colleagues apparently accepted this argument, while regretting that the Canadian public could not be made aware of the details of Canada's peace-making role. The Prime Minister, however, doubted that this role could continue without better "cooperation and understanding" by the United States and one minister "found it difficult to reconcile the various elements of Canadian policy".

If this was Walter Gordon, as it probably was, he followed up his private doubts with a public speech on May 13, in which he called upon Canadians "in all political parties ... to press the Americans to stop the bombing". Gordon claimed later that Pearson told him afterwards that "he agreed with 98% of what I had said" (Gordon memoirs, p. 284).[2] I think this is probably true, although he certainly disapproved of ministers breaking the principle of cabinet solidarity. In fact, when President Johnson and the Prime Minister discussed the subject two weeks later in Ottawa, Pearson proposed that the bombing be stopped without conditions as a preliminary to talks on a cease-fire. But this was a private view. Publicly, the Government continued to speak of a "mutually acceptable formula" for ending the bombing, thus echoing U.S. policy.

The private view became public policy when Martin told the UN General Assembly on September 27 "that all attempts to bring about talks between the two sides are doomed to failure unless the

---

[2] Walter L. Gordon, *Political Memoir* (Toronto: McClelland, 1977).

bombing is stopped". There were two main reasons for this change. Canadian opinion, including opinion within the Liberal Party, was shifting from support to concern about the war, a factor that a minority government had to take seriously. Secondly, the diplomacy of "helpful fixing", a term used in the report on foreign policy which Geoffrey Murray and I were then preparing for the Prime Minister, had brought no rewards, despite the continuing efforts of Martin to take advantage of our role on the ICSC to probe the intentions of Hanoi. Indeed, not until the spring of 1968, when the bombing was restricted, did the North agree to begin the bilateral talks.[3]

The fits and starts of Canadian policy on Vietnam during this period can be explained in part by the tensions that arose between Pearson and Martin over their respective roles in the direction of foreign policy. Despite their joint belief in the value of private diplomacy, Pearson, as leader of the Liberal Party and an old pro in dealing with the Americans, was wont to rely on his long experience of when and how to assert Canadian concerns about the uses of American power. He did this without always consulting Martin, whose reliance on the tradition of Canada as "peacemaker" he regarded with a touch of paternal condescension. Martin, in turn, had to be sensitive to Pearson's image as the "master" of foreign policy who could do no wrong in that field, while he, Martin — a political veteran — must await his final attempt to grasp the golden ring.

÷ ÷ ÷ ÷ ÷

---

[3] See the final chapter below, by Molgat, for the evolution and outcome of these talks. – Ed.

Memories of Cambodia
November 1965 – November 1968

Louise Pommet-Dyer

My contribution to this book will be about my everyday life in Cambodia, at work and at what I called home for three years.

My role as secretary to the Canadian Commissioner to the International Commissions for Supervision and Control (ICSC) was one of support. No momentous decisions to make, or important incidents to report to Ottawa; those were the domain of the Commissioner, so my free time could be devoted to learning about Cambodia and its people and enjoying life in Phnom Penh.

How did a girl born in the pretty but sleepy town of Rivière-du-Loup find herself, in the sixties, part of a Canadian peacekeeping mission in Asia? It is a long story.

* * *

I was born with itchy feet and started exploring my surroundings almost as soon as I could walk, despite verbal admonition from maman and, at times, physical admonition from papa! But my curiosity remained and was heightened when, from the large windows of my school, I was often distracted watching big ships from Europe coming up the St. Lawrence River on their way to Montreal. I daydreamt a lot and determined that, one day, I would "see the world".

In the mid-fifties I discovered air travel and thought of being a stewardess, as they were called in those days, but I was turned down for being under 21 years of age. I continued working in my home town, waiting for the magic 21, in the meantime travelling extensively within Quebec and Ontario, spending one month in New York at the head office of my then employer, followed by a whole summer at a Spanish language school in Mexico. All these confirmed that travel was for me.

Out of the blue I saw an advertisement in *La Presse*, a Montreal newspaper: the Department of External Affairs was looking for bilingual stenographers to work both in Ottawa and in Canadian missions abroad. This was indeed what I had been looking and waiting for. I applied and, after successful tests and interviews, I headed for Ottawa in May 1961, armed with one suitcase and very little money, for what I knew would be an exciting and enriching new life.

External Affairs

One of my hopes on joining External Affairs had been to go back to New York on a short posting during the United Nations session held in September. Instead, around July 1961, Personnel offered me a short posting to Laos. I am not sure what made me say no then: disappointment, fear of the unknown, too far away — I can't remember. Most of my friends thought I had been silly to refuse and although I was convinced it had been too soon for me to go to Asia, slowly the idea took hold in my head.

I did go to the United Nations session in New York that September and resumed work in Ottawa on my birthday, 8 January 1962, on which day I was called in to Personnel and offered a two-and-a-half-year posting to Rio de Janeiro. I was both stunned and delighted as I had had a soft spot for Rio — it sounded so exciting and I immediately said "what a lovely birthday present"! Indochina, once again, had to wait.

I spent a very happy time in Rio, came home at the end of 1964 and was assigned to the Minister of External Affair's office in Ottawa where I worked for one year. The winter of 1964–65 was a particularly bitter one and I did not like it much so when the autumn of 1965 rolled in I asked to be sent out, mentioning that it would be nice to go somewhere warm, "as long as it was *not* Saigon".

The 'not' must have been lost on the Personnel lady, who called me in later on and, to my astonishment, told me I had been assigned ... you guessed it, to Saigon! I said a very "definitely not" but quickly added that I would, however, consider Phnom Penh. No doubt a little piqued, the lady said Phnom Penh was also open and demanded I make up my mind that minute. Without hesitation I said yes. And that's how I found myself on my way to Indochina in November 1965 and where destiny, it would seem, was already awaiting me.

Leaving for Phnom Penh

I was briefed, given a post description and the name of the secretary I was to replace (Margaret Govan). I wrote to her to find out more about the job and living conditions, and her reply made me quite pleased indeed that I was going to Phnom Penh. I liked the idea of living in a bungalow rather than in a hotel room as was the case for secretaries in Vietnam and Laos. I decided then that, although the posting was supposed to be for nine months, it sounded so nice and interesting that I would soon ask to stay at least one year.

Monique Lefort was going to Saigon so we teamed up to travel together, stopping over in Vancouver, Tokyo and then Hong Kong to collect our visas before continuing on to Indochina. We met up with Jean-Marie Sauriol at the Hong Kong airport, also on his way to Phnom Penh and the three of us, happy but nevertheless a little apprehensive, flew away towards our new life in these exotic, yet unknown, lands for the next year.

Monique left us at Saigon airport, our first contact with Indochina. The atmosphere was what I had imagined: heat, noise, confusion, military aircraft everywhere ... I was glad I was continuing on to Phnom Penh.

Phnom Penh was just one hour away and what a contrast! It was clean, quiet and orderly, only the heat was the same. Jean-Marie and I were met at Pochentong Airport and, driving along nice avenues lined with palm trees, we were soon at the *Hôtel Le Royal* and shown to our respective bungalows.

First impressions of Phnom Penh

That night a cocktail party was being held at the Commissioner's residence to bid farewell to Margaret and welcome Jean-Marie and me. I was soon to find out that a new face was a good excuse for a party and what a terrific idea to get to know the local foreign community.

At that time, the Commissioner's residence was located above the office, in the centre of town and had, like many apartments in Phnom Penh, a large terrace where one could retire in the evening to enjoy some respite from the day's heat. Having done so, I soon found myself surrounded by quite a few nice young men who started arguing as to who was the most eligible bachelor among them. I was impressed. From inside came another young man who inquired about all the frivolity going on and, when told, declared *he* was the most eligible bachelor there. I had no idea who he was, but I was curious. I was to meet him again the next day over lunch at his apartment where he had invited the Canadian group. I was to get to know him very well and his statement was to cost him dearly!

That same week, I was invited to dinner at the chartered bank. I did not know the manager and his wife but was very pleased with the attention. I had no idea where the bank was located so I was a little nervous since I had as yet no idea of the layout of the city and this not being an official function, I was on my own, with no driver to take me there. I was told the mode of transport was by *cyclo* ('pedicab'), which I should hail either from the front of the hotel or from the street. I felt quite brave when I jumped into one and asked the driver to take me to the chartered bank. I did not realise then what 'loss of face' meant and that drivers never admitted not knowing where one's destination was, they just started pedalling. I remember quite a bit of pedalling going on, with stops here and there and anxious looks from the driver wondering whether we had arrived, with me dissolving in the seat. Somehow I got there, no doubt very late for dinner. Someone must have felt sorry for me as I remember being driven back home. After that I studied a map of the city and enough of the Cambodian language to give necessary directions — then it was the driver's turn to dissolve in the seat, but with laughter!

The Canadian ICSC delegation was the only one to have a female staff member; the other two were staffed by men only. Phnom Penh and, for that matter, the three Indochina postings, were considered "hardship" postings, suitable for men only. I did not think so from the beginning and my staying a full three years would no doubt have helped to dispel this myth if the events we know, and that are now part of history, had not happened.

A few days after my arrival the Indian delegation made a valiant effort at international friendship, hosting a little evening gathering in honour of the Canadians, and I think both Jean-Marie and Bernie (Gamache) came along. I can remember a lot of smiling going on but not much being said as the Indian accents were rather foreign to the ears of three French-speaking Canadians, with my communicating skills in English not being the best. I was glad I had gone but nobody from either side repeated the experience, and I regret it now. As far as the Polish delegation was concerned, it was 1966 and sadly those were the days when "East" and "West" did not meet.

The week after I arrived I was invited to the "Fête des Eaux", held that year in December. I was thrilled to be part of this important festival celebrating the end of the monsoon, when the waters of the Tonlé Sap reverse their course to flow back into the Mekong. I was already getting pretty adept at jumping into *cyclos* so I took one and got to my destination without difficulty this time. I much enjoyed the pageantry and the excitement of the very colourfully dressed *pirogue* crews, who vied for first place in the various races with the Head of State looking on. I was impressed at being one of the guests and will never forget that day. Unfortunately, I remember getting chilled in the late afternoon air by the river — even Phnom Penh has a winter — and coming down with a terrible cold; not a good start to my posting.

The office

After a quick tour of the office Margaret was gone and I was left to find my way. The office was not large: a small entrance/reception area, three small offices for the Canadian staff and a larger one for the Commissioner. There were four Canadians: the Commissioner, C. Webster, Jean-Marie, Bernie and myself. The three staff were neighbours at *Le Royal*, and we got along very well both in the office and socially.

A small Cambodian man was the delegation's *planton* ('orderly)', who sat in the reception area. Although he spoke French well, he was so very shy that he stood to attention whenever spoken to, and we could barely hear him. There was also a young cleaner and two drivers, one assigned to the Commissioner, the other to general duties, one of which was to drive the Canadian staff to and from work, a blessing in that tropical climate.

The driver assigned to general duties was very quiet but very fond of gambling as we found out, and he was lucky, too, in managing to pick winning numbers on a regular basis. But it seemed to work for him only for, as much as I tried, he never picked any winning numbers for me, unfortunately.

The Commissioner's driver gave us quite a fright one day shortly after I arrived. For some unknown reason, he climbed on the roof of the delegation and fell off the ladder, the Commissioner and I finding him unconscious on the ground. When he came to we realised he has suffered a very nasty break of his right arm and before we could do anything, he declared point blank he would not go to hospital but would see the local bonesetter! We had to point out to him that a bonesetter may not mend such a bad break properly and this could mean the end of his career as a driver. Finally he accepted going to hospital and, to our relief, made a full recovery and resumed his duties.

My work was not very onerous to start with: the Commissioner attended regular meetings of the three delegations, amended the minutes produced *verbatim* by the Indian delegation handling the secretariat, after which I typed the amendments and then the much-reduced version produced after a consensus had been reached. I also typed dispatches to Ottawa, kept the files and read as much as I could so as to learn about what was going on.

The Canadian government participated in the Colombo Plan and was offering scholarships for young Cambodians to study in Canada. There was also a teaching program whereby French speaking Canadian teachers were seconded to local Phnom Penh *lycées*. The Commissioner handled those two programs. All work at the delegation was done in English, except for official communications with the Cambodian government, which were done in French. I was used to working in both languages but although I spoke English fairly comfortably, I lacked confidence to enter into discussions. I often found myself at parties, listening and not saying much, at times preparing suitable replies in my head, only to find the conversation had moved on; but I persevered, gained confidence, my communicating skills improved and my shyness disappeared.

My home

My new home was a little front bungalow in the back yard of the *Hôtel Le Royal*, the best hotel in Phnom Penh, which was located in a short street having the Catholic Cathedral at one end and the Phnom ('hill)' at the other. My bungalow was next to the hotel's restaurant, *Le Cyrène* and the swimming pool, the latter lost on me in those days as I had not yet learned how to swim. It was comfortable enough although very sparsely furnished, two tiny iron beds in the bedroom and the bathroom offering only a small shower with cold water. Even in such a hot climate, a cold shower in the morning was hard to take and I tried without success to have the hotel install a hot water system. The living-*cum*-dining room at least had an air conditioner but it was not large enough to reach the bedroom and cool it properly. Yung, a young Chinese maid who had worked for my predecessor, made me very welcome and as we started work very early in the morning, it was nice to have my breakfast laid out before I left. Her attentions compensated for the shortcomings of the bungalow.

Those bungalows were very popular with people spending a little time in Phnom Penh or while waiting for a permanent residence. Later on I had a couple of rather eccentric neighbours, one of whom was a Spanish gentleman who always wore his jacket thrown over his shoulders and walked around the hotel compound with a black panther on a leash! The other was a French doctor who kept a pet tiger and was known to have had to patch up some of his dinner guests, even teasing them on arrival with a "don't worry, I am a doctor"! His wife was away, and when she came back the tiger had gone—she must have given him the choice. Needless to say that when the poor animals were taken out for their walks, I stayed well indoors. The good doctor also had quite a reputation with young people needing advice or help and the story was that careless young men would receive their jabs with the cry "ah, the wages of sin"!

A few months later Charles Aznavour came to make a film and was also a neighbour for a while, playing daily games of chess with Jean-Marie. Pity I was too shy in those days to ask him for his autograph as I was quite a fan of his.

Christmas and New Year's Eve, 1965

There was an excellent highway leading to the beach resort of Sihanoukville (Kampong Som), not very far away—maybe three hours by car. The Commissioner allowed the staff to borrow the car and driver and having arrived in December I thought it a good idea to spend Christmas at the beach. I invited Monique from Saigon and she joined Jean-Marie and me for our first Christmas in Indochina; I remember we had a lovely time although poor Jean-Marie got quite sunburnt. I decided there and then that I would pay regular weekend visits to this lovely spot with comfortable accommodation, good food and where the beach extended as far as one could see.

After Christmas at the beach in Sihanoukville, I came back for a New Year's Eve party, ushering in 1966. It was held on the terrace of No. 5 Wat Koh where a few Australians lived in a small three-storey block of flats. The large terrace on the roof was ideal for parties as in the evening it became quite cool, even to the point of having to wear a cardigan. There was music for dancing and at one end a bar and buffet had been installed. I was escorted to the party by no less than two very nice young men: Ken, and Bernie from the office.

Life in Phnom Penh

Phnom Penh was a lovely city with lots of trees, parks and flowers. It was also clean, with garbage collected daily and the streets swept, also daily, by an army of women wearing their red *kramas* (large multi-purpose scarf) around their head. So it was a pleasure to go out and about in Phnom Penh, which was also a very safe place. I can remember *cyclo* drivers always standing by the chair, cap in hand, while one got in. They could not imagine that *barangs* (meaning either 'French' or 'foreigner)' could or would want to walk in that heat, so when one was about in the city, they always made a beeline for one. We always thought some of them were spying on us as they seemed to know a lot.

For such a small city, Phnom Penh had quite a few nice restaurants, little bars and eating places. *Le Cyrène* at *Le Royal* was one of the nicest and best restaurants in town and sitting around the pool on an evening was very pleasant indeed. The most popular, however, and my favourite, was definitely *Le Café de Paris*, run by Monsieur Spacezzi, a Corsican gentleman of generous proportions with a superb voice. At first he used to frighten me as he would suddenly loom over one's table, enquiring with a booming voice whether all was in order, then bursting into song. He made the most delicious chocolate mousse, his secret recipe, which he promised to reveal once I had gone back home. Although I wrote and was told afterwards he enquired about me on a regular basis, he never sent the recipe but using the hints he had given, I worked at making my own version of what I think turned into a "Spacezzi mousse" he would have approved of. I heard he settled in Marseilles later on, a diabetic then, and sadly that he died there.

There was also *Le Venise* restaurant, run by a very nice Italian couple and *Le Bar Jean*, run by a Frenchman, called Jean naturally, who made the best *soupe à l'oignon gratinée* in town, a very satisfying meal in such a hot climate. I ran into Jean in Nouméa many years later, his health broken. He had left Phnom Penh and had opened a little bar first in Hong Kong, then in Cap St-Jacques (now Vung Tau), but somehow became a prisoner of the Vietnamese for a while after the fall of Saigon. When released, he found his way to New Caledonia.

In the centre of town was the Government's department store, called the *Magasin d'État* where, on the second floor, one could have a light lunch or afternoon tea. For a very relaxed atmosphere and a simple fare, there were also some floating restaurants on the Mekong and I can remember a very funny incident there one afternoon. Some French people were having coffee but found ants already busy in the sugar bowl. They were not impressed, called the *garçon* and requested sugar without ants. The *garçon* very nonchalantly went to the railing, picked the ants, one by one, and threw them into the Mekong. Then he replaced the sugar bowl back in front of the French people. I was laughing too much to hear what happened after that.

Quite often one would be invited out for Chinese banquets and one thing was always a puzzle: the food was delicious and plentiful, then why was it that the last dish was always a bowl of plain white rice? Really one could not swallow anything else but forced oneself, to be polite—we thought—to take a little. It was only after I left that I learned the Asian protocol in this matter—the host hoped he had served enough food to satisfy the guests so, to prove it, bowls of white rice were placed on the table hoping no one would have any. I do hope the poor hosts realised our ignorance of their customs and forgave us on that basis but I wish a little book on etiquette had been available in order to avoid many *faux pas*.

Shortly after my arrival I had started learning the Cambodian language from a school teacher who had been recommended to me. He was very good and came to my bungalow twice a week. I enjoyed it enormously and was learning the phonetic way which, I think, had been devised by the French, and I found it fairly easy. The writing, however, is quite flowery and difficult, and I did not get around to tackling it. Unfortunately, I think my timing was all wrong, I was trying to study in the afternoon when it was still quite hot and, after a few months, I found I was too tired to absorb much. I put it off to come back to it later on, but I never did, to my regret. I still have all my notes and books and look at them with nostalgia at times.

Excursions outside Phnom Penh

The reader no doubt has guessed that the "eligible bachelor" Ken had started taking me out shortly after my arrival. He was an Australian from Sydney, seconded to the Cambodian government under the Colombo Plan. The project he oversaw was to train young Cambodians to take over the running of the municipal workshops at Tuol Kork.

Life was becoming more interesting, I was settling well into my job and my leisure hours were now well occupied with exploring the city and what it had to offer, going out with Ken and, gradually, fitting into the Australian/British group. Ken had a car so we travelled around quite a bit, visiting various villages and towns nearby. My two favourites were the brass village and the silk village. It was fascinating to watch the people at work, having established their ateliers under their houses, and see the beautiful brass objects come to life and also the silk cloths being woven. Cambodian brass workers were true artists, producing superbly engraved and embossed vases, bowls, etc., while the silk weavers produced cloths of shimmering hues with lovely motifs through them woven with gold or silver threads; they were a delight.

We had a nice experience one day in a Cambodian village. Ken had been teaching English to a few of the boys from the workshops and, one weekend, they invited us to their village. The house, like all village houses, was built on stilts with a precarious-looking ladder leading to the living area. The people normally lived on mats spread on the floor, on which they ate and slept. We climbed the ladder and found that, for us honoured guests, two chairs had been carried up, on which we were made to sit while dish after dish was brought up and served to us. Thank heavens, the Cambodians like the Thais do not use chopsticks but eat their food with spoons, making it a lot easier for us to balance our dish on our laps. It was a bit embarrassing however as everyone sat on the mats around us, and only ate after we were finished. We were in a dilemma: should we eat a lot to prove we were enjoying it, or should we eat little to make sure enough would be left for the others! I wished my Cambodian had been better in order to communicate properly.

After lunch the boys' sisters took me into their room where we lay down on mats for a rest and I remember how awfully hot it was. Cambodians usually bathe twice a day so, after siesta, I was presented with a *sampot* ('long skirt)' and blouse to change into and we marched to the Mekong. Even though middle-aged and older women still went around bare breasted in their villages, they were a naturally very modest people. They always bathed dressed in a *sampot*, the men wearing theirs tied at the waist, the girls and women tying theirs over the chest. It was fun floating fully clothed with my long *sampot* billowing around me. I was also given some white chalk. At first I thought I was meant to eat it, but realised it was to be crushed and applied to one's face to whiten the complexion. Having been of an anaemic nature all my life, I was already fairly pale but obliged nevertheless. That was indeed one of my best days in Cambodia, so peaceful, the people so friendly and generous.

On another occasion a young man from Ken's work, Yin Ksan, decided to get married. There was much ado about the whole thing, with his mother disowning him, he said, because the girl was "too dark"! He got married, nevertheless, and asked us to be his "parents" for the occasion and come to his home. It was far, and quite complicated to reach, having to go there first by car, then transfer to a canoe and finally to a *cyclo*. We were well received by the bride; she was quite nice and not dark at all, after all. Again, we were presented with a feast and enjoyed a very special day. Unfortunately, not much more than a week later the fickle damsel had left poor Ksan. He told us, without appearing overly distressed, that she had been very demanding and had left him for a more virile friend of his!

An engagement party

At Easter 1966 Ken and I decided to get engaged and sent out invitations for a cocktail party at Ken's — this, of course, being an ideal excuse for another party! There had been a little whispering and wondering about us among the foreign community, so everyone flocked to the party to hear the news confirmed and to congratulate us. Everyone loves a romance and this livened up the fairly quiet Phnom Penh life. By then I thought it was time to request an extension of my posting from nine months to one year and this was granted immediately, but I had more extensions in mind as I was very happy in Phnom Penh.

Changes in the office

Soon afterwards, Commissioner Webster's tour of duty was over and he was gone. Very sadly, not much more than a year later, we were shocked to hear of his very untimely death in Europe. Commissioner Clair Nutting replaced him. He believed in delegating and as I was fairly well adapted to the office and the city by then, I found myself becoming more involved with projects and with the daily running of the office. I started administering both the Colombo Plan and the Canadian teacher projects, communicating with the Cambodian government and Ottawa on these matters. It was not always easy and consumed a lot of time and energy. It all started when a young Cambodian came over, inquiring about his scholarship. I retrieved the material, discussed it with the Commissioner, who asked me to handle it. The young man was quite anxious to leave so we made sure he was soon on his way. Later on I found out that he had two wives and no doubt had been eager to go to Canada not only to study but probably for a rest from domestic squabbling!

The Canadian teachers were an excellent bunch. One was a single girl my age, Marie-France James, and we became good friends. Even though I saw them all socially, to my regret I never managed to visit the schools where they taught. The Cambodian government was obviously pleased with this project, asking for more teachers and a larger contingent arrived around September 1966.

I suffered an embarrassing incident with one nice couple who invited me to dinner. They gave me directions and I said I would go by *cyclo*. That I did but that particular *cyclo* driver was not the brightest and after turning round for a while without finding the place, I had to go home quite upset and exasperated as I could not even apologise to them until seeing them again since neither of us had a telephone. Home telephones were a luxury in those days and not many people had them. I have a feeling that when we met again and I apologised, my explanation fell rather flat as no doubt they found it hard to believe.

New residence and new office premises

After a little while, the new Commissioner decided he did not much like living in an apartment located above the office and asked me to check the availability of houses in Phnom Penh. I cannot quite remember how I went about it but I met two lovely ladies, who were sisters, who took me to a house they had for rent. In Cambodia, as in the rest of Asia, the ladies take care of family business as a rule. The house was nice and Commissioner Nutting liked it and moved in.

The sisters, Claudine and Pauline, spoke excellent French and, as it turned out, they were married to two brothers. The brothers, Rakmoni and Pongmoni Sisowath, were Prince Sihanouk's first cousins. I became very friendly with Claudine and her husband Rakmoni,[1] a really delightful couple who had two little girls then and I saw quite a bit of them while there.

Commissioner Nutting also decided we needed bigger and better premises and through his contacts found a really nice and modern, air-conditioned office on the first floor of the East Asiatic Company, into which we moved. What an improvement! It was bright, with large windows and each of the staff had a large office with nice furniture and, in mine, there was a large sideboard to hold stationery. It was a nice sideboard, indeed, and after a while I realised "something" had made a home in it. I was keeping coffee and biscuits in it for morning tea for us and visitors and, one day, the biscuits had been nibbled at! I asked the cleaner to get a trap (more like a cage) and, sure enough, a large rat was caught. How it ever got there remained a mystery. I asked the cleaner to dispose of it and, on prodding, I found out later on that, being a Buddhist, he could not kill it, but whatever he did, the rat did not come back.

More changes in the office

A reorganisation also took place at that time, with two new local staff being employed, who spoke French and a little English. One, a bright young girl, became our receptionist when the little *planton* left us and the other, Pan, a father of nine, became our liaison officer with the Cambodian government as well as performing general duties. The office of the Canadian staff was out of bounds for local staff and this had Pan very intrigued. Until the day I left, he tried constantly to come in and have little peeks — there was really nothing to see. By then Bernie had gone and been replaced by Gene Gullason. As incidents were increasing on the Cambodia–Vietnam borders, a new position of Military Advisor was created and Major

---

[1] Tragically, they both perished at the hands of Pol Pot's *Khmer rouges*.

Gilles Bellavance, a very nice young officer, joined our little office. We became even busier.

Life at a very small mission, in a small tropical country far away from home was not meant to be easy but was made easier by the regular contacts we had with the Saigon delegation. The ICSC had access to *Aigle Azur* aircraft and weekly visits were made to Phnom Penh, Vientiane and Hanoi. A medical officer would drop in to give us our necessary shots, dispense advice and tablets, etc., as necessary. Although we were quite safe in the city, travelling into the countryside could be a health hazard, especially with malaria, and we needed to be careful. A regular supply of instant coffee and coffee whitener also came on those weekly visits, allowing our visitors to enjoy a cup of coffee with us.

A little excitement in the office

The delegation also received regular visits from a courier, who brought us official and personal mail and, among other things, took care of changing the combinations on our safe and filing cabinets. We had a funny incident on one of those visits and I hope Jean-Marie will not mind my telling it. All the combinations has been changed, duly noted and, mindful of security, Jean-Marie filed the new numbers in one of the cabinets and promptly locked it. As soon as this was done, we realised what had happened: we were locked out! Nobody had yet made separate notes of the one combination needed to open the safe and all other cabinets. The courier was recalled from his well-earned rest to see if he could remember anything; he racked his brain while we agonised over various number combinations but to no avail. The next morning a locksmith was called in but could do nothing, except suggest blowing the drawer up! We were appalled, fearing extensive damage and Ottawa's wrath but we had no choice and, to our relief, this was done, damaging only the one drawer holding the elusive combinations; they were retrieved and we resumed work with trepidation. Ottawa indeed was not amused when an invoice was sent for *"dynamiting of filing cabinet"* but work had to go on.

An extension almost gone wrong

Time was marching on, a year had passed since my arrival but three months earlier I had sought and been granted a further extension of one year. Jean-Marie, however, left and was replaced by Richard Longtin, and Gene by Ron Holding. It was sad to see my friends go but the new arrivals were friendly and competent and fit in well.

Around February of 1967 I lost a lot of weight, which I could ill afford, and became out of sorts, looking quite jaundiced. The doctor thought the local food, spices and herbs had upset my digestive system and I was told to keep off them. I consulted another doctor, who prescribed morphine. I could see I was getting nowhere so, rather worried, I flew to Hong Kong where local friends, May and SJ Chan,[2] booked me into the Matilda Hospital, high on the Peak. After a few tests, it was thought I could be suffering from tropical sprue, causing malabsorption thus loss of weight. However, after a rest in cooler weather (it was February and fairly fresh up on the Peak in Hong Kong) and a series of vitamin injections, I felt quite well again and returned to Phnom Penh.

Commissioner Nutting was immensely understanding throughout this period as my illness must have been of the utmost inconvenience to him. He was quite concerned and said that if I had another such spell he would have to send me back home for health reasons but I was quite determined to stay and made sure I watched my diet and did everything to remain well after that unpleasant episode. I am very grateful to him for his patience.

A garden wedding

Everyone was starting to whisper again—when are they going to get married? So, my health restored, to everyone's relief, Ken and I fixed May 1967 as the date. I must say I never encountered such community spirit and was overwhelmed by the interest, kindness and offers of assistance from everyone. We had thought of eloping, but we would have never been forgiven: rob the foreign community of a party—unthinkable! After much ado as to how an Australian and a Canadian could get married in Cambodia, it was ascertained that the Australian Ambassador had the power to marry us. So that was

---

[2] May worked at the Canadian High Commission and I met her and husband when honeymooning in Cambodia the year before.

settled and the ambassador, Noël-St-Clair Deschamps, quite thrilled at the idea, offered to hold the ceremony at his residence. It was perfect, with a lovely large garden, trees and lawn, leading to a wide verandah. Everyone then got into the act and we decided it would be a lot easier to let ourselves be organised. The British group arranged to fly in the Church of England Padre from Singapore so there could be a blessing. This led to Ken having to be christened on the eve of our wedding. Fred, the Padre, had asked to meet us before the ceremony and, on finding out that Ken had never been baptised, said this had to be done before he could participate. Ken obliged and with Robin and Liz Leonard as godparents, the little ceremony took place in Ken's apartment. We had secured a large, solid silver, Buddhist monk's begging bowl into which Fred nearly drowned Ken, with me in stitches but trying hard to be composed for such a solemn occasion. Pity nobody took any photos.

Everything had fallen into place: John Given, the Australian military attaché, would give me away, his wife Bobbie would take care of the reception, their daughter Christine would be flower girl and Shirley Green bridesmaid. On Ken's side, Harry Goodman, who worked on the same project as Ken, would be his best man. Mr. Nutting offered his car and chauffeur, the flowers, music and filming were taken care of by some of the guests and I commissioned a local photographer, who was seen crawling around and under bushes during the ceremony, taking a marvellous record of the whole proceedings.

I got up very early on the morning of 20 May 1967, feeling quite nervous, of course. After a visit to the hairdresser's, who did my hair and nails for free as a wedding present, I got dressed and waited for my party to arrive. I found that Shirley was even more nervous than I, so we decided champagne was in order or else we would trip on the mats on the way to the altar.

I had a panic attack when I got out of my bungalow to go to the ambassador's residence. The car and chauffeur had vanished. Knowing he had a little time, the chauffeur had decided to retrieve my mail from the office and brought me a lovely congratulatory letter from my favourite uncle, Louis Pommet, enclosing a gold sovereign he had carried throughout his time in Europe as a major during the Second World War. I was moved and thought it a good omen. We were also very spoiled by all our guests and received some magnificent presents, many of which were handcrafted solid silver objects.

Late May in Phnom Penh is the beginning of the monsoon, with the rains coming almost daily but not before late afternoon — around 4 p.m. We knew we would be safe to get married at noon, hold the reception and then make our way to the airport before the downpour. It all went according to plan, the sun shone bright and warm and both the wedding and the reception were magnificent.

Although there may not have been any clouds in the sky until 4 p.m., a couple of incidents did cloud our day. While at the reception word came that the *Villa Princière* at Siem Reap, where we had hoped to spend our honeymoon, had just been closed down for renovations. As the name indicates, the villa belonged to Prince Sihanouk who, when not needing it, rented it out. We had visited it before — it was truly luxurious and fit for a prince, indeed — but it could not be helped so we had to be content with the *Auberge des Temples*, not a bad substitute after all since it was located opposite the famous ruins at Angkor Wat.

The other incident happened at the airport. We arrived ahead of the guests who were following with champagne to continue the party before our departure. However, seeing that all passengers had checked in, the airport staff decided in a very cavalier fashion to dispatch the flight ahead of time. Despite our protestations we were made to board and off we went, leaving our guests on the ground with the sight of a disappearing aircraft in the sky! I think they sat around the airport and drank the champagne, while we had a dry flight in a converted military aircraft.

Although we flew to Angkor, we had asked a driver to bring Ken's car so we could use it while there and then drive ourselves back. The huge temples are scattered over many kilometres in the region. There was very little by way of organised tours in those days so a car was a must if one was to visit properly. Ken and I loved that area so much that we went three times in my three years there, spending close to one week each time. Although I loved both Angkor Wat and Angkor Thom, the two better known of the temples, my favourite was Bantei Srei ('Women's Temple)', so dainty and lovely. I also much admired Ta Som and what nature had done to it, with tree roots encircling it and growing on top of it, nearly crushing it in its embrace; it was awesome.

A new life

We drove back to Phnom Penh to start our new life. I left my little bungalow, saying goodbye with regret to Yung, who had been with me since my arrival, and moved into Ken's comfortable apartment on the first floor of No 5 Wat Koh. It had air conditioning, plenty of hot water and a large living room opening on to a nice balcony from where our little dog Jerry used to survey the world below.

The surroundings to my new home were quite different from those of the *Hôtel Le Royal*. At one end of Wat Koh — a very short street — were a Chinese restaurant and a Chinese cinema, vying with each other to make the most noise, particularly noticeable on Sunday mornings when we were at home. Daily at dusk a young man would walk down our street, making a strange sound by banging two wooden sticks together. We were quite perplexed for a while until a local friend told us he was the soup seller from the Chinese restaurant. I wish now we had tried it, even if just to see.

Apart from moving to a new home, my life did not alter much. After siesta now I could take my little dog Jerry for a walk, explore the city, shop or just drop by at the Mekong Jewellery for a chat with my friends Ty Vanna and his sister Bac Lang — a dangerous habit as I did not always come out empty-handed. Sometimes I would take a *cyclo* to return home and on one of those occasions I became convinced that some of the *cyclo* drivers were indeed spies in disguise. I jumped into one, saying nothing, and automatically the driver started towards the *Hotel Le Royal*. I put up my hand to show him my wedding ring and he said immediately, "Ah, Wat Koh". He turned around and took me straight to my new place of residence.

Leisure time and socialising

Everyone worked fairly long hours, six days a week, usually starting around 7 a.m. and finishing around 1 p.m., which left long evenings and Sundays free. We all had house help and the Vietnamese servants in particular were superb cooks and housekeepers — one could leave the running of the house to them. They could just as easily prepare dinner for two or six, or a cocktail party for 50 without flinching. They all helped one another and when invited elsewhere, we could be sure to find our own servants in the kitchen or serving the guests, they were such a very close-knit group. On one occasion when the party was at our place, I came home from work to hear strange noises in the kitchen. I had a peep only to find live crabs scurrying on the kitchen floor with the cook, armed with a long knife, in hot pursuit. I never looked again and did not much enjoy crabs in the shell after that!

On Sundays, the servants were off duty and it became a tradition to gather at someone's place about once a month for a curry lunch, to which I became addicted. On other Sundays everyone could be found dining in the various restaurants of the city.

Our social life became even busier as we were well integrated into the British/Australian/Canadian group. There were lots of parties as well as many official functions, which, at times, I found hard because of my malabsorption problem and also my inability to drink alcohol in the tropics. People were a little suspicious of non-drinkers so I always asked for a whisky and water served in a long glass, which was always full! What people did not know was that I hated whisky and the one glass used to last me all night as I used it only to wet my lips. No doubt many young people living in the tropics for a long time gave their liver to the service of their country!

As part of the Colombo Plan, Ken often received official invitations from the Cambodian government. Shortly after our marriage an invitation came for a dinner hosted by the Prime Minister in honour of the then Australian Leader of the Opposition, Gough Whitlam. When he and Mrs Whitlam walked in I heard very petite Madame Son Sann exclaim: *"Comme ils sont grands!"*

A special treat was to be invited to attend performances of the graceful Royal Ballet and one always hoped beautiful Bopha Devi would be the star. Daughter of Prince Sihanouk, she was a true *Apsara* ('heavenly dancer)' and one could imagine her having just walked off one of the bas-reliefs of Angkor.

Once we were invited by the then Queen Kossomak to the Palace for her grand-daughter's wedding reception held in the palace grounds. Just about everyone had been invited so by the time we got there we were frantic to find a table. We could not believe our luck to see an extremely well located table still free. Our contentment was short-lived, however, as very soon we realised this particular table stood right on top of the palace drains. By then, unfortunately, no other table was available.

Exploring the countryside

Fairly regularly at weekends we would travel to the beach — particularly that of Sihanoukville, which was linked to Phnom Penh with an excellent road — especially when we could manage to take Saturday morning off, giving us a nice long weekend. Unfortunately, returning from one such weekend we found we had been burgled, Ken lost his new gold watch and cufflinks but only the second pair of trousers from all his suits — very considerate of the thieves, we thought, to have left his suits intact. Luck had it that, although the same key also opened my side of the cabinet holding some of my nicest jewellery, the lock worked only with the key upside down and in reverse, which fooled the burglars. After that, I kept my jewellery case in the office safe.

For a change we paid a few visits to the very nice Kep resort where the motel was located up high, giving one spectacular views on the beach and the sea. Their seafood was the best, plentiful and delicious, particularly the *cigales de mer,* a kind of large prawn.

Bokor was another popular resort where we went once, located in the Cardamom range, where the air was so pleasantly cool, in contrast to Phnom Penh. There was gambling there but it was off-limits to the locals, so it was mainly frequented by Chinese and Vietnamese people. On a weekend visit I saw my dressmaker sitting at the tables, gambling away and oblivious to the world around him. I was quite worried that he would increase his prices if he lost but he did not — maybe he had been lucky.

Travelling on country roads was not always easy as dusk came quite suddenly in those tropical regions. Cambodians also had a habit of coming outdoors in the evening to enjoy the cooler weather, sitting on the edge of the paved road with their backs to it. The roads were not wide so coming around corners could be quite hazardous, with the driver having to be vigilant not to hit anyone. A funny incident happened on one such occasion: coming around a bend I heard expletives from Ken and, looking ahead, I saw a Cambodian man "walking" his water buffalo on a rope — quite a common occurrence there. The problem this time was that man and beast were each on opposite sides of the road with the rope stretched between them. Thankfully, after a horrified look, the man promptly let go of the rope.

Through Liz Broatch, an English girl living in Phnom Penh, I had met and befriended people who lived on the rubber plantation of Mimot east of Phnom Penh, almost at the Vietnamese border. They were hungry for a bit of social life and always made us very welcome, so we used to drop them a line announcing our visits. We were quite unaware of the protocol to be followed and found out while visiting one weekend when other friends suddenly "appeared", unannounced. Out host became quite agitated, revealing without realising that all visitors' names had to be approved beforehand. By whom, he did not say and we did not ask, but it was well known that this was very much an area where Vietnamese people had always lived and worked alongside Cambodians and it was suspected of being used as a refuge by the North Vietnamese. There was a war going on next door and although life seemed normal on the surface, we witnessed daily sorties of American bombers, some having dropped bombs uncomfortably close, targeting those suspected Vietnamese camps, hence the large red cross on some roofs of the plantation.

On the way back from Mimot one had to drive via Kampong Cham, also known to be home to a large Vietnamese population and, to our dismay, we discovered one day that all was not well even this close to Phnom Penh! Always an avid photographer, I never moved without my camera at the ready. Something caught my attention, rice paddies, huts, I can't remember, but I asked Ken to stop and wandered closer with my camera. I was stopped dead in my tracks by a Vietnamese, dressed in fatigues, popping out of a hut, waving a machine gun in my direction and motioning for us to keep going, without taking photographs. Not a word was exchanged but we understood only too well and were on our way very quickly. For some unknown reason, neither Ken nor I reported the incident—no doubt it was safer not to rock the boat.

Unaware of the ravages the *Khmer rouges* would later bring to the northwest of the country, and where undoubtedly they were already active, I decided it would be nice one day to try a train ride and go to Battambang. Although not particularly enthusiastic about the idea Ken obliged and we boarded this rickety train, which turned out to be very uncomfortable, slow, and hot, getting us there about lunch time, not a good time for sightseeing in that heat. Close to fainting from heat exhaustion, I asked the first *cyclo-pousse* I saw to find us a day room in a local hotel where we collapsed not seeing a thing of that city, just awaiting the next train for the return journey in the late evening. Ken had to pay the price for a whole compartment of four couchettes so we could have it to ourselves, but word got out somehow and Ken had to forcibly close the door on a couple of men hoping for a free bed in our compartment. They could not understand our desire for privacy and I concluded train travel in that region was not a good idea after all.

The Canadian/Australian Film Club

The Canadian delegation in Saigon through its military personnel was getting a regular supply of the latest movies and was sharing them with the other three posts (Phnom Penh, Vientiane and Hanoi). Phnom Penh was the first port of call and three new releases were left with us weekly. These were most welcome as, apart from dining out or attending functions, the Phnom Penh cinemas offered mainly Chinese and Indian movies as well as the occasional French movie. Our delegation had a projector, previously kept at the residence, but on moving Commissioner Nutting had left it at the office so the staff could borrow it. I carried it back and forth for a while and eventually kept it at the apartment and started inviting friends over to share the films with us. We were showing them in our large living room, leaving the doors to the balcony wide open for a little fresh air and, after some time, we realised with amusement that we had quite an audience in the street below. Soon after, however, official word came that the authorities were not at all pleased with these film showings as they could be subversive to the locals and, if I remember correctly, we were asked to put the films through customs on arrival. These films came in the diplomatic bag, were for our own personal use and left the country a week later, again in the diplomatic bag. This was definitely not a customs matter. We were shocked and not prepared to be deprived of this very innocent amusement, so we ignored this request but obliged, as far as the locals were concerned, by closing the curtains to our balcony. There the matter rested for a while.

Fraternisation between English speaking foreigners and local people was frowned upon at that time—it seems we were all considered suspicious. After a while people invited themselves to our movie shows and the apartment became too cramped and too hot. Furthermore, being of a very generous nature, our maid was dispensing freely to the guests Ken's supplies of imported beer and spirits, causing a hole in the stock and, more importantly for newlyweds, the budget—serious measures had to be taken!

Discussions took place and the Canadian/Australian Film Club was born; it would be held on the roof of our building, a day and time were fixed and local beer and soft drinks would be provided at cost. On the said night, people helped move and set up chairs, the screen and projectors. People also brought us bags of ice to keep the drinks cool in buckets. The Australian Embassy had a projector as well and put it at our disposal. It was a very well organised community effort and more and more people flocked to our film evenings. Among them was a young American girl married to a Cambodian and soon again the authorities used that as a pretext to make noises so, with regret, we had to ask that young man to refrain from attending. We had no more trouble after that but were upset at the pettiness shown; maybe we had missed the point — that the authorities were miffed for not being invited to participate.

Ken was projectionist *par excellence* and his reel changes were nothing short of a Grand Prix performance; however, always the perfectionist he was not quite satisfied. The films were in Cinemascope and viewing could be much improved, he thought, with a special conversion lens. I approached Mr. Nutting with the idea and he authorised purchase of such a lens, which we imported directly from Japan. It made quite a difference but we really needed two lenses for efficient showing and that's when a rather amusing incident occurred. The Australians offered to buy the second lens and, to simplify matters, asked me to place the order since I had organised purchase of the first one. I obliged but to my dismay the reply from Japan was that "the lens has already been supplied". I wrote again explaining I wanted a "second" lens — no, "the lens has already been supplied". I decided the Australians had better do the ordering themselves as I was getting nowhere and a second lens finally arrived. However, a while later a third lens suddenly appeared — the Japanese manufacturer's translator no doubt thinking the first lens had been lost. Should the Japanese manufacturer ever read this I am confident that enough time has now elapsed for the translator in question not to be chastised.

Work of a different kind

After the departure of Commissioner Webster I was quite surprised one day to have a Cambodian gentleman visit my office. I found out he was Mr. Phuong Margain, who supervised the production of the English edition of the monthly magazine *Kambuja*, also published in French by Prince Sihanouk. Mr. Phuong asked me to replace Mrs. Webster on the English translating team. I felt quite honoured and wondered how difficult it would be, but I knew I could not refuse. To quote Prince Sihanouk, the magazine *"filled a vital need: to make known to the world the efforts and achievements of our people and our country"*. It carried articles about achievements and recent happenings in Phnom Penh and in the countryside, reviewed books and press articles about the country, etc. It was quite an extensive magazine, containing over a hundred pages, including advertisements and some amusing cartoons — usually directed at "imperialists". To my relief, I was at first mainly given captions to translate then progressed to articles and sometimes some proofreading. This assignment lasted until my departure and helped in giving me a greater insight into my host country. An added bonus was the fairly generous stipend in local currency given for this work; I made sure I spent it well — adding some lovely gold jewellery to my collection.

On another occasion I was approached by Liz, who worked for the East Asiatic Company in whose building the delegation had its offices, asking me to do her the favour of replacing her for a month, in the afternoons only, while she went on holidays. At first I refused as I could not see how I could cope — I had become addicted to my siestas by then. But nobody else could be found who spoke French and English and seeing that she would miss out on her well-deserved holiday, I accepted a little reluctantly but enjoyed the experience very much as it was not very onerous, mainly answering the telephone and typing a few letters.

More changes in the office

Major Gilles Bellavance's tour of duty finished in the middle of 1967 and it was with much regret that we bade him farewell. His replacement was Lt. Col. Andy Woodcock, a dedicated military man with a good sense of humour. Just before the end of his posting, Richard Longtin was offered an extension that we all hoped he would take but, to our chagrin, he turned it down. After thinking about it some more he changed his mind, but it was too late as, by then, his replacement, Roger Lacroix, had been appointed.

Another romance soon blossomed. Ron Holding, our communicator, fell in love with Moira (Nicky) Nicholson of the British Embassy and after a little while they were engaged and got married at the embassy later on in the year. Ron asked Roger Lacroix to be his best man and poor Roger was more nervous than the groom, arriving for the ceremony a little the worse for wear, for which we teased him mercilessly later on.

After I had been there a little over two years — of course, by then I had requested an extension for a third year — Commissioner Nutting departed and was replaced by Richard (Dick) Gorham. I hoped that, now that I had been in the country for two years and was well settled in my job and my home, I could assist the new Commissioner even better.

The new Commissioner turned out to be a very friendly and approachable man with a wicked sense of humour and a contagious laugh and we got on extremely well. He and Lt. Col. Woodcock attended all Commission meetings, which were increasing in frequency in line with the increase in border incidents. The minutes were getting more lengthy, time consuming and requiring numerous amendments for the final version, as reaching a consensus was rarely smooth sailing. These final minutes caused their own incidents, one of which Mr. Gorham nicknamed the "paper-clip" incident.

The Commissioner and the military advisor were spending more time on field trips, verifying border incidents which, as I mentioned, were increasing in severity and quantity. Sometimes findings made for amusing reading in the minutes as, on one occasion, an old lady at the border complained bitterly about the incursion which had deprived her of her jewellery but what distressed her particularly was the loss of her gold teeth!

Cambodia was in a dilemma to keep its neutrality while not antagonising its Vietnamese neighbours, so the authorities played the incidents down or denied them. Word of incidents would reach us long before an official request to visit the area concerned was made to the ICSC. In one particular instance, it took a while before a request finally came; the Commissioners and entourage duly set off only to find a peaceful village with villagers claiming total ignorance of the purported incident. Had the villagers been rehearsed, and the damage erased? One will never know.

It was time already for Lt. Col. Woodcock to return home and his replacement was Lt. Col. Luc Chabot[3] Our communicator Ron had also gone with Nicky, having been cross-posted to Saigon, and was replaced by Roger Banville, a neighbour from Rimouski and with whose brother, Martin, I had worked in Brazil. We all seemed to get along and work particularly well together; indeed, we were a very happy family, but we were constantly reminded of the seriousness of the situation around us, at night especially, as we listened to the thuds of falling bombs at the border.

We were now well into 1968 and Ken and I thought we would stay yet another year, making it four years for me, this having been approved by Ottawa. However, we were anxiously watching the signs: the war had escalated in Vietnam and was spilling over the border with more incidents, the *Khmer rouges* were active in the northwest with Prince Sihanouk waging a merciless war against them. At one stage, a photo was even published in the local newspaper of the execution of a *Khmer rouge* traitor whom we all hoped had been Pol Pot, but it was not to be.

We loved the country and I particularly loved my job at the delegation and I was also very proud of being part of the Department of External Affairs. Leaving meant I would have to resign from *"mon père le Ministère"*[4] and this broke my heart. Another heartache was our lovely little dog Jerry. With Australia's then stringent quarantine laws we knew we could not take him and we could not subject him to months and months of quarantine in England before being able to bring him over — he was small and fragile and would not survive. But the war was indeed worrying us and we were also getting anxious to settle down — had I lost my wanderlust?

We agonised but finally decided to go in November of 1968 and made all the necessary arrangements. I don't think people believed us — we hardly believed it ourselves. Although there were plenty of small frustrations, life in Phnom Penh had been very special for

---

[3]Lt. Col. Chabot was a delightful man and I was privileged to count among his friends for over 30 years. It is extremely sad that he passed away as these chapters were being prepared and that he will not be able to read them.

[4]Expression coined by Ambassador Jean Chapdelaine when I was his secretary in Rio de Janeiro. When ready to dictate he would always ask, "What are you doing?", and very often I would reply, *"j'écris à ma mère"* ('I'm writing to my mother'). He would then add: *"Maintenant, écrivons à ton père le Ministère"* ('Now, let's write to your father, the Minister [of External Affairs]').

me and was the best period of my life. Of course, there were lots of farewell parties and some lovely gifts, and we arranged for little Jerry to move in with a British girl who lived upstairs from us. She was a little reluctant at first but we learned that she had soon fallen in love with him and passed him on to another British person on leaving. I do hope he was taken out before the events that we know and that he came to no harm.

My replacement arrived the day before my departure. She was Thérèse Rhéaume, a lovely dark-haired girl whom I met at the airport with Luc. I saw a smile on his face but that's another story, better told by Thérèse.[5]

We must have been popular as Pochentong Airport was more full on our departure than on a Sunday when half of Phnom Penh used to descend on the airport to watch the weekly *Air France* plane arrive and see who was going or coming. I was very sad indeed and my arrival in Australia was not the happy event it should have been; this time I was not on a posting, this was for good ... but already I was thinking of ways of escape — my wanderlust was not dead after all!

Epilogue: Was there Life after Phnom Penh?

Yes, there was life after Phnom Penh I am glad to say and, in a nutshell, never having been afraid of challenges, I put my heart and efforts into adapting to my new land. So, by February 1969 Ken and I had bought and moved into a brand new home in a lovely suburb. Rather concerned by the tyranny of distance I was eager to find ways of temporary escape and by March 1969 I had started work for the Australian international airline, Qantas Airways Limited. The thought of settling down in the Antipodes had been a little daunting but working for an airline would hopefully make it easier for me to continue "seeing the world", albeit as a tourist this time.

After a few months at *Qantas* I was assigned to the office of the company secretary where I felt quite at home with agendas and minutes of meetings but happily without the border incidents.

Ken and I resumed our travels, exploring the Asia-Pacific region mostly, sometimes even indulging in two trips a year and, of course, I visited Canada on a fairly regular basis.

---

[5] See below for her account of life in Cambodia. – Ed.

Disaster struck after I had been in Australia for around 15 years. What had been diagnosed in Hong Kong as tropical sprue came back to haunt me and the true nature of my malaise over the years was revealed: a non-Hodgkin lymphoma that had turned very nasty. I lost my spleen, had chemotherapy treatments for six months, wore a wig for one year and weighed 45 kilos. My feeling was one of annoyance at this waste of time; cancer was a word, not a sentence so, after ten weeks away I resumed work with my usual determination and never looked back.

I stayed on at *Qantas* almost another ten years but the job was becoming a monster and was swallowing me. I would leave home at 7 a.m. and return at 7 p.m., a merry-go-round of home — office — home so, in May 1993 I decided to take early retirement.

After a few months of leisure, however, I realised I had too much energy now that I was well and I needed to keep occupied. I had always loved languages — I could speak six by then — and remembered with amusement that Dick Gorham had written in my reference when I left Cambodia that I could speak "some" French (meaning, he assured me, *'considerable in degree'*, according to the dictionary). So I approached the Australian accrediting agency, sat for the professional translator's exam and was successful. I turned a room of our house into a little office, registered a business name and opened a secretarial and French translation office. This was fun — I was my own boss and working from home.

I thought I should join the Translators' and Interpreters' Association, attended some of their New South Wales branch meetings and, after a few months, found myself their minutes secretary. Then, in 2000 the Olympic Games came to Sydney. Great excitement seized the whole population, me included, and I put my name down as a translator. I was accepted, the only Canadian on the translating team, and was involved for six weeks as a French translator, a fact I am very proud of.

I still pack my bags regularly — that passion will never leave me. And I do not open my dictionaries as often these days; there is so much to explore in this vast Australian continent, I must make time for that. Often I think of Cambodia where this adventure started; the memories linger but I am afraid to go back. What I lived in the sixties was a dream and I don't want to wake up.

÷ ÷ ÷ ÷ ÷

Assignment to Cambodia
February 1968 – December 1969

Richard V. Gorham

During the 1950s the Department of External Affairs began inviting officers to indicate their preferences for future assignments. Included on the list of choices was service on one of the Indochina Commissions for periods of one year alone or, later, for longer periods accompanied by a spouse and children. At this time I was happily serving in Tokyo with my wife, Dorie, and two small children, but, like most of my colleagues in the service, I volunteered for a short period of duty in Indochina.

There was no response to this offer and I fulfilled subsequent assignments in the Department's Far Eastern Division from 1960 to 1963, one in New Delhi from 1963 to 1966 and a third in the Economic Division, from 1966 to 1967.

This latest assignment involved activity regarding nuclear safeguards and inspired me to hope for an eventual posting to our Embassy in Vienna, which was responsible for Canada's relations with the International Atomic Energy Agency. Dorie and I now had a family of five young children and the thought of an assignment to Indochina seemed totally out of the question.

It was with some surprise, therefore, that in November 1967 I received a telephone call from the Personnel Division enquiring whether I would be interested in fulfilling my earlier commitment to undertake an assignment in Cambodia. My immediate response was negative, pointing out that my family status and obligations had changed markedly since the 1950s, when a short-term assignment in Indochina had seemed feasible.

I was advised that this assignment would be as Head of Post in Cambodia and could involve accompaniment by my wife and family if I so desired. This represented a significant change and after glancing out the window at the beginning of a snowfall and the thought of the coming winter months I said I would call my wife to discuss the matter. The combination of an interesting career challenge and opportunity and the avoidance of a cold winter did the trick and we agreed to accept the posting, to begin in early 1968.

At that particular time the military situation in Indochina had been escalating rapidly. The United States and South Vietnam had become involved in an undeclared, but nevertheless full-scale, war with North Vietnam. It had just culminated in the North Vietnamese *Tet* offensive, which was militarily disastrous for the United States and South Vietnam and had raised the political and military stakes to a new level.

Cambodia was not a direct participant in this developing military situation and Prince Norodom Sihanouk, the Cambodian Chief of State, hoped to keep his small independent country free from the military activity taking place in the neighbouring states. He knew full well that North Vietnamese and Vietcong forces were making use of his territory and he hoped to use the International Commission as a device to limit, at least to some degree, this activity.

Unfortunately, however, such hopes did not materialise and Cambodia had become indirectly but increasingly involved in the growing conflict. Military action in neighbouring Vietnam frequently spilled over into Cambodian border zones, which were used as sanctuary areas by North Vietnamese/Vietcong forces from which to attack South Vietnam or to flee from U.S./South Vietnamese retaliation.

Protesting Cambodia's innocence and inability adequately to police its own borders, Sihanouk frequently called upon the International Commission to investigate and condemn these incidents as unwarranted violations of Cambodian territory and sovereignty.[1]

When the Cambodian government first requested that the Commission investigate an incident allegedly caused by South Vietnamese/U.S. forces, the Canadian delegation took the position that the Commission should decline to become involved on the grounds that it was not within the Commission's mandate. The Indian and Polish delegations, however, argued otherwise and voted to undertake the investigation. Legal experts in the Department of External Affairs took the view that a majority of the Commission having decided to make an investigation, Canada was obliged to participate and should

---

[1] On previous occasions when Cambodia had requested that the Commission investigate incidents allegedly caused by Thailand or Laos, it had declined to do so on the grounds that such investigations were not within its mandate.

endeavour to make the investigation as factual and legally accurate as possible.

With the benefit of hindsight and experience I believe that this legal interpretation was a mistake and that we should have refused to participate in any investigation which was, in our judgment, not within the Commission's mandate. However, the precedent having been set to accept the majority decision, we continued to participate, following the Department's directives.

Experience soon proved that establishing the facts was easier said than done. To begin with, the Commission was being asked to investigate an incident which had taken place at least 48 hours previously. It had no independent means of transport and was thus taken to the scene by Cambodian military authorities. At the scene the Commission was presented with a structured presentation by Cambodian military officers, complete with maps and diagrams, shown a variety of military artifacts allegedly found at the scene and presented with witnesses who invariably declared that it was a totally unprovoked attack by South Vietnamese/U.S. forces and that there were never any North Vietnamese/Vietcong forces in the area. Information from the South Vietnamese/U.S. side usually claimed that the incident involved a military action involving forces from both sides of the conflict.

At first, such investigations were undertaken by an Investigating Team made up of representatives of the three delegations (Canada, India, Poland), who would prepare an investigation report, initially drafted by the Indian secretariat, which would be referred to the South Vietnamese authorities for comment. Subsequently, the investigation report plus any South Vietnamese comments would be considered by a meeting of the three Commissioners, who would eventually prepare a report, at times unanimous but more often than not an Indian–Polish majority report endorsing without question the Cambodian allegations and a Canadian minority report arguing that the facts did not justify such conclusions.

During the investigations and the subsequent deliberations the Polish delegation and, all too often, the Indian delegation as well, would go to great lengths to ignore or reject any facts or information which tended to indicate North Vietnamese/Vietcong presence or activity involved in the incident. This attitude seemed to be shared by the Cambodian authorities, who hoped that a Commission presence would mitigate North Vietnamese/Vietcong activity without formally denouncing it. During a discussion shortly after my arrival, my Polish colleague acknowledged that in some cases there was North Vietnamese/Vietcong involvement in the incident but he would do his utmost to prevent the Commission from accepting or reporting such a reality. He also assured me that he would deny ever saying such if I were to mention it.

In these circumstances, to conduct meaningful investigations and reach factual conclusions proved very difficult and frustrating for the Canadian delegation, which was often accused of trying to cover up or minimize U.S. involvement. In my experience the United States never sought to deny totally its involvement in any of the incidents investigated, but only asked that the Commission set forth all the facts in an unbiased manner.

The Commission's final reports were considered confidential and were presented to the British and Soviet Foreign Ministers, the co-Chairmen of the Geneva Conference, for further consideration and action. In most cases there was no further consideration and certainly no action, with the result that the international community had very little factual knowledge of the inadequacies of Commission investigations nor of the frustrations of the Canadian delegations in trying to make the investigations thorough and factual.

During a 1969 visit to Phnom Penh by Arthur Menzies, a respected Far Eastern expert in the Department of External Affairs, he commented to me that if Canada should ever become involved in another truce monitoring organization we should insist that its proceedings be open to public scrutiny, as is the case of United Nations. This thought stayed with me and, a few years later when I was the official spokesman for the Department of External Affairs, it was the inspiration of what came to be called the "open-mouth policy" followed by Canada when it was a member of the replacement Commission established in 1973 to monitor and assist the short-lived peace agreement which enabled the United States to withdraw from Vietnam.

Over time the size of the Commission and of each delegation was gradually reduced. By the late 1960s the Commissioners themselves constituted the Investigation Team and would then sit as a Commission to deliberate their own report of their own investigation, which had been drafted by the Indian secretariat.

In addition to the frontier incidents involving Cambodia, another factor was that South Vietnam and the United States were convinced that neutral Cambodia was serving as a supply route for sea shipments from China of Chinese or Soviet military equipment to North Vietnamese/Vietcong forces. U.S./South Vietnam protests and representations to Prince Sihanouk were countered by his declarations of innocence and his inability to police all sea ports and border crossing points, followed by a request that the International Commission should monitor all sea shipments coming into the major port of Sihanoukville.

As a result the Commission did, in 1967, undertake such a monitoring exercise, which came to nought because admitted Chinese shipments of arms were declared exempt from investigation since they were claimed to be destined for the use of the Cambodian Army. The Canadian delegation had urged that the Commission inspect such shipments and judge whether they were appropriate or necessary for the small Cambodian Army and verify whether they were properly stored in Cambodian military depots. These efforts were resisted by the Indian and Polish Commissioners, who argued that such investigations would constitute an illegal interference in Cambodia's domestic affairs and would clearly be beyond the Commission's mandate.

Subsequently, the United States proposed, and Prince Sihanouk agreed, that the International Commission should monitor the Cambodian–Vietnamese border by helicopter patrols to detect and prevent North Vietnamese/Vietcong military activity. The United States offered to provide the helicopters and Canada, as a Commission member, agreed to provide the necessary air and ground crews. By the time of my appointment in early 1968 as Commissioner, the Department of National Defence had already taken steps to designate the necessary personnel and have them briefed, inoculated and ready on stand-by for this task. I thought that the Canadian delegation would soon have a small air force as part of its composition!

Prince Sihanouk, while declaring he was in favour of such helicopter patrols, asserted that he could not accept helicopters from the United States because he had publicly renounced receiving any economic assistance from that country. He suggested that the United States donate the helicopters to the International Commission rather than to Cambodia. However, this idea provoked long, tedious legal and political objections by the Polish and Indian delegations that the Commission had no mandate to receive such equipment from the United States, which had not been a signatory of the Geneva Agreements that had created the Commissions. The net result was that the proposed border supervision by helicopters never came to pass and the Canadian delegation never added the anticipated small air force to its composition. Thus, the challenges facing me in undertaking the assignment as head of the Canadian delegation to the Commission were rather daunting.

However, of more immediate concern were the family and domestic arrangements for Dorie, myself and our children to undertake the proposed assignment. It soon became apparent that while there could be educational arrangements in Phnom Penh for our three youngest children, such was not the case for my teenage son and daughter. With considerable reluctance, therefore, we decided to place my son in Ashbury College in Ottawa and my daughter in Netherwood School in Rothesay, New Brunswick and have my brother in Ottawa and my sister in New Brunswick act as guardians.

This was a heart-wrenching situation which was difficult for all members of the family. In early January my wife escorted our daughter to New Brunswick and got her properly admitted to the school and we installed our son in Ashbury College in Ottawa. We then left Ottawa in early February with our three younger children, had a brief stop in Tokyo to visit old friends and then met in Hong Kong with my Commission predecessor, Claire Nutting, who briefed us on the Commission, Phnom Penh and the society of which we were about to become a part.

The Hong Kong stop-over enabled us to do a great deal of shopping for tropical wear clothing as well as a couple of white linen/silk suits for me, which were the Cambodian *de rigueur* formal dress. I also purchased a pair of custom-made dress shoes. (I still use the shoes but the tropical clothes and the white suits seem to have shrunk in size over the years!)

We arrived at Phnom Penh in early February 1968 and were met at the airport by officials of the Cambodian Foreign Ministry, by Lt. Col. Andy Woodcock, the delegation military advisor, and by Mrs. Louise Dyer, the delegation secretary. Mrs. Dyer was a Canadian who had been assigned to Phnom Penh a year or two previously. She had married a resident Australian involved with an Australian aid project and provided valuable insights and assistance based on her experience of Phnom Penh.

The other members of the delegation staff were a Canadian administrative clerk, a Canadian communicator, a Cambodian secretary, a Cambodian administrative clerk and two Cambodian drivers. Later during my assignment the Department of National Defence assigned a sergeant clerk to assist the military advisors.

In most cases the Canadian personnel were on one-year assignments — early in my tour, Lt. Col. Woodcock was replaced by Lt. Col. Chabot, who in turn was replaced by Lt. Col. Bouffard. Mrs. Dyer was replaced by Thérèse Rhéaume, who later married Lt. Col. Chabot after they had both returned to Canada.

After arrival we moved immediately to the delegation residence and started to get used to a new climate, a new life-style with Cambodian and Vietnamese servants, new language problems, new friends, new adventures and the usual challenges of culture shock adjustment.

A first task was to arrange for schooling for our three young children until such time as they could be accepted in a French *lycée* in Phnom Penh. We were able to engage a young British girl to supervise their work under an Ontario correspondence system and a six-hour per week audio-visual French-language program.

A second task was to adjust to the fact that mail from Ottawa proved to be a very slow and uncertain process, especially the Paris–Saigon leg, because of the military dangers at Saigon and civic unrest and strikes in Paris. As a result, during our first six weeks in Cambodia, we received only two letters from home. There were equal delays for our children in boarding schools to receive letters from us. Only after mid-March were we able to exchange letters with home on a reasonably regular basis, thanks to a routing change from Ottawa–Paris–Saigon–Phnom Penh to Ottawa–Vancouver–Hong Kong–Phnom Penh, which I instituted.

These communication delays were particularly grievous and hard to take as we could not keep adequately in touch with our children in boarding schools and we received news of the deaths of my wife's mother and my sister's husband only after the funerals had taken place.

Another frustrating communication problem we faced was the lack of taxis in Phnom Penh that one could summon to go from one place to another. Although I had an official car and driver at my disposal it was often difficult to provide transportation for Dorie and the children and to conduct official business at the same time. To cope with this sutuation I had ordered, prior to my departure from Ottawa, a personal Peugeot station wagon from France. However, for one reason or another it did not arrive in Phnom Penh until August — seven months after ordering! Once we had another set of wheels, life became much more manageable for the whole family.

Coping with communication delays, the climate, the new lifestyle in a strange community, language barriers, etc., were daily challenges for both my wife and our children in adjusting to our new environment. Indeed, even before our arrival the whole process of placing two of our children in boarding schools, closing up our household in Ottawa, leaving Canada in mid-winter and arriving in a semi-tropical climate in Cambodia presented various physical and emotional strains on all of us.

Our first diplomatic function shortly after our arrival was an evening garden reception at the Soviet Embassy to celebrate Soviet Armed Forces Day. During the course of the evening one of the guests called me to attend to my wife, who was not feeling well. Dorie told me she feared she was about to faint. Hoping to avoid such a situation in the grounds of the Soviet Embassy we headed for the exit but Dorie collapsed en route. The Soviet Ambassador and his staff were most helpful. Dorie was carried up to the Ambassador's air-conditioned dining room and laid on the dining table.

A Soviet doctor involved with a Soviet aid program attended her and proposed an injection. Having been brought up on Cold War suspicions of KGB truth serums I objected. The doctor, who spoke no English but did speak French and certainly better than I did, asked me "Quel âge a-t-elle?" I intended to reply "quarante ans" but instead, in my concern and confusion, mistakenly said "quatorze ans". The doctor looked surprised and asked in an incredulous tone "Quatorze ans?" Assuming that he was thinking that she looked older than forty years I forcefully asserted "Oui, quatorze ans!" after which there was no further discussion, Dorie revived and we were able to leave.

It was only after reaching home that I suddenly realized my linguistic blunder. I later apologized to the Soviet Ambassador, who, incidentally, had once served in Ottawa, and thanked him for the assistance rendered. To this day, however, I wonder how many times the doctor, living somewhere in the Soviet Union, might reminisce about his days in Cambodia and about the Canadian husband who insisted that his mature wife was only fourteen years old and wondering if the Canadian climate had something to do with it!

During the first several weeks after our arrival there was very little Commission activity, which I found rather frustrating, but I occupied my time by reading all the back files of the delegation, calling on other ambassadors and Cambodian officials and getting to know my Commission colleagues — V.V. Paranjpe, the Commission chairman and head of the Indian delegation, and Tadeusz Mulecki, the head of the Polish delegation. Dorie was busy making our house into a home, getting curtains installed, studying French, calling on ambassadors' wives and looking after the children's education and activities.

Our closest friends were members of the British, Australian, and German embassies, a number of Canadian teachers and members of the foreign business community. We also enjoyed reasonable social contacts with our Indian and Polish colleagues on the Commission, but our standing disagreements on Commission operations served to prevent any close friendships. Friendships with Cambodians were difficult to establish, partly because of the language barrier, but mostly because Prince Sihanouk and his government were now frowning upon close relationships between Cambodians and the foreign diplomatic community.

The Department of National Defence had established a practice of sending 16mm versions of feature Hollywood films, which the Canadian delegation arranged for regular film showings and which proved a most welcome social activity for all concerned. We also made trips to the seaside, our first such venture resulting in the whole family getting terribly sunburned.

Another pleasant early diversion involved a formal outing arranged by Prince Sihanouk to a seaside area of Cambodia, flying part way by DC-3 aircraft and then by boat to a secluded lagoon for a swim and then supper. This proved to be the first of several such outings arranged by Sihanouk for the foreign diplomatic corps and Commission members, which enabled him to demonstrate gracious hospitality, musical talent (he often sang at dance concerts he hosted), humour and political gamesmanship.

Other highlights were the visits to Cambodia in April and May by the President of Indonesia and by Haile Selassie, the Emperor of Ethiopia, with formal airport arrival and departure ceremonies, sports complex extravaganzas and formal state dinners.

I was very much impressed that at the airport arrival ceremonies Prince Sihanouk acted as his own Chief of Protocol and introduced us all individually to his distinguished guests. This was indicative of the degree to which the Prince was knowledgeable about everything that was happening in his country.

* * *

Finally, on May 5, 1968, the Commission got some work! It was invited to investigate an incident which had taken place at a border crossing post called Bavet on the highway linking Phnom Penh to Saigon. It was alleged that the fortified South Vietnamese post just across the well marked border had wilfully and maliciously opened fire on the Cambodian post and caused considerable damage but, fortunately, no serious casualties. Following the established format of an Indian–Polish vote and a Canadian objection we proceeded to the scene.

From the evidence on the ground it was clear that the Cambodian border post had been under military attack and had suffered damage. When we asked whether any North Vietnamese/Vietcong were in the vicinity witnesses assured us that there were none and that the incident was just an effort by South Vietnam to inflict damage on the economy of Cambodia. It seemed like an open and shut case but later in Phnom Penh I received reliable information that the incident had in fact been caused by the Vietcong troops taking over the Bavet post and initiating an attack on the South Vietnamese post, which then retaliated with assistance by U.S. helicopter gun ships.

This was my initiation into the inadequacies of Commission investigations and the denial by the Cambodian side of any involvement of North Vietnamese/Vietcong personnel engaged in a military skirmish with South Vietnamese/U.S. forces. It was to be the pattern of events in all the subsequent frontier investigations the Commission was asked to undertake.

Another lesson I learned from this first incident was the importance of having some knowledge of the significance of the military artifacts often presented to the Commission as evidence. During the

Bavet incident we were shown remnants of small rocket-like projectiles. When I asked my military advisor of their significance he confessed ignorance, noting he had not seen the results of military action since the Second World War.

To correct this deficiency I subsequently arranged for an extensive briefing by the U.S. side as to what would likely be found at the scene of mortar, artillery, machine gun or aerial rocket attacks. I returned from this study with a bag full of various bits of shrapnel which enabled me to make a more informed judgment of subsequent incidents under investigation.

During this briefing I was also shown an impressive variety of modern military equipment and military ordinance developed to detect and kill an enemy. When I asked why, with all this detection and destructive material, the U.S./South Vietnamese forces were not winning the war, it was explained to me that the North Vietnamese did not "play fair" because they did not use easily detectable equipment such as tanks, steel helmets, etc!

Subsequent to the Bavet investigation the Commission was called upon to investigate eight other border incidents during the course of the 1968 summer and fall. The usual pattern was that the Commissioners and their military advisors were taken to the scene, accompanied by a large entourage of foreign military attachés, diplomats and occasional media representatives.

At the scene we would be presented with the alleged facts and shown various items of evidence such as pieces of equipment of U.S. origin, evidence of bullet holes, etc., and the bodies of persons killed, and also invited to interview witnesses. There was never any doubt that some sort of military action had taken place which had caused physical damage and destruction to dwellings and deaths and injuries to Cambodian citizens. However, determining the actual cause and sequence of events was always much more difficult.

Comments by witnesses were sometimes contradictory. On one investigation a witness was asked whether he had seen any aircraft involved. He acknowledged that he had and that the aircraft was distinguished with a white star. A second witness, a few yards distant from the first, also acknowledged that he had seen an aircraft but distinguished by a red star. Later, at the Commission meeting, the Polish Commissioner laboriously argued that a white star seen from a certain angle as from the position of the second witness would appear red.

On some occasions the Commissioners were treated to a meal after the investigation, but on most occasions we each brought along our own picnic lunch. The Polish Commissioner usually shared an ice-cold bottle of Polish vodka and canned anchovies while I provided some cold beer. We always enjoyed watching the Australian military attaché and his sergeant, who would set up folding chairs and a table with a linen table cloth, plates and cutlery and a carafe of wine, dining in elegant style in contrast to the rest of us picnicking on the ground!

Our personal highlight of that summer was the arrival of our son and daughter from their boarding schools for the school holiday period, which brought all our family together. Thanks to the generosity of the local Shell representative we were able to spend two weeks in a fine villa at the seaside resort village of Kep which he had rented from the owner, who was Prince Sihanouk's wife, Monique. We also visited the nearby village of Sihanoukville and its beautiful white sand beaches, went to the magnificent temple ruins of Angkor Wat or spent afternoons at the swimming pool of the Phnom Penh *Cercle Sportif*.

On one occasion we were invited to attend the premier showing of a film entitled *Le Petit Prince*, made by and starring Prince Sihanouk and his wife, Monique. We brought along our two oldest children who accompanied us in the receiving line to meet Sihanouk. I was impressed when he commented approvingly that we now had all our five children together—another example of the degree to which the Chief of State was kept informed.

The film left a good deal to be desired in terms of technical and artistic merit but one felt it diplomatically necessary to extend some words of praise. My wife very cleverly handled the situation by praising Sihanouk for the beautiful scenes of Angkor Wat, while I made a riskier comment of asking how he had ever found the time to make such a film!

Over the next few months visiting dignitaries were routinely treated to a showing of this film after which praises were diplomatically made to Sihanouk. When the wife of the German ambassador mentioned that she had just attended her fifth showing I asked her how she had responded. I was impressed when she told me that she had bluntly told Sihanouk that she did not like the film. However, she confessed that when he asked why, she responded diplomatically that it was because in the film Sihanouk had parted from his wife Monique and she knew that in real life he could never do such a thing!

To enhance their relationship with the Chief of State a number of ambassadors from the socialist countries would often write to him expressing in exceedingly unctuous terms their praise of his policies and accomplishments only to be embarrassed to discover their letters published a few days later in the local newspaper.

In another effort to ingratiate themselves to the Chief of State some of the socialist countries proposed that Sihanouk should organize an international film festival to be held in Phnom Penh in November 1968 and at which Sihanouk's own films could be featured. After I had enquired whether such a festival involved all countries represented in Phnom Penh, it was announced that in response to my "request" Canada would also be invited to participate and enter a film in the festival. I was pleased, therefore, that the National Film Board agreed to enter the excellent animated Norman McClaren film *Pas de Deux*.

Each diplomatic mission in Phnom Penh was invited to nominate individuals to act as judges of the films being shown at the festival. As I had no expertise in such matters I nominated Pierre and Diane Lanteigne, two CIDA-sponsored Canadian teachers in Phnom Penh who had had some film experience in Montreal. Shortly before judging day they came to my office in some concern to report that despite the technical and artistic inadequacies of Sihanouk's film, several of the countries represented proposed to award him a First Prize and they wondered how they should vote.

I responded that I had nominated them to exercise their own judgment and if they deemed Sihanouk's film unworthy of a prize they should vote accordingly. However, because of the possible diplomatic repercussions I said I would seek Ottawa's blessing for my proposed course of action. There being no response by judging day they voted against Sihanouk's film. Not only were there no diplomatic repercussions, but the Canadian entry of *Pas de Deux* won a prize.

There were, however, some internal repercussions. The day after the film judging I received Ottawa's instructions that we should vote for Sihanouk's film regardless of its technical and artistic inadequacies. I responded with a message that "fortunately your instructions arrived a day too late for I would have been ashamed to implement them". This brought a stern letter from headquarters that my message had not been well received and such flippancy should not be repeated!

As part of his efforts to have international support for the integrity of his nation Sihanouk had appealed for other nations to make a formal declaration of recognition of Cambodia's frontiers. After much legal consideration in the Department for an appropriate wording, I was authorized to present to Sihanouk on September 2, 1968 Canada's formal recognition of the "territorial integrity of Cambodia within its present frontiers". Sihanouk greatly appreciated this gesture, which was given prominent praise in the local media.

There was an active United Nations Mekong River development project in Cambodia called the Prek Thnot project in which Canada was involved. In my capacity as a Canadian government representative in Cambodia I attended various meetings concerning this project and, finally, on September 9, 1969 I signed and presented to the Cambodian government a Canadian donation cheque for two million dollars. This remains the largest cheque that I have ever signed or even held in my hand!

In the fall of 1968 Sihanouk began making noises about wanting the Commission to investigate any areas in Cambodia in which the United States claimed North Vietnamese/Vietcong forces were present. However, neither the Indian or Polish delegation showed any interest in pursuing the matter, claiming to be waiting for a specific request.

In October 1968 the Commission was asked to investigate the alleged defoliation of a Cambodian sugar plantation in the area of Memot, which was widely believed to be a Vietcong sanctuary. Surprisingly, the Polish Commissioner declined to participate, arguing that he was unwell and that his military attaché was not competent. However, after several days' delay during which any Vietcong in the area probably evacuated, he relented and the Commission undertook to investigate.

I had learned from a resident Belgian agronomist that the sugar plantation in question had suffered from bad management and inadequate irrigation not from any defoliation, which claim had been made to cover up this failure. Thanks to the Polish delay I was able to obtain some pertinent information from Canada about sugar cane, irrigation, etc. During the investigation my military advisor and I startled our Commission colleagues by systematically and professionally measuring the height of the canes and the distance between leaves, etc., collecting leaf samples and soil samples for subsequent analysis. The whole investigation degenerated into a farce, with the Polish delegation vigorously pointing out any speck of dried grass along the roadway or the occasional dead tree in a peasant's back yard as evidence of defoliation and the Indian chairman simply at a loss for words. The Commission never did meet to pursue the matter further.

By the end of 1968, working and living conditions in the Commission had been improved vastly with the installation of a direct Phnom Penh–Hong Kong–Ottawa telex line, which resolved our previous communication problems. We also acquired replacements for our out-moded typewriters so that Lt. Col. Chabot and I could type our own messages and provide an electric typewriter for my secretary. We also obtained tape recording equipment and a polaroid camera to assist us in the conduct of our investigations. Finally, I was also able to rent a very pleasant seaside villa in Kep, which enabled the family to enjoy vacation outings.

Unfortunately, 1969 brought forth new personal problems. Being away from the family and in boarding school in Canada proved unacceptable for my son and it became necessary for him to join us in Cambodia in February. Boarding school also proved unacceptable for my daughter and we decided to have her stay in Cambodia as soon as her school year ended. This required a search for a larger residence to accommodate the whole family. At about the same time it became necessary for the delegation to move to new premises, which created various frustrations of moving, installing air conditioners, furnishings, and telex and waiting 31 days for telephones.

I was pleased that we were able to establish the delegation at a choice site close by the Independence monument in Phnom Penh and where the Canadian flag could be clearly seen the whole length of the boulevard. After considerable frustrations and delays we eventually got comfortable, efficient and secure office accommodations set up. With all our children at home together and settling down to a satisfactory educational routine the assignment was proving to be quite comfortable. I had, therefore, suggested to the Department an extension of my posting to the summer of 1970. This was readily granted (with the caveat that possible departmental budget restrictions might alter assignment situations) and we began to plan a nice sea voyage to Canada for leave in the summer of 1970.

By 1969 Commission activity had begun to slow down with some investigations cancelled because the site was allegedly "too dangerous" or because the Polish delegation was reluctant to participate, presumably out of concern that we might find clear evidence of North Vietnamese/Vietcong activity.

In the spring of 1969 my military advisor was privately given by the French military attaché a copy of a very surprising internal Cambodian government report commenting that the Commission was proving inadequate for Cambodia's purposes partly because of the Polish delegation's unwillingness to expose North Vietnamese/Vietcong activity, partly because of the Canadian delegation insistence on credible facts and partly because of the Indian delegation's lethargic conduct of Commission business. The report suggested that the time may have come for the Commission to be invited to leave.

In May 1969, Sihanouk, apparently under pressure from members of his government to do something about the increasing North Vietnamese/Vietcong presence in the country, made a speech, fully reported in the Cambodian media, that 10,000 North Vietnamese troops were within Cambodia's borders and he hoped that when hostilities ended they would return home to Vietnam.

I proposed to the Indian chairman of the Commission that he call a meeting to consider an investigation of what appeared to be a clear violation of Cambodia's frontiers by North Vietnam and a matter clearly within the Commission's mandate. Weeks went by before he called a meeting, at which he claimed that the Commission could not undertake an investigation because it had no transportation facilities or equipment. The Polish Commissioner argued that the Commission did not undertake investigations on the basis of press reports. I responded that a public speech by the Chief of State was surely not a "press report", at which he countered that the Cambodian Foreign Ministry should make a formal notification of the speech and a request for an investigation. I asked the Foreign Ministry to provide such notification but was told that was unnecessary because Sihanouk's speech had been adequately reported in the media. When I asked whether he would make the same statement to the Indian and Polish delegations he responded that he would if they asked him to. The result was that nothing developed.

Later in the autumn the report given to us privately by the French Embassy appeared, word for word, in the local media. I was surprised to be told by the Soviet Ambassador that he understood that the Cambodian government had given the document to the Commission chairman several months ago. When I challenged the chairman to explain why he did not inform the other members of the Commission his lame excuse was that it had been given to him in his capacity as head of the Indian delegation and not as chairman. It is a matter of regret that he had not seen fit to inform me of this matter when he first received it. It is of even greater regret that the government of India did not see fit to inform our High Commission in New Delhi or our department in Ottawa of this significant matter concerning the Commisssion.

The Commission situation was now becoming more dramatic and on October 7, 1969 the Cambodian government officially informed the Commission that because of the financial burden of maintaining the Commission Cambodia would like the Commission to terminate by the end of the year. My telex to Ottawa requesting instruction how to react to this matter resulted in a very brief message on October 9 stating that because of instructions I was about to receive concerning departmental budget reductions I could advise the Cambodian government and the Indian and Polish delegations that Canada would have no difficulty in responding to the Cambodian request.

On October 13, 1969, I received instructions to inform the Cambodian government that, in view of budget restrictions at home, the Canadian delegation would leave Phnom Penh as soon as possible and that our Commission representation would be handled henceforth by the Canadian delegation in Saigon. The same situation would prevail with respect to the Canadian delegation in Laos.

From a professional point of view I was delighted to deliver this message but would have been happier if we had cited the reason as being because we were fed up with the farcical role of the Commission rather than budgetary reasons, especially as the major cost of the delegation was paid by the Commission. Ottawa sympathized with my position but instructed that the budget reasons would prevail.

From a personal point of view, however, having just re-located the delegation office and our residence, having got our two older children settled and our family happily together I was not enamoured by the thought of packing up and moving again to Ottawa or elsewhere.

Over the next few weeks Sihanouk began to back-track slightly, hinting that if someone would help to pay the Commission expenses it might be allowed to stay. The Indian government, the Soviet government and others urged Canada to reconsider. This added another element of personal uncertainty and confusion as we now did not know whether we would be leaving or not. Nevertheless, we proceeded to destroy files and make other arrangements to leave while anxiously awaiting some word from Ottawa as to our next destination. Frustrating days went by with no communication from Ottawa on this subject. Finally the first message received related to instructions to transfer government property to the Canadian delegation in Saigon and a cryptic and infuriating instruction to "count the silverware".

Subsequently I was finally informed that, after closing the mission, I should return to Canada for an undisclosed Ottawa assignment. This presented us with new problems. The tenant who rented our house in Ottawa was secure in his tenancy until the next summer so we had to face the prospect of searching in mid-winter for a place to live.

On November 16, Prince Sihanouk hosted a very gracious farewell dinner for us. Our Australian colleagues hosted a farewell reception for us and we hosted our own farewell reception as a last function at our delegation office.

Dorie and the five children departed for Canada on December 1 and arrived in Ottawa a day or two later, with one sick child, inadequate winter clothing and no place to live. Within a very short space of time, however, my wife was able to locate and rent suitable accommodation, clothe the family for winter life and prepare for the Christmas season—a truly commendable achievement in very difficult circumstances!

I remained in Cambodia progressively closing the delegation, shipping government property to Saigon, destroying files, destroying communication cypher equipment (smashing the mechanical devices and dumping the debris in the Mekong River), getting involved with a visit by Cyrus Eaton, and waiting to discover whether the Commission was to continue or disband.

Finally, the decision was taken that the Commission should adjourn *sine die*, meaning that it would continue to exist legally until such time as it was called back into action or finally terminated. Thus, on January 3, 1970 the Commission voted unanimously to adjourn *sine die*, which proved to be the last act of the International Commission of Cambodia and it faded into history.

By this time our delegation had been reduced to four Canadians — myself, an administrative clerk, Lt. Col. Bouffard and his sergeant, who all took up residence for the last few days in the Phnom Penh *Hôtel Le Royal*, after which we were to proceed to Saigon and onward.

One of the specific tasks of the military sergeant was to ensure that all delegation members had up-to-date visas for North Vietnam, South Vietnam, Laos or Thailand in case there was a need for any of us to visit any of those countries on short notice. During the wind-down of the delegation I frequently requested and received assurance that all of our visas were up to date. We had arranged for many friends to toast us farewell at the airport with champagne when we discovered as we were checking through to obtain our boarding passes that the South Vietnamese visas for the sergeant and the administrative clerk had expired by one day! Consequently the Air Vietnam official refused to issue them boarding passes!

Time was of the essence and there was no way I was going to leave Cambodia with two members of my staff still there. I quickly commandeered a car and sped to the residence of the Japanese Ambassador, who acted as South Vietnam's representative in Cambodia, and arranged for a one-day extension of the visas, returned to the airport just in time for us all to board the airplane *sans* champagne and with much teasing from my friends!

It had been my desire to send a final message to Ottawa with some sort of memorable text, Biblical or other, and I had asked some friends for suggestions. A British friend suggested that, since the Director of our Far Eastern Division in Ottawa was a former Saigon Commissioner, Blair Seaborn, my final message should be "Seaborn I'm airborne". That was the message I sent to terminate my 23-month assignment in Cambodia and to achieve a small place in history as the last resident Commissioner in the ICSC in Cambodia.

Ma vie au Cambodge
octobre 1968 – décembre 1969

Thérèse Rhéaume-Chabot

Lorsque l'on m'a offert un poste au Cambodge, j'ai dû, tout d'abord, vérifier le lieu dans mon atlas. Toutefois, j'étais prête à aller n'importe où. Comme j'étais le deuxième choix et que la première personne avait déjà utilisé plusieurs semaines du temps alloué pour les préparatifs, j'ai dû faire tout en vitesse. J'avais eu des réactions aux injections, sans toutefois m'absenter de mon travail et j'avais même trouvé le temps de m'acheter de beaux vêtements pour le voyage. Bien que je doutais d'arriver à tout faire, mes valises étaient bouclées à temps et le Ministère des affaires étrangères a même accepté un excédent de bagages.

Je partais à l'aventure, l'esprit ouvert, avec l'intention de me réjouir de l'occasion de travailler en Asie. De Vancouver à Tokyo, j'étais la seule femme parmi plusieurs hommes d'affaires en première classe et je fus la coqueluche du moment. De Tokyo à Hong Kong, je ne voulais que dormir, au désespoir de l'agent de bord qui désirait que je fasse honneur à ses petits plats. À Hong Kong, même si j'arrivais à une heure du matin, je me sentais parfaitement en sécurité. Pendant les trois jours qui suivirent, je fus escortée par quelques membres de la délégation canadienne dans les magasins et les restaurants. Je quittais Hong Kong éblouie, emportée par l'exotisme et munie d'un deuxième beau trousseau.

En atterrissant au Cambodge, le doute me saisit et je me suis demandée ce que mon aventure me réservait. À mon grand étonnement, j'étais accueillie par le Commissaire lui-même, M. Richard Gorham, sa femme, l'attaché militaire et les autres membres de la délégation. La petite secrétaire ne tenait pas pied sur terre. Après une réception en mon honneur, l'attaché militaire se chargea même de me conduire à l'*Hôtel Le Royal*. Lorsque je présentai mon passeport au préposé, je croyais sentir que le Lt.-Col. Luc Chabot pouvait lire mes coordonnées au-dessus de mon épaule et comme j'étais dans la trentaine avancée, je me suis dit "... maintenant qu'il a vu mon âge, s'il est libre, ce n'est pas à moi qu'il va faire la cour … " À mon insu, la première impression avait été bonne et comme dans tout bon roman, le dénouement se dévoile à la fin.

Pour moi, le Cambodge c'était le paradis. Il faut dire qu'en 1968 et 1969, lors de mon séjour, la guerre rageait au Vietnam mais uniquement sur la frontière et dans la jungle du Cambodge. Dans la capitale, nous vivions donc en paix. Pays tropical, du soleil tous les jours; des plages de sable blanc désertes; une ambiance de travail agréable, grâce au Commissaire; une bonne qui voyait à toutes les tâches ménagères et qui cuisinait de petits plats français; vivre parmi des autochtones qui avaient les mêmes désirs que moi, du confort dans la paix. Et de plus, avoir l'occasion de visiter une des merveilles du monde, les temples de Angkor Wat et les longs weekends, pouvoir visiter d'autres pays avoisinants tels la Thaïlande, le Laos et le Vietnam. Pouvais-je en demander davantage? Toutefois, j'ai mis environ trois mois à m'habituer au rythme ralenti des cambodgiens en général et de leur façon de nier quelque chose en hochant la tête du haut en bas. Les communications personnelles et téléphoniques exerçaient souvent ma patience pour leur manque de clareté et rapidité. On mettait également souvent beaucoup de temps à réparer l'équipement.

Comme je me levais à l'aube pour les nouvelles à la radio en anglais en provenance de l'agence de presse "Tass", en attendant mon chauffeur cambodgien, de mon balcon je voyais passer les moines bouddhistes en quête de leur nourriture de la journée. En face, j'apercevais la buanderie des occupants étalée sur le trottoir pour sécher au soleil. Et le soir, à gauche, je humais les odeurs de la cuisine cambodgienne et le jacassement gai des habitués m'était agréable.

Un soir, comme je me sentais hardie pour explorer, je m'aventure dans les rues, me fiant sur mon sens d'orientation. Lorsque je décidai de rentrer chez moi, je signale au conducteur du cyclo-pousse mon intention de me prévaloir de ses services et je lui donne, ce que je croyais être les bonnes directions. Il roulait d'une rue à l'autre et je ne reconnaissais toujours pas mon domicile. Après une heure de route, je devins de plus en plus inquiète. À souligner que le pédaleur est à l'arrière du passager. Enfin, quelques minutes plus tard, nous nous engageons dans la bonne rue. Ouf! grand soupir de soulagement, je suis enfin chez moi saine et sauve. Il va sans dire que le cycliste a reçu un très bon pourboire.

Sur le même sujet de rémunération, apparemment je payais ma bonne trop pour ses services et on m'a accusée de créer un précédent. J'ai suivi ma conscience et je n'ai porté aucune attention à ces propos.

Une deuxième exploration de la ville m'a apporté une expérience différente. Un soir, en rentrant à la brunante, j'ai senti que j'étais suivie par un type en motocyclette et ce, pendant une bonne demi-heure. Toutefois, je connaissais la route maintenant. J'ai eu la chair de poule pour une période qui m'a paru très longue, mais en fin de compte ma rentrée fut saine et sauve. Était-ce la police secrète qui s'enquerrait de mes allées et venues? Après tout, je vivais dans un état policier.

Je dormais toujours avec les fenêtres ouvertes et une fois pendant la nuit, un bruit m'a réveillée et en ouvrant les yeux, j'ai vu l'ombre d'une personne qui marchait sur mon balcon. Le bruit que j'ai fait en retour l'a détourné. Un admirateur, un voleur, un agresseur? Dorénavant, les fenêtres de mon balcon étaient toujours verouillées pendant la nuit.

J'ai été choyée par le Commissaire M. Gorham car, comme mon unité à l'*Hôtel Le Royal* n'était pas adéquat, il m'a trouvé un appartement très confortable. À souligner que les coûts de mon hébergement étaient aux frais du gouvernement cambodgien ainsi que de la Commission. De plus, il me prenait tous les matins pour aller au travail.

Comme le pays est petit et que le corps diplomatique l'était aussi en proportion, je participais souvent aux dîners et réceptions.

Lorsque le Canada a décidé de se retirer de sa fonction de gardien de la paix, avant la fermeture du bureau, le Prince Sihanouk a invité notre délégation à dîner au Palais royal et j'étais assise presqu'en face de lui. Ce fut pour moi un grand honneur. Comme il est de petite taille, les invités cambodgiens devaient toujours s'incliner en sa présence, afin que leurs têtes ne dépassent la sienne. Soirée mémorable!

Lors d'une visite au Vietnam, j'ai eu l'occasion de monter dans un hélicoptère américain et du haut des airs j'ai pu constater la destruction. Ce qui m'a également frappée, c'est l'ambiance dans le "mess" des soldats à Danang. Je sentais qu'ils vivaient entre la vie et la mort.

Avant de quitter, j'ai remis ma démission au Ministère des affaires étrangères, car le Lt.-Col. Chabot m'avait demandé en mariage.

Je suis partie avant la fermeture officielle, laissant le Commissaire sans secrétaire. Je souhaite qu'il m'a pardonnée.

Nous nous sommes mariés en 1971 et il s'est éteint lors de la préparation de ce projet, soit le 3 avril 2001. Comme l'un de ses passe-temps était l'écriture, s'il n'avait pas été si malade, il aurait fourni une contribution très intéressante au "Projet de l'Indochine".

Au Canada, en défaisant mes malles, j'ai constaté qu'il me manquait une pipe à vapeur et une couverture de laine. La pipe avait probablement servi à fumer de l'opium et j'y tenais à titre de souvenir typique de l'Asie et bon sujet de conversation lors de nos "parties" au Canada. Je souhaite que les emballeurs ont obtenu une somme qui leur a profité au moins.

Une courte carrière à l'étranger, mais fascinante.

The Sequel:
Canada Does it Again in Vietnam
April 1968 – May 1973

Daniel Molgat

Initially, Canadian participation in the old International Commission for Supervision and Control (ICSC) after the Geneva Conference 1954 had been a surprise. This was followed by a measure of satisfaction during the first few years of its operations. There then ensued a long period of frustration and, eventually, by the late 1960s a good deal of anger.

Trying to avoid a repeat performance (1968–1973)

Pierre-Elliott Trudeau became Prime Minister in April 1968, at a time when it was becoming clear that the Americans and the North Vietnamese were trying to reach a cease-fire. In the national election campaign, it seemed that Vietnam, and indeed foreign policy in general, were not subjects uppermost in the minds of Canadians. The new Prime Minister was known to be sceptical of Canada's past "helpful fixer" role and efforts were begun to fend off the prospect of having Canada drawn once again into participating in another supervisory commission which it would be difficult to refuse. Accordingly, the objective was to avoid being invited to do so unless the arrangements and terms of reference for such a body were likely to make it effective. On Ottawa's instruction, such representations and warnings were repeatedly given to the State Department by the Embassy throughout the late 1960s and early 1970s.

In Ottawa, policy steps were also taken to avoid the prospect. In September 1969 a memorandum to cabinet was submitted by the Departments of External Affairs and National Defence on the possibility that Canada might be asked to participate in a new commission. It was approved by full cabinet on January 15, 1970 and the Embassy in Washington was instructed to inform the U.S. authorities of the Government's decision.

Marcel Cadieux had just been named ambassador to the United States; under instructions from Ottawa, he delivered the message to the U.S. Administration. Its essential point was that the Canadian government would not consider participating in any future commission that it could not regard as holding real promise of effectiveness and, specifically, that one essential condition would hinge upon its reporting responsibilities. The Canadian government would require that such a commission be mandated to report to a continuing political authority such as the UN that could consider taking action upon its reports, rather than relying upon the parties to the conflict themselves to deal with reports to the effect that one of the parties was in violation of the agreement. This concept of a "Continuing Political Authority" was to prove central to the Canadian government's approach when the prospect of participating in a new commission materialized three years later.

A balloon goes up, and then deflates (1972)

Discussions, and then negotiations, between the United States and the Democratic Republic of Vietnam dragged on for many months, in the course of which our Embassy in Washington dutifully reminded the State Department that Canada's participation in any future supervisory commission should not be taken for granted. As for the futile Commission already in existence, as late as August 7, 1972 the Embassy was reporting to External Affairs that it had formed the impression that the U.S. government would find it quite acceptable if the Commission were to adjourn *sine die*. Canada was not disposed to propose such an adjournment, but on September 5, 1972 the Department of External Affairs instructed the Canadian delegation to the ICSC in Saigon that if India or Poland were to make such a proposal, the delegation should support it.

Then, rather suddenly, events began to move with surprising (and sometimes unnerving) speed, and the negotiations between the United States and North Vietnam seemed to be moving toward a conclusion. Marcel Cadieux reported to the Department about Dr. Henry Kissinger's negotiations with North Vietnam, the welcome news that he believed that a cease-fire or terms of a settlement would be announced before November 7. On October 24, 1972 (Dr. Kissinger having just returned from Vietnam) Cadieux reported somewhat alarmingly to the Department on a conversation with

William Sullivan, Deputy Assistant Secretary for East Asian Affairs. Sullivan had said that while the United States understood Canada's wish not to be taken by surprise, the State Department was unable to discuss what was likely to emerge from Dr. Kissinger's negotiations in the way of international supervision of a cease-fire. The following day Cadieux met with Marshall Green, Sullivan's superior, to underline the importance of our knowing in advance about any aspects of a Vietnam settlement in which Canada, as a member of the existing Commission, might be involved. Green replied that Secretary of State William Rogers had told him just before the meeting that things had not reached the point where there was anything to discuss on these aspects.

On October 26, 1972, Secretary of State Rogers told Cadieux that he was optimistic that a cease-fire would soon be achieved. He spoke very broadly of the outlines of a possible agreement and said that it envisaged a four-member commission composed of members "that would be agreeable to both sides". The same day, Dr. Kissinger gave a press conference on the expected agreement in the course of which he mentioned that it contained "a very long and complex section on international supervision".

Little information as that was, it was of course more than the U.S. had been prepared to tell Canada in official conversations. Consequently, External Affairs instructed the Embassy to find out more and to express to the U.S. authorities "our serious reservations about the role apparently envisaged". Indeed, a telegram of October 28 from the Department to the Embassy in Washington made those reservations clear. It said that while much was still unclear, as the Department understood it, the arrangement envisaged was very complicated, that Canada's ability to influence it was very limited, that the composition of the proposed commission was unpromising, that the long-term viability of a cease-fire was doubtful, and that success of a peaceful political settlement in Vietnam was even more doubtful. The State Department's response to the Embassy's request for more information had been thin and, on October 30, External Affairs told the Embassy to inform the State Department that it could not give the State Department much comment because it had been unable to obtain from the U.S. authorities "all the information necessary to fill in the blanks in the proposition".

As soon as that message was conveyed the pressure rose. On October 31 Under-Secretary of State Alexis Johnson told Cadieux that the Canadian government's response to possible participation in a supervisory commission was required "within two days". Sullivan added that signature of an agreement was expected within days, that a Canadian decision not to participate would mean having to search for another country willing to serve as an alternative, and that this could delay the signature or implementation of a cease-fire agreement.

This situation had naturally led to an intense process of study and discussion in Ottawa, with the involvement of the Embassy in Washington and our delegation to the old ICSC in Saigon. A task force was set up in the Department, with participation from National Defence, composed largely of officers with experience in the Indochina Commissions. On the basis of the information that was available from the Americans, the general judgment of the participants in the task force was that the supervisory commission envisaged did not meet Canada's criteria and that the Government should inform the Americans that Canada could not agree to participate. The military representative on the task force shared that view and judged that the scale envisaged for the operation would place unreasonable strains on the officer personnel resources of the Canadian Army.

Some members of the task force even groped (as civil servants probably should not have done) for "political" as opposed to "policy" reasons for refusing. The Liberal government had just emerged from the November 30 general elections with its representation in the House of Commons reduced to 109 members, equal to the Official Opposition. There was some question as to whether Prime Minister Trudeau would decide to lead a minority government or if Robert Stanfield, as leader of the Official Opposition, would be asked to form a government. Some officials on the task force argued that this offered good political reasons for informing the United States that the Government could not agree to participate in the commission.

Political realities, however, decided otherwise. The Secretary of State for External Affairs, Mitchell Sharp, judged that Canadian opinion would not understand or accept a decision by the Government that might have the effect of presenting an obstacle to a cease-fire in Vietnam and to U.S. disengagement from that country.

In addition, the Chief of Defence Staff, General J.A. Dextraze, informed the Under-Secretary of State for External Affairs, A.E. Ritchie, that notwithstanding the considered official view of his representative on the task force, in his opinion a refusal to participate would not be consistent with the mandate and mission of the Canadian Armed Forces.

The balloon deflates

Both the temperature and the pressure soon fell, because in December 1972 the negotiations between the United States and North Vietnam broke down, and the United States engaged in large-scale bombing of the Hanoi–Haiphong area. Negotiations resumed in the first week of January 1973 and on January 5 Mitchell Sharp, addressed the House of Commons on the Vietnam situation. He said that Canada welcomed the cessation of U.S. bombing at the end of December: "We found it very difficult to understand the reasons for that bombing, or the purpose that it was intended to serve. We deplore that action". He welcomed the resumption of negotiations, and went on to discuss the prospect that a cease-fire agreement might be concluded in which Canada would be invited to join a supervisory commission. He noted that Canada had been engaged in such supervision in Vietnam for more than eighteen years and that it had proved to be "a thankless task" but that it had been indicated to us that Canada would be acceptable to all the parties as a member of a new body. He said that Canada would wish to play a constructive role in assisting a peaceful political settlement "if it held the promise of success" and that if invited to do so Canada would consider the invitation sympathetically and constructively.

However, he went on to say that the Government had "an obligation to ensure that Canada's contribution would be a real and effective one, and to ensure that Canada's attempt to contribute to peace not be reduced once again to impotence". He set out a number of conditions upon which the Government would base its judgment on whether or not to participate in a new supervisory commission:

1. That the provisions for the operation of the new organization be workable and offer real prospects of effectiveness;
2. that all belligerent parties be bound by the agreement;

3. that there be a "continuing political authority" that would assume responsibility for the settlement and to which the commission or any of its members would have access. Canada, he said, would prefer that such an entity be provided for in the initial agreements, but failing that Canada would consider that it could be established by the international conference that we understood would be convened thirty days after a cease-fire;
4. that members of the commission have freedom of movement and observation in the demilitarized zone and throughout South Vietnam, and have the necessary logistic support;
5. that Canada be invited to participate by all of the parties concerned.

If all the essential requirements were satisfied except the requirement for a "continuing political authority" Canada would be prepared to consider serving for a minimum of sixty days during which time the Government would assess the outcome of the international conference. If no such entity were established or if, having been established, it ceased to exist, Canada would have to reserve the right to withdraw from the Commission at any time.

When all relevant texts became available, he said, the Government would examine them in the light of the criteria and conditions he had just set out. He made a further statement that had important implications for the manner in which the Canadian delegation conducted itself once Canada did become a member of the new Commission. Drawing upon the lessons of Canadian frustration in the 1954 Commissions, he said that Canada would not allow itself to be frustrated as a member of such a new Commission by a rule of unanimity. We would regard such a Commission to be a forum whose proceedings would normally be open to the public, and even if that could not be agreed we should not regard the Commission's proceedings as being confidential or privileged in any way unless they were unanimously agreed to be so, and we would consider ourselves free to publicize the proceedings as we saw fit.

The "open-mouth policy" was born. It would later attract much attention and comment.

Mitchell Sharp's statement to the House of Commons was based upon a good deal of work by his department and the Department of National Defence. An informal working group in External Affairs, composed largely of veterans of the earlier Vietnam Commission, had developed a draft protocol for an international supervisory commission. The document was given to the United States and later to the Vietnamese. Drawing on the experience of the 1954 Commissions and the reasons for their ineffectiveness, the protocol set out detailed provisions that the working group considered to be important to achieve the effective functioning of a new commission. While the U.S. and Vietnamese parties negotiated an agreement, the Department watched and waited to see the extent to which the negotiating parties were prepared to provide for a supervisory commission that could be effective in its supervisory role.

Here we go again

The U.S.-Vietnamese negotiations proceeded. On January 23, 1973 Marcel Cadieux reported that Secretary of State Rogers had spoken with him about the agreement with North Vietnam and had given him that part of the text which dealt with an international supervisory commission, to be called the International Commission for Control and Supervision (ICCS), presumably to distinguish it from its ill-fated predecessor, the 1954 International Commission for Supervision and Control (ICSC). With what was perhaps intended to be a rebuff to India, the members of the Commission would be Canada, Hungary, Indonesia and Poland. The other documents in the agreement, State Secretary Rogers said, were "not yet ready". Cadieux reported that Rogers tried to suggest that our concerns were substantially met in the agreement but he went on to say that Rogers' claim was not persuasive, especially in respect of a continuing political authority. Rogers asked Cadieux that Canada go to three-day stand-by for the deployment of personnel to serve on the ICCS.

The same day Cadieux sent a telegram to the Department commenting on the prospect that lay before us from the point of view of Canada's relations with the United States, entitled "How and when can Canada get out of Vietnam?" With his long experience of the Vietnam Commission, first as a member of the Canadian delegation in the Commission itself in Vietnam and subsequently as Legal Advisor and later as Under-Secretary of the department, Cadieux had no illusions. He was acutely aware of the ineffectiveness of the Commission in its last decade, of the difficulties that participation in the Commission had caused to other aspects of Canada's foreign policy such as in our relations with India, of the debilitating effect of our involvement on the personnel resources of the Departments of External Affairs and National Defence, and of the corrosive effect it had had upon the morale and idealism of personnel of both departments. However, his immediate responsibility was for Canada's relations with the United States.

In his telegram he considered the degree to which it seemed likely that, in an agreement to end its involvement in the Vietnam war, the U.S. would satisfy the Canadian government's conditions for participating in a new supervisory Commission. He concluded that "it is a good guess that the final package will be less than fully satisfactory to us". He then turned to the question of the effects on Canada's relations with the United States by accepting or refusing the invitation to participate in a new supervisory commission. His conclusion was that, in the short term, acceptance could not be expected to generate practical benefits with respect to a more benign U.S. approach to other problem areas in our bilateral relations. On the other hand, he thought that a refusal might well engender resentment and hostility in the White House and would not be well understood in U.S. public opinion or in the U.S. press. He went on to express doubts about the possibility of agreeing to only join a commission with reservations or with an escape clause, which he thought would cause serious unhappiness in Washington. Nevertheless, he agreed with a view conveyed to him by External Affairs that if Canada agreed to participate it might place a two-year limit on its participation. On balance Cadieux' conclusion was that if Canada was invited to participate in a supervisory commission for a cease-fire agreement it should do so. After all, he argued (referring to Canada's continued participation in the ineffective Commission since 1954) "we have justified our continued participation on the premise that a time might come when the parties wanted international assistance in supervising a new cease-fire".

Canada was still not committed to participate, beyond having said that our existing staff of the Canadian delegation in Vietnam would be available to assist in the initial stages of the "peace process". At the same time, the logistical and personnel requirements of our possible participation had obliged National Defence and External Affairs to make contingency preparations for joining the ICCS. Moreover, Secretary Rogers had asked that Canada go to three-day stand-by for the deployment of personnel to serve on the ICCS, and we did in fact move remarkably quickly. The cease-fire agreement was signed in Paris on January 27, 1973, and Canada informed the signatories that it would serve on the new Commission for an initial period of sixty days. At 3:30 a.m. on January 29, the head of the Canadian delegation to the ICCS, Ambassador Michel Gauvin, arrived in Saigon. On the same aircraft were his Senior Political Advisor, Vernon Turner, as well as General Duncan McAlpine and an advance group of the military contingent that would be under his command. Deployment of the rest of the 290-strong Canadian delegation, military and civilian (to Saigon and to six other far-flung locations in South Vietnam) followed quickly.

External Affairs' choice of Michel Gauvin for the position was significant. Gauvin was an experienced Foreign Service Officer, several times an ambassador, and formerly a wartime and much decorated military officer in the *Régiment de la Chaudière*, who had been awarded the DSO for gallantry in combat. He was known for his judgment, toughness, and outspokenness. Gauvin was an ideal choice to conduct an "open-mouth policy" of "saying it like it is". But he placed a condition on accepting such a difficult role: the Department had to provide as his deputy a Foreign Service Officer in whom he had particular confidence: Vernon Turner, who had served with him in 1956 on the first Vietnam Commission, the ICSC. Similarly, Turner was prepared to accept the assignment on a number of conditions, including that his wife be allowed to join him when local circumstances permitted. The Department agreed to the requests of both men, and the team was formed.

Canada's determination to have the Commission work effectively seemed not to be entirely matched by that of others. When Gauvin arrived in Saigon at 3:30 a.m. on January 29, he found that although the first meeting of the Commission was due to take place at 8:00 a.m. that same day, no arrangements had been made for such a meeting to be convened. Gauvin proposed that the meeting take place at 10:00 a.m. and undertook that the Canadian delegation would make the arrangements for the meeting on the premises of the former Canadian delegation to the 1954 Commission. The meeting did take place there on Gauvin's schedule, but it found a relative void in the arrangements for its necessary liaison with the three Vietnamese and American parties. The cease-fire agreement had provided for the establishment of a four-party Central Joint Military Commission (CJMC)[1] with which the ICCS would work. When Gauvin tried to arrange a meeting with the CJMC for the following day, January 30, so that the ICCS could begin to get on with its work, he found that there was no-one with whom to meet.

This, unfortunately, was only a foretaste of the frustrations to come. As the Commission deployed its regional teams and as it slowly succeeded in beginning to function, the frustrations began to mount. The Commission's interlocutors, provided for in the agreement signed in Paris, were ineffective. The Commission's four-party teams in Saigon and in the six regions received complaints of alleged violations of the agreement by both sides, but for the Canadians the investigative and reporting situation was reminiscent of the worst times of the 1954 Commission: when the complaint was against the South Vietnamese or against the Americans the team could usually agree to investigate it, but when the complaint was against the North Vietnamese or their South Vietnamese proxies the four-party team often could not agree to investigate the complaint because of opposition from its Hungarian and Polish members. When all four national participants did agree to investigate a complaint against the North Vietnamese or their South Vietnamese proxies, it would find it impossible to agree on a report supporting the complaint, again because of Hungarian and Polish opposition. Because of that same opposition the Commission and its teams found it impossible to make their discussions open to the media and the public, as the Canadians had wished. If the Commission did report, there was no "continuing political authority" to which it could do so: only the four parties in the Central Joint Military Commission.

The "open-mouth policy" then came into play. Gauvin was under instructions from Ottawa to be open and public about what went on in the Commission, and he was regularly seen on the world's television screens (but, as time went on, chiefly on Canada's screens) saying what was going on. This was not popular with his Hungarian and Polish colleagues or with the North Vietnamese and their allies, nor was it agreeable to the Americans, because it created a series of unsettling impressions: not only that the Commission was

---

[1] The four parties being the Democratic Republic of Vietnam, the Provisional Revolutionary Government of South Vietnam, the Republic of Vietnam, and the United States.

not functioning as the Paris Agreement of January 27, 1973 had provided, but that perhaps not all the signatories to the agreement had ever intended or expected that the Commission would do so; not only that the Paris cease-fire agreement itself was not effective, but that perhaps not all the signatories had ever intended that the Paris Agreement itself would be. The fact was that in the midst of a cease-fire the Vietnam war was still being waged.

From the point of view of achieving a more effective "control and supervision" role for the Commission, there was still one hope: an international conference was to be convened one month after the cease-fire agreement was signed. It was somewhat theatrically and grandiloquently intended to perform the rather shallow role of "acknowledging" the agreement signed on January 27 and to "guarantee" the ending of the war. But in that latter role it was possible that it could be used to advance Canada's purpose. The conference duly convened in Paris on February 27, 1973, attended by the four parties to the January 27 agreement, the Secretary General of the United Nations, the permanent members of the UN Security Council, and by Canada, Hungary, Indonesia and Poland as members of the Commission. The Canadian delegation was led by Mitchell Sharp. He made it clear in advance that his main objective at the conference was to have it establish a "continuing political authority", preferably the Secretary General of the United Nations, to which the Commission could report — without a requirement for unanimity — with a view to deciding what action could be taken if those reports indicated that the cease-fire agreement was not being observed. At a dinner the night before the opening of the conference, the Canadian delegates told their American colleagues plainly that if Canada's concerns on that central point were not met, no one should count upon Canada's remaining long as a member of the Commission.

As the international conference proceeded it became clear to Mitchell Sharp that Canada's concern did not have much support among the other participants, and that some participants were firmly opposed to it. The North Vietnamese delegation in particular was clearly unhappy with the participation in the conference of the Secretary General of the United Nations, and seemed determined to ensure that the UN should have no role. There was an instructive incident in that regard as the conference got down to work. A committee on legal affairs was established by the conference, but the UN

Secretary General's representatives were not included in its membership. The Canadian delegation took the initiative of co-opting two members of the Secretary General's legal staff to sit with it in the section of seats allotted to Canada in the committee's meeting-room, though it was agreed that they would not speak. The committee duly began its work until the North Vietnamese delegation asked for a recess. During the lengthy recess the Canadian delegation was informed that it had come to the attention of the North Vietnamese delegation that extraneous participants were seated with the Canadian delegation and that the committee would not reconvene until those persons were removed.

For Canada, the crucial issue was to have established a "continuing political authority" so that the Commission could break out of a sterile situation in which it could only report formally to the warring parties on its observation of the cease-fire. As the conference drew toward its close it became clear that this would not be achieved. The international media was present in very large numbers and, finding the conference proceedings rather dull, focused on a question: would Canada wash its hands of the whole thing and announce that it would withdraw from the Commission? As the conference ended, the Canadian delegation issued a press release. The frenzied interest of the journalists was such that, as Mitchell Sharp's press officer walked into the press room holding a sheaf of copies of the press release, he was mobbed by journalists trying to snatch copies from him before he reached the rostrum. He held his sheaf of press releases tightly, and one journalist was so eager to obtain an advance copy that he bit the press officer's hand in an effort to pry one from his grip.

The outcome that Canada was announcing, however, was less dramatic than some of the media had hoped for. Mitchell Sharp's effort to achieve the establishment of a "continuing political authority" had produced only agreement that the Commission would provide its reports to the Secretary General of the United Nations and to the governments represented at the conference.[2] In any event this circulation of reports would not be expected to lead to any action in response to findings of violations of the cease-fire. If any such action seemed necessary, it would require reconvening the conference

---

[2] As the work of the Commission unfolded subsequently, it does not appear that any such reports were ever agreed upon or issued.

itself, and this could be done only if North Vietnam and the United States jointly requested such a reconvening, or if at least six of the countries participating in the conference requested it. This was not enough to satisfy Canada's requirements, but nor was it so starkly negative as to justify withdrawing from the Commission. Instead, Mitchell Sharp expressed doubt that these arrangements went far enough in meeting Canada's essential conditions, and doubt that they would work. In his final statement to the conference, he said that Canada would suspend judgment until it had had an opportunity to review carefully the new arrangements in light of Canada's experience on the Commission.

He took that review seriously. On March 12, he flew to Indochina and visited Saigon, Vientiane and Hanoi until March 18. In the course of that visit he had discussions with the political leaders in those countries and had lengthy talks with Michel Gauvin and Vernon Turner, with both General McAlpine and some of his senior officers, with some of the External Affairs officers who were leading the Commission's regional teams, and with more junior members of the Canadian delegation. The trip was not without some dangers: in Hanoi the airfield had been bombed by the United States some months before and was still incompletely repaired. There was some question as to whether the remaining length of usable airstrip was sufficient to permit the landing and take-off of the Canadian Forces Boeing 707 in which he was flying.

Sharp had several purposes in his trip to Indochina. He wanted better to understand the attitudes and intentions of the Vietnamese parties with regard to the agreement, to the cease-fire, to the political and military future, and to the Commission and its functioning. He wanted to understand whether and to what degree they attached importance to Canada's continued participation in the Commission. He also wanted a better understanding of what was happening in South Vietnam and of what the future might hold. On the one hand, he was aware of American views of the "peace process" that were relatively optimistic and that suggested that Canada should "stay the course". On the other hand, he had Gauvin's view from Saigon that the cease-fire was not effective, that the Commission was not functioning effectively, and that it could not be made to function.

He did not return to Ottawa with a very optimistic assessment. On the day of his return from a gruelling trip and a long trans-

Pacific flight he appeared before the Standing Committee on External Affairs and National Defence of the House of Commons. He said that despite Canadian efforts the Commission was not fulfilling its role, and that the U.S. and Vietnamese parties had not even put in place the Joint Military Commissions that were essential to the cease-fire, which in any event was not being observed. He said that he did not consider that Canada should be expected to go on playing its part for a protracted period.

By then Canada had been participating in the new Commission for almost two months. Michel Gauvin's very first report from Saigon on February 1, 1973 was still ringing in the ears of those in External Affairs who were dealing with Vietnam. We shall do, he had said, "everything... through leadership and initiatives" to make the Commission effective, so that "when we... have had enough, we will be free to withdraw with honour and with no... need for excuse".

Canada's undertaking to serve on the Commission for an initial period of sixty days was about to expire, and the issue of whether or not to withdraw from the Commission was arising pressingly. If the only criteria for decision had been observance of the cease-fire, the prospects for effectiveness of the Commission, and satisfaction of Canada's requirement that there be a "continuing political authority", the decision to withdraw would have seemed evident. But there was a further South Vietnamese political factor in play. The Paris Agreement of January 27 had provided that general elections be held in South Vietnam, to be supervised by the Commission, and that a somewhat farcically named "National Council of National Reconciliation and Concord" would organize the elections. There had been no visible progress in establishing such a body, but it could be argued that the two South Vietnamese parties needed a little more time to achieve movement toward a political solution of that kind, and that if they succeeded in doing so the role of an un-disrupted Commission would be important.

On March 27, 1973, Mitchell Sharp announced the Government's decision: Canada would extend its participation in the Commission for another sixty days. If, by the end of that additional period, there had not been a substantial improvement in the situation in Vietnam or some signs of an imminent political settlement, Canada would announce its withdrawal from the Commission by May 31, with a grace-period of up to thirty days to allow the parties to the agreement to find a replacement for Canada. In Canada's remaining time as a member of the Commission, he said, its delegation would continue to play its role fully: Canada would not take part in a "charade", and it would not condone inaction when it believed that action was required.

There followed no improvement in the situation in Vietnam nor any signs of a political settlement and on May 29 he announced the decision of the Canadian government to withdraw from the Commission (the only qualification to that decision was that Canada would be willing to consider extending its participation temporarily if, as seemed unlikely, general elections were held in accordance with the Paris Agreement of January 27, 1973.) That decision was badly received in Washington. While the official public reactions of Dr. Kissinger and of the State Department were simply regretful but understanding, Prime Minister Trudeau's *Memoirs*, published twenty years later, revealed that President Nixon's reaction had been angry and rather intemperate.[3]

As events unfolded, Canada's departure at the end of July caused no major disturbance to a Commission that was in any case dysfunctional. Canada was replaced by Iran.

* * *

For almost twenty years Canada had played a role in Indochina that it had never desired nor sought, and from which neither the Government nor Canadian public opinion ever drew much satisfaction. There had been good reasons for Canada's accepting to play that role. In 1954, it was to assist in a process that facilitated the disengagement of France from a lost war. In 1973 it was to facilitate the disengagement of the United States from a lost war. In both cases, the objective was consistent with Canada's foreign policy and appeared to be in consonance with the wishes of most Canadians.

At long last, the task was over.

÷ ÷ ÷ ÷ ÷

---

[3] Pierre-Elliott Trudeau, *Memoirs* (Toronto: McClelland, 1993).

Index

17th parallel, *map*, 4, 16

Agence France Press (AFP), 36, 37, 79
Aigle Azur, 16, 51, 76, 109, 135
Anderson, David, 89
Angkor Wat, 16, 51, 55, 138, 140, 161, 171
Anh, Le Duc, 50
Anh, Nguyen Van, 91, 97

"Bacon", 88, 89, 93, 96, 106–108, 111
Baie d'Along, *map*, 51, 72
Banville, Roger, 147
Bao Dai, 18
Bauer, Bill, *photos*
Beaulieu, 28
Belgium, 2
Bellavance, Gilles, 135, 145
Binh Xuyen, 24–26
Blanchette, Arthur E., xiv, xv, xvii, 1, 3, 45, 53, *photos*
Bouffard, Clément, 156, 168
Bridge on the River Kwai, 79
Britain, ix, xvii, 1, 3–5, 48, 103
Broatch, Liz, 141, 145
Bundy, McGeorge, *photos*, 104, 110
Byrne, J.S., 109

Cadieux, Marcel, 175–177, 180, 181
Camp des Mares, 10, 49, 51, 90
Campbell, Peter, 36
Canadian International Development Agency (CIDA), 59, 162
Cannon, Lucien "Brodie", 90
Cap St. Jacques, *map*, 16, 24, 25, 51, 55, 96, 130

Caron, Janine, 40
Carter, Tom, 51, 67
Central Joint Military Commission (CJMC), 183, 187
Chabot, Luc, xviii, 147, 156, 164, 170, 172
Chapdelaine, Jean, 147
Childs, Marquis, 118
China, xvii, 1–3, 5, 47, 48, 50, 60, 64, 88, 93, 110, 112, 114–116, 118, 119, 154
Chou En-lai, 2
CIA, 45, 87, 104, 114
Collins, Ralph, 114
Colombo Plan, 1, 38, 40, 59, 60, 127, 131, 133, 140
Cooper, Chester, 87, 88, 104
Cox, Gordon, 89, 90

Delworth, Tom, 89, 91, 105
"demilitarized zone" (DMZ), 4, 16, 48, 179
Democratic Republic of Vietnam (DRVN), 74, 83, 92, 94–96, 98, 99, 101, 104, 106, 107, 111, 175, 183
Deschamps, Noël-St-Clair, 137
Devi, Bopha, 140
Dextraze, J.A., 178
Diem, Ngo Dinh, 18–20, 24–26, 31, 50, 82, 85, 115
Dien Bien Phu, 29, 31, 47, 70, 113
Dong, Pham Van, 92, 93, 98–102, 106, 111
Dulles, Allan Foster, 114
Dulles, John Foster, 114, 115

Dyer, Ken, xviii, 131, 132, 136–144, 147, 148, 155

Eaton, Cyrus, 168
Eden, Anthony, 2
Ellsberg, Daniel, 93
Esmonde-White, Larry, 90
External Aid Office (CIDA), 49, 59

Fall, Bernard, 74
Fixed Inspection Teams, 6, 7, 13, 16
Food and Agriculture Organization (FAO), 60
Ford, J., *photos*
Fortier, D'Iberville, 43
France, ix, 1–5, 9, 11, 21, 25, 31, 45, 48, 53, 55, 60, 64, 66, 118, 157, 188
Francis, J. Ross, xv, xvii, 32

Gamache, Bernard, 125, 126, 129, 134
Gauvin, Michel, x, xi, 14, 182, 183, 186, 187
Geneva Agreements, 3, 4, 6, 12–14, 16, 19, 21, 35, 47–49, 71, 86, 95, 96, 103, 105, 120, 155, 175, 177–179
Geneva Conference, ix, xiii, 1–6, 20, 45, 55, 103, 113, 114, 153, 174
Giap, Vo Nguyen, 29, 50
Given, John, 137
Goodman, Harry, 137
Gordon, Walter, 120
Gorham, Richard (Dick), xvii, xviii, *photos*, 146, 149, 150, 170, 172
Govan, Margaret, 124
Green, Marshall, 176
Green, Shirley, 137
Greene, Graham, 47, 89
Gullason, Gene, 134, 136

Hôtel Le Royal, 57, 65, 124, 126, 127, 139, 168, 170, 172
Hatheway, Bob, 105, 112, 113
"helpful fixer", 117, 119, 121, 174
Hill, Lois, 43
Ho Chi Minh Trail, 4, 45, 66, 68
Hoa Binh Hotel, 28
Holding, Ron, 136, 145–147
Holmes, John, 6, 52
Hooton, Frank, 72, *photos*
Hungary, ix, xiv, 8, 41, 180, 184

ICSC Cambodia, xvii, xviii, 4, 58, 59
ICSC Laos, xvii, 4
ICSC Vietnam, xiii, xviii–xx, 3–5, 15, 20, 85
India, ix, xiv, 2, 5, 19, 48, 56, 58, 64, 110, 113, 120, 152, 166, 175, 180, 181
Indonesia, ix, xiv, 8, 114, 180, 184
International Commission for Control and Supervision (ICCS), ix–xi, xiv, xviii, 8, 14, 180–183
International Commissions for Supervision and Control (ICSC), ix, xiii, 2, 3, 5, 7, 10, 13, 15, 47–51, 57, 63, 68, 85, 87, 92, 95, 99, 108, 109, 111, 118, 120–122, 125, 135, 146, 169, 174, 175, 177, 180, 182

Jackson, David, 92, 99, 102, 109
James, Marie-France, 133
Johnson, Alexis, 100, 177
Johnson, David, *photos*
Johnson, Lyndon, 7, *photos*, 87, 98, 99, 106, 107, 117–120
Jurgens, Kurt, 55

Kampong Som (Sihanoukville), *map*, 55, 128, 129, 141, 154, 161
Kennedy, John F., 117
Kep, 55, 141, 161, 164

Khanh, Nguyen, 88, 95, 97
Khmer rouge, 55, 56, 134, 142, 147
Kissinger, Henry, 100, 175, 176, 188
Kosygin, Alexei, 104
Ky, Nguyen Cao, 97

La Couture, Jean, 68, 69
La Presse, 123
Lacroix, Roger, 145, 146
Lam, Mai, 92
Langley, Jim, 40
Lanteigne, Diane, 162
Lanteigne, Pierre, 162
Lau, Ha Van, 92, 99, 102, 103, 111
Lefort, Monique, 124, 128
Lodge, Henry Cabot, 85, 90, 91, 100
Longtin, Richard, 136, 145

MacLaren, Roy, P.C., xvii, 47, *photos*
Mai, Bo, 102
Marler, Herbert, 101
Martin, Paul Sr., 3, 40, *photos*, 86, 87, 100, 101, 107, 110, 115, 117, 119–121, 147
Massey, Vincent, 33
Matheson, Ardath, 32
McAlpine, Duncan, x, 182, 186
McCabe, Robert, 113
McCardle, Jim, 88
McGaughey, Charles Eustace, 30
McNamara, Robert, 100
Menzies, Arthur, 114, 153
Michalski, S., 57
Michener, Roland, 110
Minh, Ho Chi, 18, 20–23, 26, 29, 31, 50, 68, 92
Mitchell, Lee, 51
Mobile Inspection Teams, 6, 7, 12, 13, 16
Molgat, Daniel, xviii, 174
Molotov, V.M., 2
Mulecki, Tadeusz, 158
Muoi, Do, 50

Murray, Geoffrey, 121
Métropole Hotel, 11–13, 15, 28, 74, 82

Nadeau, Norma, 89
NATO, xviii, xx, 8, 10
Nicholson, Moira (Nicky), 145, 147
Niemh, Sok, 61, 62, 64
Nixon, Richard, 100, 188
Nol, Lon, 56
Nutting, Claire, 133, 134, 136, 137, 143, 144, 146, 155

Oglesby, Roy, 59, *photos*
"open-mouth" policy, x, 153, 179, 182, 183

Paranjpe, V.V., 158
Pardy, H.G., 109
Paris Agreement 1973, ix, xiv, 8, 14, 153, 180, 182–184, 187, 188
Paris Conference, x, 184
Pas de Deux, 162
Pearson, Geoffrey, xviii, 117
Pearson, Lester B., 3, 7, *photos*, 86–88, 92, 100, 110, 115–121
Pentagon Papers, 93, 108
People's Army of Vietnam (PAVN), 11–13, 18, 72, 92
Perkins, V.J., 109
Phumisarah, Norodom, 62
Pol Pot, 56, 61, 62, 147
Poland, ix, xiv, 2, 5, 8, 12, 41, 48, 56, 120, 152, 175, 180, 184
Pommet, Louis, 137
Pommet-Dyer, Louise, xviii, *photos*, 122, 155, 156
Pope, Tom, 88
Prek Thnot project, 163

Rae, Saul, 11
Rahman, "Ishi", 95
Republic of Vietnam (RVN), 68, 183

Rhéaume-Chabot, Thérèse, xviii, *photos*, 148, 156, 170
Ritchie, A.E., 115, 178
Roberts, Peter, xiii, xix, 105, 112
Robertson, Terence, 107, 108
Rogers, Louis, 88
Rogers, William G., ix, 176, 180, 181
"Rolling Thunder", 104
Ronning, Chester, 2, 114, 119, 120
Rozee, Jack, xv
Rusk, Dean, *photos*, 86, 87, 107, 115, 116, 119

Sauriol, Jean-Marie, 124–126, 128, 135, 136
Schioler, John, xix, 67, *photos*
Seaborn, Blair, C.M., xiii, xix, *photos*, 85, 107, 112, 118, 168
Sharp, Mitchell, P.C., xi, xiv, 8, 108, 177–179, 184–187
Sihanouk, Norodom, 4, 53, 55, 56, 59, 60, *photos*, 134, 138, 140, 145, 147, 151, 154, 158, 159, 161–163, 165–167, 172
Singh, Ghanshyam, 58
Small, John, 114
Smith, Arnold, 87
Smith, Jean, 41
Smyser, Dick, 100
Souphanouvong, Prince, 35, 45
Souvanna Phouma, Prince, 35, 37, 45
Soviet Union, xiii, xviii, 1, 3–5, 45, 47, 48, 60, 103, 115, 158
St. Laurent, Louis, 3, 23
Stanfield, Robert, 177
Street Without Joy, 74
Suez, xiv, 47, 110
Sullivan, William, 87, 88, 110, 176, 177
Suramarit, Norodom, 55, 62, 64

Taylor, J.H., C.M., xx, 15, *photos*
Taylor, Maxwell, 100
Temple University, 115, 117
Tet offensive, 151
The High and The Mighty, 76
Trinh, Nguyen Duy, 106–108
Trudeau, Pierre-Elliott, 30, 110, 174, 177, 188
Turner, J. Douglas, 109
Turner, Vernon G., x, xv, xx, 10, *photos*, 182, 186

U Thant, 101
UNFICYP, 83
United Nations (UN), x, xviii, 1, 2, 8, 38, 72, 101, 117, 120, 123, 153, 163, 175, 184, 185
United States, ix, x, xiii, xiv, 2, 5, 7, 8, 30, 45, 47, 48, 50, 56, 60, 66, 70, 83, 86–88, 93, 98, 99, 101, 103, 105, 107, 108, 114, 115, 118, 120, 151, 153–155, 163, 175–178, 180, 181, 183, 186, 188
U.S. Military Assistance Advisory Group, 7, 48, 70, 89, 102, 103, 105, 115
U.S.S. *C. Turner Joy*, 98
U.S.S. *Maddox*, 98
USSR, ix, xix, xx, 50

Vietcong (Viet Minh), ix, xi, xiv, 4, 8, 18, 26, 66, 70, 85, 96, 97, 103, 115, 151–154, 159, 163, 165

Webster, C., 126, 133, 144, 145
Westmoreland, William C., 100
Whitlam, Gough, 140
Woodcock, Andrew, 145–147, 155, 156

The Golden Dog Press

This volume was produced using the TeX typesetting system, with Bitstream's Charter fonts.

www.ingramcontent.com/pod-product-compliance
Lightning Source LLC
Chambersburg PA
CBHW060951230426
43665CB00015B/2160